Polemic

ESSAYS FROM
THE ENGLISH INSTITUTE

Since 1944, the English Institute has presented work by distinguished scholars in English and American literatures, foreign literatures, and related fields. A volume of papers selected for the meeting is published annually.

Also available in the series from Routledge:

Polemic
Critical or Uncritical

edited by
Jane Gallop

Routledge
New York • London

Published in 2004 by
Routledge
270 Madison Avenue
New York, NY 10016
www.routledge-ny.com

Published in Great Britain by
Routledge
2 Park Square
Milton Park, Abingdon
Oxon OX14 4RN
www.routledge.co.uk

Routledge is an imprint of the Taylor & Francis Group.

10 9 8 7 6 5 4 3 2 1

Library of Congress Cataloging-in-Publication Data
Polemic : critical or uncritical / edited by Jane Gallop.
      p. cm. — (Essays from the English Institute)
   Includes bibliographical references.
   ISBN 0-415-97227-2 (hardback : alk. paper) — ISBN 0-415-97228-0 (pbk.: alk.
paper)
   1. Literature, Modern—20th century—History and criticism. 2. Books and
reading. 3. Polemics. I. Gallop, Jane, 1952- II. Series.
   PN771.P66 2004
   809'.93384—dc22
                              2004014175

Contents

Acknowledgments

This volume, by its very genre, depends upon the work of many people. Most visible of course are the thoughtfulness and eloquence of the authors here included. Less visible but much appreciated has been their willingness to revise in a timely manner.

None of this would have existed without the four people who planned the panels for the 2002 English Institute: Jonathan Crewe, Claudia Johnson, Gayatri Chakravorty Spivak, and Michael Warner. A good number of people worked to make that event possible and to help with the transition from event to volume. I cannot single out all those people but they include Mary Beth Wilkes, Conference Coordinator of the English Institute, and the Board of Trustees and Supervisors who selected the papers for the volume.

Finally, I simply could not have edited this volume without the labor and intelligence of my assistant, Kelly Klingensmith.

Introduction

Jane Gallop

The first paper at the 2002 English Institute (September 20–22) was Amanda Anderson's "Argument and Ethos." According to Anderson, in contemporary literary and cultural studies, "ethos has suffered a kind of exile from theoretical work." The particular "kind of exile" ethos suffers is not really an absence from theoretical argument, but rather a peculiar sort of presence: "no matter how disavowed . . . it tends to come back in shadow forms, haunting the debate." Anderson calls for "a fuller acknowledgment of the insistent presence" of ethos in our arguments.

While I find Anderson's argument about ethos lucid and persuasive, I want at the same time to acknowledge that, along with its astute argument, "Argument and Ethos" brought something else into the English Institute. What the title of that paper terms "ethos" also appears under another name. In order to better capture the shadowy presence that haunts our arguments, Anderson refers to it not only as "ethos" but also as "character." And although it is not exactly what Anderson means by "character," still the word seems to portend the odd fact that "Argument and Ethos" ended up bringing into the English Institute not only its cogent argument but also two characters who tended to come back in shadow forms through the next three days, haunting our reception of the diverse papers presented.

One of these characters is named Habermas. Loosely based on the actual German philosopher Jürgen Habermas, in Anderson's essay he appears most memorably not in her attentive, sympathetic version of him but in the role he's given in the oft-told tale of his "famous" debate with Foucault. While Anderson does not subscribe to this portrayal of Habermas—indeed she critiques it as caricature and misrepresentation—in order to represent the debate and the place of ethos in it, she gives us a vivid sense of Habermas's unfortunate role in that scenario: "As it did in the earliest days of the 'debate,' the name 'Habermas' often continues to provoke a knowing weariness in the literary field, one which defines a certain consensus about what Habermas signifies—plodding style, an embarrassing optimism of the intellect, and dangerous complicity with the Enlightenment."

In bringing this "Habermas" to our attention, Anderson moves us to a truer, more complex appreciation of Habermas; her careful argument convincingly lays the flat, stock character to rest. Yet the caricature she has evoked, nonetheless, persists beyond her paper. Later that day, I found myself recalling that Habermas character as I listened to Amy Hollywood describe an allegorical figure named Reason.

Hollywood's paper is about a fourteenth-century dialogue written by a woman mystic. The historical period and the genre that Hollywood considers are both remote indeed from the topic of Anderson's paper, but Hollywood's Reason sure acts and sounds a lot like Anderson's "Habermas."

Reason is a character in a dialogue with Love, the Soul, and a number of minor interlocutors. The dialogue repeatedly enacts Reason's limitations in understanding what Love and the Soul are saying; Reason is continually flummoxed by what strike her as contradictions. As Hollywood puts it, "Reason is the foil"; her particular role in the dialogue[1] is not to get it.

Just so, "Habermas" as portrayed in the debate with Foucault doesn't get it. Like Reason, he is stymied by his interlocutor's apparent incoherence and self-contradiction. In the story Anderson analyzes, Habermas is in fact "the foil."

There are a number of ways we might account for such a resemblance. According to Anderson, Habermas "was alleged to be simply on the side of Reason." Those producing the Habermas caricature are, like Hollywood's fourteenth-century mystic, critical of Reason's limitations. The Habermas caricature might be so catchy precisely because it draws on a long literary/philosophical tradition with a stock type for dim-witted Reason.

The resemblance also suggests the possibility that accounts of "famous" intellectual debates may be the contemporary version of medieval allegorical dialogue. The two figures in an oft-recounted debate may—despite their historical existence—function rather more like allegorical figures.[2] The contemporary genre could be understood as, like allegory, a way of dramatizing intellectual problems, of working out arguments by means of character.

At the 2002 English Institute, we had an opportunity to consider another such twentieth-century debate. Immediately after Anderson spoke, we heard Louis Menand's paper on Pauline Kael and Andrew Sarris. Sarris there seems a lot like Hollywood's Reason. Hollywood writes: "Reason cries out in pained incomprehension ('For Gods' sake, Love, what can this mean?' is a continual refrain . . .)." At the English Institute, Menand's paper was entitled "What Was That All About?"; the question characterizes Sarris's position. As Menand puts it, Sarris "never really got it."

As we listened to Menand talking about Sarris and Kael, we remembered Habermas and Foucault from the previous paper. The resemblance however was hardly uncanny. Both Menand and Anderson had been invited to speak on the panel organized by Jonathan Crewe on Polemic. Jonathan had proposed Polemic as the topic for the Institute's customary genre panel. The similarity between Anderson's and Menand's characters suggest that polemic may well be a genre.[3]

If we think within this genre framework, it might suggest another explanation for the resemblance between Sarris and Habermas (as well as that between Kael and Foucault). Menand says of Kael: "Her disciples were everywhere. She knew that she had won." Anderson is likewise examining a field in which Foucault's "disciples" are "everywhere." Considering the generic similarities, we might conclude that in the wake of a polemic, the loser takes on a certain character—a bit dim and perplexed about what the winner has said.

If the loser looks plodding and limited, the winner on the other hand is elusive and charismatic. Menand's paper allows us to appreciate Kael's panache, her wit and sense of timing; Anderson's quotations likewise give us a sense of Foucault's style and charm. Menand emphasizes how large a following Kael had, how widely she was admired; Anderson not only highlights Foucault's devoted following but critiques the distorting effects of their admiration. If Anderson's reading of Habermas is dedicated to correcting the reductive caricature, in relation to Foucault she wants to correct the "cult of personality" and what she calls the "charismatic fallacy."

Like its "Habermas," the Foucault evoked in "Argument and Ethos" became an "insistent presence" at the English Institute, "coming back in shadow forms" in our reception of later papers. Not only in Menand's account of another twentieth-century polemic, but also in a paper on a topic seemingly remote from Anderson's concerns. Just as we recalled Habermas while we listened to Amy Hollywood talk about poor Reason, a day later we might have thought of Anderson's Foucault-as-cult-figure while Helen Deutsch regaled us with stories about the ways followers have for two centuries worshipped Samuel Johnson.

Whereas Anderson's paper is about the shadow presence of character in contemporary argument, Deutsch's paper takes us pretty far away from argument and square into the realm of character. Johnson here is not so much an author as a character, explicitly treated as one by Deutsch. A character in Boswell's *Life of Johnson* of course, but also more broadly in the legends, anecdotes, myths and rituals prized by his devoted followers. Analyzing Johnson as a literary character, Deutsch defines him by tradition and genre (romance), understanding him through placing him in literary history.

In Deutsch's paper, Boswell is a character too, Johnson's straight man, sounding at times a bit like an uncomprehending Sarris/Habermas figure but, quite unlike them, enjoying his puzzlement as a sign of Johnson's superiority. This passing resemblance between Boswell and Sarris suggests a certain relation between the two kinds of characters, defeated adversaries and followers. Where the polemical loser is pained by his incomprehension of the dominant figure; the devoted follower is stirred by his incomprehension to greater admiration.[4] Given this relation, it is interesting to remark that Anderson's paper pits Habermas not so much against Foucault but against Foucault's "admiring commentators."

In Anderson's critique of the Foucaultians, there is a suggestion that their relation to him is religious. Words she uses like "charismatic" and "cult" derive from a religious context, and she reminds us that David Halperin has written a book called *Saint Foucault*, an "avowed hagiography." While the odd Foucaultian might write "hagiography," the Johnsonians, Deutsch shows us, regularly treat Johnson's remains as relics. What in Anderson's account of the Foucaultians is but a shadow of religion becomes in Deutsch's analysis of the Johnsonians a full-blown "secular religion."

Anderson bemoans the "cult of personality" and the "charismatic fallacy" in the followers of Foucault; Deutsch accepts and even values the very same things in Johnson's followers. Anderson's perspective is what we call critical; it dislikes fallacy and suspects belief. Deutsch's perspective is part of the 2002 English Institute's attempt to explore other ways of reading beyond the critical, what Michael Warner calls Uncritical Reading.

*****

Although "Argument and Ethos" was the first paper, the 2002 English Institute began to take shape ten months earlier, in December 2001, when the Board met to plan the conference. At that meeting, Michael proposed as a panel what he first called Pious Reading. There was not a lot of enthusiasm for that topic among us, until he retitled it as Uncritical Reading, making it clear that what he was interested in were ways of reading that we rule out of bounds by our disciplinary norm of critical reading. Instinctively receptive to anything that promises to call into question our limitations and blind spots, we immediately liked this topic of Uncritical Reading.

Our collective response to the two versions of his topic bears out what Warner in this volume says about our disciplinary formation. Our commitment to the critical makes us (like Anderson) suspicious of the pious; our commitment to the critical also makes us want to embrace the uncritical once we see it as our blind spot. (Hollywood's paper concludes dramatically with the paradox of this second response: "perhaps my allegiance to critical reading demands the annihilation of critical reading.")

In "Uncritical Reading," Warner writes: "The most obvious candidates for such a program of 'uncritical' reading are various styles of religious reading, but they are not the only ones." Although at the meeting Michael had begun by thinking of modes of religious reading (hence his invitation to Hollywood, a scholar in religious studies), we could see that his broader rubric included the panel Claudia Johnson had proposed on Author-Love. Understanding Author-Love as a species of Uncritical Reading, we chose to have two panels to explore types of reading transgressive of the critical. (Deutsch's paper was part of the

Author-Love panel, and it actually leads us to understand Author-Love as a kind of religious reading).

Besides panels with formal papers, the English Institute has for a number of years included a roundtable where we discuss a short text that those attending are asked to read. At the planning meeting for the 2002 Institute, Gayatri Spivak proposed Kant's "What Is Enlightenment?" for the roundtable. As we were envisioning two panels to explore what lay outside our critical norm, it seemed apropos to return to Kant and the formulation of our ongoing sense of the critical.

English Institute 2002 was shaping up to consider the Critical and the Uncritical, to reconsider and perhaps reopen what Warner calls "the axis of opposition fundamental to our institutional role." We then began wondering if we could come up with a genre panel to fit somehow with this larger topic; it was at this point that Jonathan Crewe proposed Polemic. We welcomed the topic with a sense that it somehow fit, but the terms of the fit were never articulated.

As I look at the papers now gathered together in this volume—three on Uncritical Reading, three on Polemic—I am more than ever convinced that the two topics fit together. The papers resonate with each other as they did in September 2002 but all the more so. Yet as editor of this volume, it falls to me to articulate the fit we felt but no one explained.

The first title I thought of for this volume was "Critical, Uncritical, Hypercritical." That formulation placed Polemic on the far side of critical, at the opposite extreme from uncritical. After reading over the papers, my assistant Kelly Klingensmith, having heard this provisional title, commented that Polemic seemed rather to be another form of uncritical reading.

If the central topic of this volume is a reconsideration of the opposition between critical and uncritical reading, the central question of the volume may be where along that "axis of opposition" do we place polemic: is it critical or uncritical?

*****

In part, it depends on what we mean by "critical." The most common meaning of the word is "inclined to judge severely, given to censuring." "Uncritical" would then mean "disinclined to judge severely," accepting. In this sense, polemic is definitively, undoubtedly, critical. While polemic is a mode of writing or speaking, it is also a mode of reading: one side reads the texts or discourse of the other side, finding errors and incriminating evidence. Polemical reading is extremely critical.

This definition ("inclined to judge severely") suggests that "critical" already means hypercritical; polemical reading would then be the epitome of critical reading. But although this definition is by its familiarity unavoidable, it is not the only, not even the primary definition of "critical" operating in this volume.

Starting with Warner's "Uncritical Reading" and consistently through Hollywood's and Deutsch's explorations of uncritical reading, "critical" refers to a disciplinary norm, to the model of reading appropriate to academic literary critics. Warner distinguishes this meaning of "critical" from the more usual sense of the critic as judging: "Critical reading is very different . . . from what the critic (in the usual sense) does. Indeed, someone who reads just to decide whether she likes something is more likely to be counted by us as an uncritical reader. The critical posture seems not to be the thumbs-up-thumbs-down decision . . . . More critical than the critic, we keep our thumbs where they are."

"More critical than the critic": In a certain way, our disciplinary notion of the critical might be called hypercritical. This distinction between our professional notion of critical and the more usual notion not only divides these two senses of the critical but exiles one of them out into the uncritical. If the critic-in-the-usual-sense is uncritical because of her inability to keep her thumbs to herself, the polemical reader would undoubtedly join her. The polemicist sticks his thumb out and points it down.

"Uncritical Reading" traces our professional idea of critical reading back to the text Gayatri wanted us all to read for English Institute 2002, Kant's "What Is Enlightenment?" Warner finds in Kant's text a contrast between two sorts of reading, critical reading and "replicative" reading. Critical reading is an example of independent thinking; the other sort of reading, the one Kant condemns as immature, "reli[es] on external authority."

Thinking of our papers, we can see Deutsch's Johnsonians and Anderson's Foucaultians practicing this sort of replicative reading. The critical reading Kant promotes is the opposite of such reverential reading; the critical attitude is the opposite of devotion, adoration, and love. Rather than attachment to an author as authority, critical reading is meant to lead to independence from authority.

Ever since Kant, Warner tells us, "critical reading has been identified with an ideal of critique as a negative movement of distanciation." This idea of critical reading as distanciation is seconded by Deutsch through her repeated use of the phrase "critical distance." As Warner articulates it however, we can begin to see this independence from authority bifurcate into two different stances: "critical reading has been identified with . . . a negative movement of distanciation, *whether of disengagement or repudiation* [emphasis added]."

While it always takes its distance, critical reading may simply disengage or on the other hand it may actively repudiate. The second mode, "repudiation," is what I would call polemical reading. If we follow Warner's formulation here, we can see the polemical as included in the critical, but we can at the same time see it as a separate type, a second, more aggressive, sort of distanciation.

Warner's contribution to this volume is followed by Hollywood's (originally presented as part of the Uncritical Reading panel Warner organized). Hollywood begins with an attempt to determine the meaning of "critical," situating it, as Warner does, within an academic discipline. While she carefully attends to the various specific meanings of "critical" in the history of her discipline, the overall effect of Hollywood's paper is to frame the opposition between critical and uncritical so as to parallel "the dichotomy between reason and love." Critical reading is on the side of reason (which fits the connection to Kant) and opposed to love. (Deutsch's paper likewise contrasts critical distance with admiration and author love.) The critical is the opposite of admiration, devotion and reverence; and so is the polemical. Thinking of our original three panels, polemic seems easily the opposite of author love.

Having formulated the axis of opposition as between reason and love, Hollywood however goes on parenthetically to suggest that the dichotomy is not just between reason and love but between "reason and the passions, reason and emotion." Love is definitely on the side of the uncritical, but what about passions we might see as the opposite of love? the emotions that impel a stance as strong as "repudiation?" the aggressive, adversarial passions which underwrite polemical reading?

Should the critical attitude be devoid of all passions, not just the reverent but the aggressive as well? Polemical reading is literally critical with a vengeance. This passion *for* the critical might disqualify the polemical from the normative model of critical reading.

While we all subscribe to critical reading, in what Warner calls "a ready consensus," the polemical has among us at best a controversial status. In this volume, Anderson and Spivak concur with Foucault in their dislike of polemic, their sense that polemic distorts argument, warps the critical. Crewe on the other hand champions polemic, defending it against Foucault's condemnation. Crewe cites polemic's crucial place in the history of criticism: "without feminist, queer, or postcolonial polemics, some of it ad hominem, there would be no academic fields corresponding to those designations. Without polemic directed at the New Critics . . . there would be no institutionalized post-structuralism in the U.S. academy."

Despite its undeniable value for the progress of our discipline, polemic, as Crewe puts it, "has a bad name in the humanities academy." The same disciplinary formation which commits us to the critical might want to rule the hypercritical out of bounds. Perhaps because its thumbs-down posture is too much part of the stance of the common critic from which the academic critic would distinguish himself. Crewe says that academics think "polemic belongs to the sphere of public journalism," which is the place where we are likely to find what Warner calls "critics (in the usual sense)." Or perhaps its shady reputation in our profession stems from something else Crewe's paper brings to our attention—polemic is entertaining.

*****

We at the English Institute certainly experienced this entertainment as we listened to Anderson quote Foucault and especially Menand quote Sarris. In his contribution to this volume, Crewe goes back to sixteenth century England, to the Marprelate controversy which he claims established "the enduring 'entertainment value' of print polemics." The Marprelate authors "made religious controversy openly a form of popular entertainment." Crewe connects this popular entertainment in the early modern print economy with the commodification of polemic in contemporary journalism, broadcasting, and certain exemplary academic careers.

According to Crewe, the Marprelate authors made polemic entertaining precisely by means of character: "by personifying themselves and their adversaries, they recast such polemic as robust comedy." This introduction of character into argument explains as well the "entertainment value" of contemporary accounts of twentieth-century debates, why we found ourselves at the English Institute enjoying Kael's attack on Sarris and Anderson's memorable characterizations of Habermas and Foucault.

It was undoubtedly the entertainment factor which prompted me to begin this introduction by focusing on character rather than argument. The entertainment at the 2002 English Institute was not just limited to our consideration of polemic. Hollywood's and Deutsch's explorations of uncritical reading were not only scholarly, cogent and insightful; at times they made us laugh.

And then there was Spivak's extemporaneous performance at the roundtable that closed the English Institute. Awed by the breadth of her knowledge, struggling to follow her difficult and important argument, we were at the same time entertained by what I would call Spivak's character, or maybe ethos.

At the end of this volume you will find a conversation with Spivak. In June 2003, I flew to New York to tape that conversation in the hope of capturing somehow both the argument and the character of Spivak's roundtable performance. In our transcribed conversation you will see that not only were we working to get that difficult argument down (she to articulate it, I to follow it), we were also amused, we were laughing.

Entertainment would seem to belong to the uncritical. Our disciplinary norm of critical reading opposes us not only to the reverent, but also to the entertaining. The thumbs-up/thumbs-down of the nonacademic critic belongs to the world of entertainment.

In Deutsch's paper, as in Warner's, the entertaining is the uncritical. But through her reading of the esteemed Johnson scholar Bertrand Bronson, we can see criticism's inability to exorcise the entertaining character that haunts our critical reading. Rather than an opposition between critical and uncritical, Deutsch's paper envisions the uncritical as the critical's shadowy double. (Warner too refers to "the enormous shadow of uncritical reading.") While Deutsch's and Anderson's images of shadows and haunting might suggest something threatening, these are the same uncritical aspects that those of us sitting there at the Institute last year experienced as entertaining.[5]

Menand's paper considers most directly this question of entertainment. Whereas we customarily oppose the "serious" and the "entertaining," Kael was not buying that opposition. "Kael's contention that 'serious' movies should be entertaining turned out to be," Menand tells us, "an extremely useful and widely adopted critical principle." Whereas "entertaining" would seem to belong with the uncritical, here it in fact becomes a critical principle. One that demands a different understanding of the relation between the "serious" and entertainment.

Like English professors advocating critical reading, what Menand calls "educated people" are suspicious of "entertainment."[6] Kael's triumph, as Menand sees it, was to "make popular entertainment respectable" to educated people. What Menand following Kael finds at the movies is "entertainment for educated people." What we at the English Institute found in Menand's paper as we laughed at Kael's wit (and Menand's too) was also "entertainment for educated people."

Anderson and Deutsch, despite vast differences between their positions, concur that argument cannot—however much it might want to—be separated from character. Their papers together, along with all the essays presented here, suggest that is good news indeed. In September 2002 we heard papers as entertaining as they were serious. Entertainment for educated people, and even beyond that, entertainment for educating people. These papers taught us a lot, from their impressive historical scholarship to their lucid theoretical interventions; they also had us laughing.

Notes

1. "Her": Reason is a female character in the medieval dialogue. Reading and rereading Hollywood, I was each time confused by the feminine pronouns to refer to "Reason," leading me to realize that I expect Reason to be a male character.
2. Of course, actual allegories often include historical figures.
3. In a note to his contribution to this volume, however, Crewe now denies that polemic is a genre ("Can Polemic Be Ethical?: A Response to Michel Foucault," note 7).
4. As I write this, I find myself wondering about my own character in the conversation with Spivak at the end of this volume. Definitely feeling like the straight man, I am in fact both pained and admiring when I feel like I don't understand.

5. Ghost stories are of course a genre of popular entertainment. Although I have been concentrating here on the laughter response (for reasons perhaps of emotional preference), entertainment produces a variety of sensations, including the thrill of fright.
6. Menand's "educated people" can be connected with the *Gelehrt* in Kant's "What Is Enlightenment?" (see Warner and Spivak).

1
Uncritical Reading

Michael Warner

I

Students who come to my literature classes, I find, read in all the ways they aren't supposed to. They identify with characters. They fall in love with authors. They mime what they take to be authorized sentiment. They stock themselves with material for showing off, or for performing class membership. They shop around among taste-publics, venturing into social worlds of fanhood and geekdom. They warm with pride over the national heritage. They thrill at the exotic and take reassurance in the familiar. They condemn as boring what they don't already recognize. They look for representations that will remediate stigma by giving them "positive self-images." They cultivate reverence and piety. They try to anticipate what the teacher wants, and sometimes to one-up the other students. They grope for the clichés that they are sure the text comes down to. Their attention wanders; they skim; they skip around. They mark pages with pink and yellow highlighters. They get caught up in suspense. They laugh; they cry. They get aroused (and stay quiet about it in class). They lose themselves in books, distracting themselves from everything else, especially homework like the reading I assign.

My work is cut out for me. My job is to teach them critical reading, but all these modes of their actual reading—and one could list count-less more—will tend to be classified as uncritical reading. What does it mean to teach critical reading, as opposed to all other kinds of reading? Are there any other kinds that can or should be taught?

Different teachers might have different ideas of how to do critical read-ing, but the axis of opposition is fundamental to our institutional role. Whether we are propounding new criticism, deconstruction, or cultural studies, our common enterprise is to discipline students out of their uncritical habits into critical reading—whatever we mean by that. Critical reading is the folk ideology of a learned profession, so close to us that we seldom feel the need to explain it. My own department requires of all entering graduate students a course called "Critical Reading." We don't specify anything about what will be taught in the course; how could we? The assumption is that any of our faculty can be trusted to convey the general idea—and no one should be burdened with expressing it.

The Cornell English department webpage begins with what I take to be a typical mission statement: "The Department of English teaches analytical and critical reading; lucid and effective writing; and studies in the values and problems of human experience and culture." Like most institutional prose, this proclamation is so careful to avoid controversy and *kulturkampf* that it wraps itself in banality. True, it is a consequential banality: because the critical profession has come to understand itself primarily as teaching "analytical and critical reading," some other justifications for the profession—notably the task of transmitting a prestigious heritage or canon—have proven difficult to sustain, once they have come to be seen as uncritical. But for the most part what is striking about this language is the apparent consensus behind it. And although the self-conception of the discipline seems perversely antagonistic to all the ways our students actually read, it has worked quite well—at least throughout the twentieth century—to legitimate the profession. With very different inflections over the past century, the normative program of critical reading has allowed literature departments to sell themselves as providing a basic element of education, despite a widely felt disenchantment with the idea of literature, which students in a technologically changing climate increasingly encounter as archaic.

Clearly, the idea resonates far beyond our own professional class. As we never tire of demonstrating, modern literature is itself full of fables of bad reading. Don't read like Quixote, like Emma Bovary, like Ginny Weasley. The rich overdetermination of such fables in modernity allows us to imagine ourselves as the bearers of a heroic pedagogy, the end of which is not the transmission of a canon or the catechistic incorporation of facts and pieties, but an open future of personal and collective liberation, of full citizenship and historical belonging. To quote another revealingly bland rallying cry: "Critical literacy means making one's self present as part of a moral and political project that links the production of meaning to the possibility for human agency, democratic community, and transformative social action."[1] We are here, we like to tell our students, to save you from habits of uncritical reading that are naive, immature, unexamined—or worse. Don't read like children, like vacation readers on the beach, like escapists, like fundamentalists, like nationalists, like antiquarians, like consumers, like ideologues, like sexists, like tourists, like yourselves.

Critical reading is evidently dense with social meaning; but its significance for modernity seems difficult to pin on any empirically describable practice of reading. Why is it apparently the case that any style of actual reading that we can observe in the world counts as uncritical? And how could it nevertheless seem that professors of literature regard the critical attitude as a necessary implication of reading itself? A suspicion begins to suggest itself: Is critical reading really reading at all? Is it an ideological description applied to people who are properly socialized into a political culture, regardless of how (or whether) they read? Or, granting a little more in charity: Is it not so much a reading practice as a notional derivative from a prior, uncritical reading that it must posit in order to exist? Is it a style of rereading, or discourse about reading, rather than reading per se?[2] Does it name the kind of liberal openness to self-questioning and reflective explicitation that could theoretically take any practice of reading as its occasion? Or is it more like a discipline, seeking to replace the raw and untrained practices of the merely literate with a cultivated and habitual disposition to read by means of another set of practices? If so, can those styles of reading be anatomized, or placed in a history of textual practice? If the latter, is this reading culture one of the formal-historical conditions of what counts as critical reason? A heroic pedagogy can be founded on textual techniques because of an imputed relationship between the practice of reading and critical reason, but what is that relationship?

The enormous shadow of *un*critical reading suggests another set of problems as well. Within the culture of critical reading it can seem that all the forms of uncritical reading—identification, self-forgetfulness, reverie, sentimentality, enthusiasm, literalism, aversion, distraction—are unsystematic and disorganized. Uncritical modes of reading, it would seem, are by definition neither reflective nor analytic. They must therefore prove untenable—i.e., transmute into the material of critical reading—when summoned to the bar of examination. Uncritical reading, it would seem, is naive; by its nature it cannot attain the coherence of a normative program of reading. It cannot constitute a real rival to what is called critical reading. Hence the ready consensus: If the choice is between critical and uncritical reading, who could be for the latter?

But what if it isn't true, as we suppose, that critical reading is the only way to suture textual practice with reflection, reason, and a normative discipline of subjectivity? If we begin to understand critical reading not simply as the coming-into-reflexivity of reading, but as a very special set of form relationships, then it might be easier to recognize rival modes of reading and reflection on reading as something other than pretheoretically uncritical. The most obvious candidates for such a program of "uncritical" reading are various styles of religious reading, but they are not the only ones. (An interesting point of comparison would be pornographic reading, which becomes a developed and familiar practice in the period of critical reading's ascendancy.)[3]

We tend to assume that critical reading is just a name for any self-conscious practice of reading. This assumption creates several kinds of fallout at once: It turns all reading into the uncritical material for an ever-receding horizon of reflective self-positing; by naturalizing critical reading as mere reflection it obscures from even our own view the rather elaborate forms and disciplines of subjectivity we practice and inculcate; it universalizes the special form of modernity that unites philology with the public sphere; and it blocks from view the existence of other cultures of textualism. In these ways it could be called a mistake or an ideology, but of course it is also the internal viewpoint of a culture with its own productive intensities, its own distinctive paradoxes, enabling even this essay, for better or worse.

Among the critics who have noticed the importance of what is usually left unthought as uncritical reading is Eve Kosofsky Sedgwick. In a suggestive polemical essay published as the introduction to *Novel-Gazing*, she argues that the dominant modes of academic criticism have drifted into an essentially paranoid suspicion of textual attachment.[4] Sedgwick's polemic targets a specific set of academic movements; but I suspect that most of what she excoriates as paranoid could be described as an extreme case in which norms of the critical have hypertrophied and become conspicuous. For reasons that might be various—such as the competitive positioning of professional discourse, which invites us to ensure that our own critical reflections will be more critical than those of our anticipated, imaginary critics—the critic adopts a projectively aggressive defensiveness in relation to the object of criticism.

Sedgwick identifies as the basic elements of paranoid reading (1) an anticipatory aversion to surprise, taken as the only security of knowledge; (2) a mimetic reflexivity in which the critic is seen as making explicit a latent or hidden reflexivity in the text; (3) a strong insistence on seeing everything in the terms of its central suspicions; (4) an interest only in negative affects; and (5) an apparently boundless faith in the efficacy of exposure. All of these can be seen as heightened versions of one or another normative project of the critical per se, though the degree of exaggeration is more visible in some, such as (4). The first, an anxiously anticipatory knowingness, is often hard to distinguish in practice from ordinary critical distance—at least when distanciation is taken as the necessary route to knowledge that is threatened by attachment, incorporation, or involvement, and where the object of analysis is credited with some anticipation of the critic's attempt to get distance on it. The second, an eliciting of a latent reflexivity attributed to the object, is a close cousin of a Romantic critical assumption I will return to later in connection with an observation by Walter Benjamin. The last, a faith in criticism as an act of exposure or demystification, is an article of faith in public-sphere forms, related to what I have elsewhere called a principle of supervision. In paranoid criticism it has become an imaginary and unmediated exposure, a power of mere knowingness. This faith in exposure is often implicit in what goes by the name *critique*.

In making her polemic against critical criticism, Sedgwick also seeks to articulate, legitimate, and promote a loose array of alternative commentary forms among queer academics, which she groups under the name "reparative reading." Reparative reading styles in her view have in common a rhetoric of attachment, investment, and fantasy about their textual occasions. For Sedgwick, these represent ways of reading that have been avoided or stigmatized as uncritical. They are certainly not preoccupied with critical distance toward their interpretive objects. But is reparative reading a structured program of reading or explication? For the most part Sedgwick describes it as local, detailed, and unsystematized. Even the patterns she singles out have this partial character, such as a willingness to describe fragments or passages without a total schematization of the text. For this reason, Sedgwick's reparative reading seems to be defined less by any project of its own than by its recoil from a manically programmatic intensification of the critical. It is not so much a method as (principled?) avoidance of method.

A rather different picture of critical reading and its uncritical other can be glimpsed in the work of anthropologist Saba Mahmood, even though Mahmood is not especially concerned with texts. Where Sedgwick sees an exaggerated criticism being countered by partial projects of attachment and reverie, Mahmood in a very different context draws a contrast between a critical ethic and another, rival system, often deemed uncritical, but equally organized and methodized as an ethical project. In a searching analysis of the women's mosque movement in Egypt, Mahmood shows its practical and ethical matrix is systematically misrecognized by feminists for whom the pursuit of autonomized agency through critical reflection is taken to be the only legitimate form of subjectivity. Mahmood works with women who aspire to be "slaves of God." This apparent abnegation of agency in fact turns out to be pursued by an elaborate program of reflection, ritual practice, mutual correction, commentary, reasoning, habit-formation, and corporeal discipline—in short, a cultivation of piety. Mahmood argues that piety in this context cannot be seen as an uncritical attitude, or a survival of premodern tradition, or passivity, or unreflective conformity; it must rather be seen as an ethical project (where "ethical" is understood in the terms of the later Foucault) that has as its end a particular conception of the human being. This conception is fundamentally incommensurable with that of critical citizenship. And here Mahmood draws a further conclusion. It is not enough to do a critique or critical reading of the piety movement, for this leaves unquestioned precisely what is at stake: namely, the way the enframing of knowledge as critical presupposes a project for being a certain kind of person. The standard of the critical, Mahmood suggests, could and should be parochialized in turn as an ethical discipline of subjectivity rather than as the transparent medium of knowledge.[5]

How could we extend Mahmood's insight about the critical to an understanding of critical reading and its relation to other, putatively uncritical modes of reading? Mahmood does not herself analyze the textual arts. But she does note as germane to her analysis that the pietists' preference for recitation as a mediation of Quranic text has to do with the cultivation of a dilated temporality to interrupt mundane time and reframe daily routine. Recitation and audition, in other words, are taken in this context to be techniques or arts for the inculcation of virtuous habits—not as a putatively primordial "orality" that would be the residual other of literacy. The important point in Mahmood's analysis, though, is not just a different technique of text-processing, or a different attitude about the text object, but a different kind of subject to which the technique is oriented.

Critical reading and uncritical reading, in this analysis, would need to be distinguished not so much on the basis of different technical methods, nor as reflective and unreflective versions of the mere processing of text artifacts, but as contrasting ways in which various techniques and forms can be embedded in an ethical problematic of subject-formation—in the case of critical reading, one oriented to freedom and autonomous agency against the background of a modern social imaginary. In the contrast between critical liberal secularism and the piety of the mosque movement, the difference can be very deep indeed, in a way made newly salient by the current political climate. But where cultures of textualism and their ethical projects are not thrown into such vivid contrast by the context of englobing struggles, it might be easy to miss the nuances by which reading practices are embedded within and organized by ethical projects for cultivating one kind of person or another. The broad contrast Mahmood draws between secular criticism and a specific tradition of Islamic piety, in other words, might be only the beginning, leading us to recognize that a great variety of text practices and ethical projects have been consolidated as, or assimilated to, the picture of critical reading—with everything else being left unthought as uncritical.

To pose the problem of critical and uncritical reading in this way is to ask new questions about what counts as critical, what it might be shorthand for, what distinct projects might be caught up in the tar of the uncritical, and how different ethical orientations might inflect different arts of commentary or practices of text-objectification and text-realization. This of course is a vast project. It is not my intention to undertake it here in any thorough way. I can neither give a full analysis of the kinds of agency and subjectivity that have at various points been classed as critical or uncritical, nor show in detail how they have been correlated with different textual arts. But I can try to suggest some ways that these questions can reframe existing scholarship in the history and theory of reading. In the remainder of this essay I revisit some of the main topoi in recent studies of the history of reading in order to pose, rather than answer, this question: how have various arts of commentary and practices of text-rendering come to be linked to the ethical projects organized on the axis of the critical and the uncritical? And what might we see in this history if we did not take critical reading as an invisible norm?

II

Surprisingly, given the volume of recent scholarship on the history of reading, I have found no history of the protocols and norms for a discipline of critical reading as such. Maybe this should not be surprising. Since literary critics tend to think of critical reading as the necessary form of any self-conscious reading, they seldom imagine it as the kind of practice that might have—as I think it does—a history, an intergeneric matrix of forms, a discipline. Histories of reading have been dominated either by inquiries into the material forms of texts or by the sort of simple classifications that can be made by outside observers without reference to the normative orientations of readers (e.g., "extensive" versus "intensive" reading, silent or vocalized, etc.). It is not immediately clear how a history of what counts as critical reading might be imagined, or what alternative reading disciplines might be misrecognized as uncritical.

Thanks to the energies of some very inventive historians of the book, however, there is a large literature that might be related to this topic. These historians have produced a new paradigm in which reading is understood as a highly variable practice, intimately related to the material organization of texts. They have denaturalized many of our assumptions about what it means to read. And this is essential in grasping what critical or uncritical reading could mean, since the mental image of critical reading seems to require at minimum a clear opposition between the text object and the reading subject—indeed, critical reading could be thought of as an ideal for maximizing that polarity, defining the reader's freedom and agency as an expression of distance from a text that must be objectified as a benchmark of distanciation.

This is precisely the sort of assumption about what texts are and how readers approach them (including this idea that texts are objects that readers "approach") that the new historians of reading dispute. They have shown that centuries of innovations in the formalization of easily navigable texts lie behind such a picture. Guglielmo Cavallo and Roger Chartier, in their survey of the new histories of reading, note that there is evidence from as early as the fourth or even fifth centuries BCE of "a reading style capable of reading 'through' a text and permitting attentive consideration, examination and probing of what was being read."[6] The great library of Alexandria, they note, gives evidence of specialized practices of entextualization and the rationalization of access:

> It was universal because it was dedicated to the preservation of books of all ages and from the entire known world; it was rational because the books it contained were to be reduced to order and to a system of classification . . . that enabled them to be arranged according to author, work and content. That universality and rationality, however, were directly dependent on writings that could be evaluated critically, copied, put into a book, categorized and placed with other books. (10)

Our history might evidently be a long one, if we think of critical reading this broadly. But what does "evaluated critically" mean here? This story usefully emphasizes the material conditions for the objectification and segmentation of discourse that are presupposed by the ideal of critical reading; and the contributors to Cavallo and Chartier's book add many more, such as the triumph of the codex format in antiquity to the elimination of *scriptio continua* in the late Middle Ages.

This scholarship has the great advantage of reminding us that what we call critical reading presupposes forms for textual objectification and a web of social relations around text objects. When ancient Greeks appointed readers—in some cases slaves—whose task was to vocalize texts of laws or monuments so that auditors might reflect on them, it would not have seemed obvious that the act of reading itself had a critical orientation.[7] A great many techniques of entextualization have to be laminated together to enable the free movement of critical evaluation in relation to its objects.[8] But did critical evaluation appear as the inevitable meaning of the new procedures of text-objectification? And could that mean the same thing for the monks of Alexandria and for modern students?

The modern idea of critical reading clearly draws on a very old tradition that has gone under other names for most of its history. Martin Irvine sees the textual culture of Western Europe as having had a remarkable continuity for more than 1,200 years in the *artes grammaticae* of the learned. Most of the forms of entextualization that are now simply taken for granted in the word *text* developed over this long history of *grammatica*, with its fourfold division of the *scientia interpretandi*: *lectio* (rules for construing and reciting); *enarratio* (rules for interpretation, including tropes, topics, syntax and semantics); *emendatio* (rules for authenticating and correcting); and *iudicium* (evaluation).[9] The modern idea of critical reading reorganizes this tradition, enfolding the last three of the four categories. And there are many features of the scholarly textual culture that of course came to be paradigmatic of uncritical reading. For example, the performance of critical reading as a mode of free agency requires that it not be seen as a strict application of rules, in the manner of *grammatica*. But because *grammatica* formalized a fundamental relation between a systematized analytic metalanguage and its codified entextualized objects, critical reading could modify the metapragmatic framework while maintaining most of the older forms of textual objectification. The modern idea also continued the pattern in *grammatica* of imagining the specialized techniques of literacy as the model of a much broader normative program—the first of the liberal arts. "Learning, interpretation, and religious understanding," Irvine writes, "were all defined in the terms of the large field of discourse that spread out from the practice of grammatica in schools, libraries and scriptoria."[10]

What we mean by critical reading obviously has deep roots, some phases of which (such as humanist philology) have been studied with more attention than others.[11] The phrase *critical reading* itself, though commonly taken by us to indicate a natural kind of reading—right, reasonable, free, and good, but often not much more specific than that— is, however, a relatively recent coinage, its current sense being difficult to find before the eighteenth century. It can be clearly seen in Romantic aesthetic philosophy, where already it is fused with the concept of the

work of art. This was demonstrated in a brilliant work by the young
Walter Benjamin:

> The immanent tendency of the work and, accordingly, the standard for
> its immanent criticism are the reflection that lies at its basis and is
> imprinted in its form. Yet this is, in truth, not so much a standard of
> judgment as, first and foremost, the foundation of a completely differ-
> ent kind of criticism—one which is not concerned with judging, and
> whose center of gravity lies not in the evaluation of the single work but
> in demonstrating its relations to all other works and, ultimately, to the
> idea of art. . . . Criticism of a work is, rather, its reflection, which can
> only, as is self-evident, unfold the germ of the reflection that is imma-
> nent to the work. . . . For the value of a work depends solely on whether
> it makes its immanent critique possible or not.[12]

With this conception of art, Romanticism deepened the ideal of
critical reading, as opposed to any other kind of reading, making it
seem like the unfolding of the necessity of art itself. From this point
the adjective *critical* acquires a new salience.

This conception rests, however, on earlier developments, such as the
apparent universalization of the critical role in the public sphere.[13] Its
importance to our pedagogy almost certainly has to do with even later
developments, in the late nineteenth and early twentieth century, since it
explicates and makes possible the kind of discourse that constitutes the
profession itself. The critical reading we teach, in other words, might be
largely projected from our own circulatory practices. I suspect it is indeed
an essential element of critical reading that the reader be imagined as a
producer of discourse. Critical *reading,* in this context, means a discipline
of *commentary,* projected as immanent to reading. But a real explanation
must go farther; the self-interest of professionalized critics is insufficient
to explain how a profession oriented to the teaching of critical reading
could justify itself as a necessity to nonprofessionals.

Obviously, more is at stake than mere text-processing, at one
extreme, or the virtuosic textualism of professional critics, at the other
extreme. Because the techniques of distanciating knowledge are tied to
a subjectivity-forming ascesis toward freedom and have come to define

agency in modern culture, a discipline of critical reading can draw on the widest cultural-historical meanings of critical reason. We can see this in Immanuel Kant's "What is Enlightenment?," which derives so much from the idea of critical reading. "It is so easy to be immature!" he exclaims in the second paragraph. "If I have a book to have understanding in place of me . . . I need not make any efforts at all." Kant contrasts this immature, replicative reading with the public use of reason, of which his supreme example is "a man of learning addressing the entire reading public." His assumption, evidently, is that the readers of that public must read differently from the immature person.

The effort that Kant thought readers should make in order to read for themselves takes on, for him, the coloration of the rest of his project; critical reading is an image of a certain kind of critical reason. And that association has left its imprint. Kant's English translators used the French word *critique* to translate the German word *kritik*, thus creating within English a difference between *criticism* and *critique*. This may have been done to capture the special sense of *kritik* in Kant as (in Walter Benjamin's phrase) "an esoteric term for the incomparable and completed philosophical standpoint"; but its subsequent usage is much broader.[14] Ever since, critical reading has been identified with an ideal of critique as a negative movement of distanciation, whether of disengagement or repudiation. (Ironically this might be most true within cultural studies, which often prides itself in anti-Kantianism.)

There is a great deal of continuity between Kant's picture of critical reading and dominant ideologies of reading in twentieth-century public culture, as can be seen in such manuals as *How to Read a Book*, the 1940 classic by Mortimer Adler and Charles Van Doren, or more recently *How to Read and Why*, by Harold Bloom. Adler and Van Doren call their model "active reading," and they make it clear that they intend a whole style of personality and culture to flow from the practices that they recommend. It is, quite clearly, a *discipline*. Just as Kant exclaims that, "If I have a book to have understanding in place of me . . . I need not make any efforts at all," so Adler and Van Doren write that "to pass from understanding less to understanding more by your own intellectual effort in reading is something like pulling yourself up by your bootstraps."[15] For Bloom as well, the problem of reading is essentially one of individual self-positing. His book opens with this declaration: "It matters, if individuals are to retain any capacity to form their own judgments and opinions, that they continue to read for themselves."[16]

Kant suggests that the difference between his two models of reading is that between a reliance on external authority and the maturity-bestowing exercise of independent thought—a difference, in other words, within the individual. But if we were to inquire into the history of this normative program, surely we would want to cast our net a little wider than the individual reader. The new histories of reading suggest that a vast cultural matrix is condensed into, and taken for granted as, critical reading: complex practices of entextualization and explicit metadiscourse (archives, annotation, indices, debate genres, commentary, summary and paraphrase, critical essays, professional scholarship, research). These allow reading to be understood as realizing a set of normative stances (especially critical distance, reflexivity, and explicitness, but generally others as well, such as independence, irony, or subversiveness) that in turn produce kinds of subjectivity (autonomy, individuality, freedom, citizenship, enlightenment) structured by a hierarchy of faculties.[17]

One might be forgiven, given the derivation of the word *critic*, for thinking that critical reading is oriented to judgments of value, to sorting worth. Critical reading, one might think, would be reading that reflects on its own aesthetic judgments. But one would evidently be wrong. Professionalized literary criticism has for the most part given up the business of taste-making; that has been turned over to unprofessionalized book reviewers. Critical reading is very different, it seems, from what the critic (in the usual sense) does. Indeed, someone who reads just to decide whether she *likes* something is more likely to be counted by us as an uncritical reader. The critical posture seems not to be the thumbs-up-thumbs-down decision of aesthetic judgment. (Benjamin notes this in the passage quoted above.) Aesthetic judgment is practiced in countless domains; but when was the last time you heard solemn injunctions to practice critical gardening, or critical hairstyling?

To some degree the separation of criticism from taste can be seen already in the Aristotelian conception of the *kritikos*. Aristotle methodically distinguishes his critical judgment from the taste judgments of audiences or the publics of popular contests. Criticism is the practice of the few, not of the many. The critic's work, as Andrew Ford summarizes it, "is not to evaluate the moral or ethical value of particular poems, but to derive from an examination of all forms of poetry the principles governing each kind and determining its proper pleasure."[18] The critic thus comes into being as the counterpart not only of the work, but of the audience. Nevertheless Aristotle uses the term *kritikos* to describe a man of judgment in general, and it is skill in judgment that makes literary criticism a mode of ethical life and citizenship. The modern ideal of critical reading means something quite different. Like Aristotle's, it also entails—more explicitly in some cases than in others—an ethical personality and a model of citizenship. But it has to do less with habits and skills of judgment than with openness to criticism. Indeed, one of its hallmarks is the reservation of judgment.

Despite the differences between the ancient and modern understandings of the critical role, much can be learned about the nature of critical reading from Ford's historical account, *The Origins of Criticism: Literary Culture and Poetic Theory in Classical Greece*. Ford's insight is that the main constituents of literary criticism—the idea of genre, the conception of poesis as artifact-making, formal criteria of value—reorganized the archaic song and performance practices that criticism purported merely to describe. Thus the earliest recorded judgments of worth about song have to do with appropriateness to context, where song is primarily understood as ritual performance in an ethical environment of context-specific obligations. Gradually such performances came to be reclassified as belonging not just to their immediate occasions but also to formally defined classes of comparable performances: genres. The new mode of judgment entailed both gain and loss, since the ethical context of judgment—in which assessing song was a matter of determining the nature of the social occasion and one's proper comportment in it—could now be provisionally set aside.

For those who were willing, in certain contexts, to dispense altogether with moral and ethical considerations in assessing artistic merit, the loss of these criteria was compensated for by making linguistic form expressive in itself. "Song" had become "poetry," and poetry was a special art of using language, the paradigmatic example of what we have called since the eighteenth century "literature."[19]

The process by which performances were objectified, classified, entextualized, systematized as genre, and circulated (as, for example, in

contests) was long and conflicted. By the time of the schools it result-
ed in a special mode of evaluation, systematically distinguished from
ordinary judgments of ethical appropriateness or taste, practiced by
sophists and philosophers. The increasing use of writing for song texts
obviously played some role in the process, but it would be extremely
reductive to think that the transformation could be explained by such
simple categories as "oral" and "written." The emergence of the critic
required new conceptions of what a text was, what class of things it
resembled (skilled artifacts), how it was related to a producer (poet),
how it might be classified apart from its performance context. In each
case, earlier conceptions had to be displaced in order to make room for
new, critic-friendly categories such as genre. "It is Romantic to think of
some fall from pure unstructuredness into genres," Ford writes; "what
the fourth-century literary theorists did was transform traditional religious and social structures that had had implications for form into literary and formal structures that had implications for society and
religion."[20] What Ford's analysis helps us to understand in concrete
detail is that the role of the critic is not merely reading—that is, a relation between a knower and a text. It presupposes a complex history of
entextualization and a reordering of social occasions.

Adler and Van Doren demonstrate this unwittingly throughout *How
to Read a Book*. At one point, for example, they offer a summary of four
"rules" of analytical reading:

1. Classify the book according to kind and subject matter.
2. State what the whole book is about with the utmost brevity.
3. Enumerate its major parts in their order and relation, and outline
   these parts as you have outlined the whole.
4. Define the problem or problems the author is trying to solve.[21]

Anyone who attempts to gain critical distance on a text by means of
such rules must be equipped with well-codified notions such as "book"
and "author"; an assumed realm of discourse in which things are classified "according to kind and subject matter"; genres of propositional summary ("state what the whole book is about with the utmost brevity") and
a language ideology in which such derivative genres can be seen not as
wholly separate texts but restatements of the same meaning, thus

abstracting meaning from textual form; a vigorously delineated sense of
totality ("outline these parts as you have outlined the whole"); an
assumption that the text-object was created by the same canons of organization; and so on. Each of these steps posits a prior stage of reading, as
the source of the comprehension that equips us to do all these things.
(You must read the book before you can classify it by subject matter, for
example.) The rules themselves are not about reading per se, but about
the manipulation of a whole battery of entextualizing frames and form
relationships. All of this apparatus must exist at least notionally as means
to establish precisely a gap between critical knowledge and the prior,
uncritical reading it posits, while also asserting that what is achieved is
just "reading"—albeit of an especially rewarding and useful kind.

The more we learn about the history of reading, the more we learn how
peculiar this formation is. For example, the culture of reading that rests
on the idea of grasping the totality of a text might turn out to be a relatively minor episode in the overall history of reading. In a remarkable
recent essay, Peter Stallybrass describes the importance of various styles of
discontinuous reading. Like the idea of the text as totality, these frag-
menting practices were enabled by the codex format, which allows readers to jump around in texts fairly freely, with indices and bookmarks and
fingers wedged between pages. One very prestigious example would be
the reading of scripture. John Locke once complained (in *A Paraphrase
and Notes on the Epistles of St. Paul*) that the custom of printing scripture
in verse/chapter divisions prevented common readers from grasping the
sacred text as a whole.[22] But Stallybrass shows that Locke's idea was something of an innovation, and one that ran counter to the institutional practice of bible reading in church services. During the heyday of the genre of
the novel, he suggests, the continuous paging through of a single text
came to be taken as the normal way of reading, but this was not the case
in earlier periods, and in the current development of screen literacies it
may no longer be true. "When cultural critics nostalgically recall an imagined past in which readers unscrolled their books continuously from
beginning to end, they are *reversing* the long history of the codex and the
printed book as indexical forms. The novel has only been a brilliantly per-
verse interlude in the long history of discontinuous reading."[23]

In imagining that one might try to grasp the Bible as a textual whole,
the better to position oneself as its understanding reader, Locke was

extending some recent innovations in scriptural commentary—the beginnings of what would eventually come to be called the Higher Criticism. (See Amy Hollywood's essay in this volume for an account of how classical scholarship and scriptural exegesis converged in that history.) He was probably influenced in some measure by Spinoza's *Theological-Political Treatise,* published in 1670.[24] Spinoza was well aware of the novelty of the method he there proposed for reading the Bible:

> Now to put it briefly, I hold that the method of interpreting Scripture is no different from the method of interpreting Nature, and is in fact in complete accord with it. For the method of interpreting Nature consists essentially in composing a detailed study of Nature from which, as being the source of our assured data, we can deduce the definitions of the things of Nature. Now in exactly the same way the task of Scriptural interpretation requires us to make a straightforward study of Scripture, and from this, as the source of our fixed data and principles, to deduce by logical inference the meaning of the authors of Scripture.[25]

Text can be assimilated to natural objects, and thus become data for the detached analysis that is here explicitly modeled on scientific method. As Spinoza continues, it becomes clear that the codex format is necessary to his method. His second rule (following the necessity of philological understanding of ancient languages) is as follows:

> The pronouncements made in each book should be assembled and listed under headings, so that we can thus have to hand all the texts that treat of the same subject. Next, we should note all those that are ambiguous or obscure, or that appear to contradict one another. Now here I term a pronouncement obscure or clear according to the degree of difficulty with which the meaning can be elicited from the context, and not according to the degree of difficulty with which its truth can be perceived by reason. For the point at issue is merely the meaning of the texts, not their truth. (88)

The ensuing analysis demonstrates vividly the sort of athletic collation necessary to analyze the contradictions, discrepancies, figurational patterns, shifts of address and pronominal usage, narrative redundancies and digressions, and other textual features that become the "data" of understanding. He does dwell on particular passages—worrying over what could be meant by the expression "God is fire," for example—but the agency of interpretation is everywhere manifested by movement between passages, like the movement necessary to realize that "God is fire" contradicts other claims and must be understood in a special sense. Spinoza's method thus foregrounds his own (critical) agility of movement, including a physical movement back and forth among numbered and indexed pages in a fixed sequence, at the same time that it backgrounds an ideal of (uncritical) continuous reading.

In his reading of Jeremiah, that backgrounded ideal is the standard against which the text can be shown to fail, since Jeremiah begins narratives, drops them, gives multiple versions of the same story, loops back in apparent self-forgetfulness, "continuing to pile up prophecies with no regard of chronological order, until in chapter 38 he resumes what he began to relate in chapter 21, as if the intervening fifteen chapters were a parenthesis," and so on. This is the sort of thing you can say about a text given the ease of discontinuous textual checking needed to discover the text's apparent corruption. A great deal of page-turning and note-taking must have been involved in this project of evaluating the sacred text as a whole. It is the method of a scholar provided with ample learning, time, industry, paper, and finding aids.

Compare Spinoza's reading of Jeremiah to that of his close contemporary, Mary Rowlandson. She, too, manipulated the codex format of the Bible in a way that she understood as enjoined upon her in the sincere effort at understanding. While held captive by an Amerindian war party in the woods of New England in the winter of 1676, she took up the Bible that had been given her by one of the Indians, opened its pages at random, and read what she understood to be the passages presented to her eye by Providence:

> I opened my Bible to read, and the Lord brought that precious scripture to me, Jeremiah 31.16. Thus saith the Lord, refrain thy voice from weeping, and thine eyes from tears, for thy work shall be rewarded, and they shall come again from the land of the enemy. This was a sweet cordial to me, when I was ready to faint, many and many a time have I sat down, and wept sweetly over this scripture.[26]

Rowlandson is just the sort of reader about whom Locke complained; the sense of the whole is not an aim of her reading. Sincere understanding, for her, does not require analytic collation, linguistic comparison, contextual framing, or any other effort at detachment from the rhetoric of address. The relevant unit is the verse. This might have something to do with the practice of memorization, since the verse divisions of scripture were convenient gobbets for internalization. But there is a richer normative program behind this apparently arbitrary selection as well. Her way of reading is enframed by the assumption that the text is everywhere uniformly addressed by God, in the vernacular, to the believer. Rowlandson performs the same ritual repeatedly throughout her captivity, and makes it clear that opening the Bible and lighting on a passage is, for her, the way to allow God to direct her reading. The apparently random movements offered by the codex format are the medium not of critical agency but of providential direction. The chance opening of the pages helps to ensure that her reading will *not* be an expression of her agency.

Of course, that does not mean that it is passive, either. Quite the contrary: it requires repetition, incorporation, and affective regulation. She sits down and weeps, and within the framework of her reading protocol this way of taking the text to heart is a necessary activity of understanding. Nor was Rowlandson's method entirely naive. It was supported by an extensive and self-conscious literature of devotional manuals on the reading of scripture. As one scholar of that literature notes, "Going over the same biblical passages, putting oneself through the stages of the redemptive order, rereading favorite manuals again and again, produced a cumulative effect that our twentieth-century desire for novelty fails to comprehend."[27] An elaborate edifice of theology, of type and antitype, lies behind the (to us) unfathomable idea that second-person address in the verses of Jeremiah could be taken as directed immediately to a weeping hostage in the woods of an Anglo-American colony.

Rowlandson's reading of Jeremiah foregrounds the elemental dyad of God and the soul as the situation of address. It is a situation rich with activity. Recognition of the text by the reader is among other things the medium of God's agency in comforting and reviving her, and of her agency in obeying, placing trust, suppressing self, etc. She construes the text as immediate demand upon her, and upon her emotions. (It is sometimes argued that this kind of ethicalization of address is typical of manuscript culture, but quite apart from the fact that Rowlandson was reading a printed Bible it would be hard to sustain the causal claims implied in that analysis.)

Spinoza, too, sees existential demands being placed on the reader by divine truth. But for him the situation of address in which divinity discloses itself to the soul requires that he objectify the text's situation of address, its orientation to context, its historical occasion, the limited capacities of its original addressees, and so on. The critical reader must be prepared to extract the text from a context deemed to be its primary situation; in extreme versions texts can be judged in what is taken to be a context of no context. At any rate, the critic's judgment is not in the first instance about context-appropriateness. Interpretation has been in this limited sense de-ethicalized; though in Spinoza's case only by introducing a new ethical agency of interpretive objectification. Paradoxically, Spinoza's reader becomes more responsible by considering himself less directly addressed.

To readers in the discipline of modernity, one of these ways of reading Jeremiah will count as critical, the other as uncritical. What is the difference? The answer to that question must have to do not just with the material object—though the physical Bibles in question already objectify a great many assumptions about text, held in common by both readers—but with the enframing, metapragmatic construal of the situation of reading, including the agency and affective subjectivity of the reader, the ends and means of reading, and the encompassing relationships of reading practice, the way the text is organized indexically around its reading. All of this is immanent to reading, an imaginary and therefore partially unconscious grasping of the situation of reading itself.

Scholars of literature are however seldom prepared to recognize in their own materials anything that they would have to describe as uncritical reading. So the ritual gesture, when confronted with a Rowlandson, is to show that this apparently uncritical reading really was critical in some sense or another. Thus Rowlandson can be said to read the way she does as a strategy for subverting ministerial authority, or as a means of self-positing.[28] When critical reading is established as a global language of value, such maneuvers become necessary to rescue texts for any canon, even the anticanonical canon. We are very good at assimilating texts and authors to the normative ideals of our own critical activity. But those normative dimensions of her reading practice that cultivate piety—precisely in the suppression of what we would call critical distance or agency—must be ignored or explained away.

So one of the deepest challenges posed by rival, uncritical frameworks of reading is recognizing that they are just that, rival frameworks. The very specific culture of critical reading is not the only normatively or reflexively organized method of reading, to which all others should be assimilated. Because the historiography is still emerging, and because the tendency to project critical reading as the necessary implication of reason or agency is so great, we do not even know as much as we would like about what the alternative frameworks have been, are, or might become in a future of screen literacies. Uncritical reading is the unconscious of the profession; whatever worlds are organized around frameworks of reading other than critical protocols remain, for the most part, terra incognita.[29]

Any attempt to trace the history, extent, and limits of the culture of critical reading will face methodological issues that will force us to go beyond the current state of the history of the book. The new history of reading usefully defamiliarizes the picture of reading as the mere processing of preconstituted text, and leads us to consider the practices of entextualization. The "materiality of the text" has become something of a slogan for this project. But what needs to be defamiliarized is not just the materiality of the text. The history of reading encompasses the normative construal of the reading situation—including the agency of the reader—as an element of that reading situation. A history of "critical reading" in particular, therefore, would have to include rather more than the protocols of text-processing, cross-referencing, and citation that Spinoza so beautifully exemplifies; it would have to describe the way in which reading subjects can be imagined to assert their own agency and freedom in relation to maximally objectified texts.

In Spinoza's case a significant part of that situation is right on the surface; he himself makes it clear that the basic interpretive posture behind his analysis is one that he expects not just of the erudite philosopher, and not just of the reader of scripture, but of the subject in a society of mutual benefit. He imagines a social order that is constituted out of individual acts of judgment, from the bottom up. Texts considered as quasi-natural objects serve as the foil for readers who can extract themselves from the immediate situation of address, exerting their own agency. Those readers are in relation to each other by means of derivative discourses of argument and analysis, so their reading can be at once the medium of internal differentiation and the common reference points in a world of difference. The *Theological-Political Treatise* is indeed remarkable for the clarity with which its exegetical method is explicitly linked to a picture of a market-based republican social order. That, of course, should not prevent us from seeing that in other ways the picture of agentialized subjectivity in critical reading is a structuring element in the social imaginary behind the treatise.[30]

Indeed, treatise form itself—as exemplified in the *Theological-Political Treatise*—presupposes a certain reading culture, in which book-length texts are taken as systematized arguments to be attributed *in toto* to their authors as intellectual property, such that we can say, "In Spinoza we find *x,*"; or, "Spinoza holds that *x,*" and so on.[31] As Pierre Hadot has recently pointed out, this conception of treatise form represents a watershed in the metaconception of philosophizing. As philosophy came to be more and more identified with this specialized textual form following Descartes, philosophy came to stand less and less for a counternormative way of living and became more and more an architecture of propositional property.[32] The texts of philosophy came less and less to be artifacts of dialogue or scripts of spiritual exercise, and came instead to be models of objectifiable systematicity. In this role they began to serve as the ideal self-image of philosophizing—though of course philosophical writing could only play this role once texts had been conceived as intellectual property and as navigable totalities offered to readers for the performance of their own critical agency. In countless such ways, the entextualizing activity of the critical reader always lies beyond the grasp of critical reading.

A systematic inquiry into the form-relationships of critical reading, in addition to opening up inquiry into the alternatives currently glossed as uncritical, might also help to break through a number of impasses in contemporary thinking. The discipline of subjectivity enjoined upon the critical reader, for example, is one thing that is often missed in contemporary critiques of the Kantian tradition, or of the critical reason that he is thought to exemplify. Perhaps the mistake here is to identify a Kantian metalanguage with the culture he sought to codify, crediting him with too much. There is certainly a tendency in the liberal tradition to identify critical reason with something that cannot be given content, that is not a cultural form in itself, but that is conceived as mere negative potential, a kind of perpetual openness to further criticism. By the same token, critical reading can be imagined in negative terms as well, as reading that is open to reflection on its own presuppositions, for example. The importance of this receding horizon of critique to the culture of critical reading might help to explain why it seems so difficult for anyone to define or codify critical reading; to do so would be to expose oneself to further criticism, and thus fail to exhaust its meaning. This normative language is consequential and not to be waved away as trivial. But it distracts attention from the equally important reality that critical reading is a historically and formally mediated practice, with an elaborate discipline of subjectivity, and one that now confronts rivals as it has done in the past. That practice—as the example of Spinoza suggests—is by no means coextensive with the Kantian or neoKantian glossings of it. And the rich intensities it affords are obscured both by its own normative self-conception and by the most common criticisms of it.

For example, Bernard Williams faults the Kantian conception of critical reason for what he sees as its essentially characterless disengagement. His comments would apply, *mutatis mutandis*, to some of the most powerful self-conceptions of critical reading:

> This ideal involves an idea of ultimate freedom, according to which I am not entirely free so long as there is any ethically significant aspect of myself that belongs to me simply as a result of the process by which I was contingently formed. If my values are mine simply in virtue of social and psychological processes to which I have been exposed, then (the argument goes) it is as though I had been brainwashed: I cannot be a fully free, rational, and responsible agent. Of course, no one can control their upbringing as they receive it, except perhaps marginally and in its later stages. What the ideal demands, rather, is that my whole outlook should in principle be exposed to a critique, as a result of which every value that I hold can become a consideration for me, critically accepted, and should not remain merely something that happens to be

part of me. It presupposes a Platonic idea of the moral self as characterless. . . . If the aspiration makes sense, then the criticising self can be separated from everything that a person contingently is—in itself, the criticising self is simply the perspective of reason or morality.[33]

Whether this is an accurate objection to liberal philosophy I leave to others. What interests me here is that the endlessly receding ideal of critical reason described by Williams arises from a historically rich culture of reading in which the critical activity is anything but empty, characterless, or unmediated. The rigorous extraction of oneself from the ethical demands of direct textual address, for example, requires a manipulation of intergeneric relationships that can only seem characterless once they have become second nature—as to most of us they have. Critical reading is the pious labor of a historically unusual sort of person. If we are going to inculcate its pieties and techniques, we might begin by recognizing that that is what they are.

Notes

1. Henry Giroux, "Introduction" to Paulo Freire and Donaldo Macedo, *Literacy: Reading the Word and the World* (South Hadley, MA: Bergin and Gervey, 1987), 15.
2. Barbara Johnson speculates on this possibility in *The Critical Difference* (Baltimore: Johns Hopkins University Press, 1980), 3–4 and *passim*.
3. See Jean Marie Goulemot, *Ces livres qu'on ne lit que d'une main* (Paris: Editions Alinea, 1991), trans. by James Simpson for some reason as *Forbidden Texts: Erotic Literature and Its Readers in Eighteenth-Century France* (Philadelphia: University of Pennsylvania Press, 1995).
4. "Paranoid Reading and Reparative Reading; or, You're So Paranoid, You Probably Think This Introduction is About You," in *Novel-Gazing: Queer Readings in Fiction*, ed. Eve Kosofsky Sedgwick (Durham: Duke University Press, 1997), 1–37.
5. Saba Mahmood, *Politics of Piety* (Princeton: Princeton University Press, 2004). The idea that the disciplines of piety should be not simply understood to be criticized but understood in a way that will parochialize the knower's assumptions is one that for Mahmood represents a higher and better understanding of critique: "Critique, I believe, is most powerful when it leaves open the possibility that we might also be remade in the process of engaging another's worldview, that we might come to learn things that we did not already know before we undertook the engagement" (36–37).
6. Guglielmo Cavallo and Roger Chartier, eds., *A History of Reading in the West* (Amherst: University of Massachusetts Press, 1999): introduction, 9.

7. Jesper Svenbro, "Archaic and Classical Greece: The Invention of Silent Reading," in Cavallo and Chartier, *History of Reading*, 37–63.

8. Here I owe much to Michael Silverstein and others. See *Natural Histories of Discourse,* ed. Michael Silverstein and Greg Urban (Chicago: University of Chicago Press, 1996).

9. Martin Irvine, *The Making of Textual Culture: 'Grammatica' and Literary Theory, 350–1100* (Cambridge: Cambridge University Press, 1994).

10. Irvine, *Making of Textual Culture,* p. 461.

11. See Anthony Grafton, *Defenders of the Text: The Traditions of Scholarship in an Age of Science, 1450–1800* (Cambridge, MA: Harvard University Press, 1991).

12. Walter Benjamin, "The Concept of Criticism in German Romanticism," *Selected Writings, Volume 1: 1913–1926*, ed. Marcus Bullock and Michael Jennings (Cambridge: Harvard University Press, 1996), 116–200, quotation at p. 159.

13. On the changing social meaning of the critic's role, see Joan Dejean, *Ancients against Moderns: Culture Wars and the Making of a Fin de Siècle* (Chicago: University of Chicago Press, 1997), 31–77.

14. Benjamin, "The Concept of Criticism in German Romanticism," p. 117.

15. Mortimer J. Adler and Charles Van Doren, *How to Read a Book* (1940), rev. ed. 1972 (New York: Simon and Schuster), 8.

16. Harold Bloom, *How to Read and Why* (New York: Scribner, 2001), 21.

17. In *Publics and Counterpublics* I have argued that one of the most important frameworks for allowing reading to count as the use of reason in Kant's sense is in fact an intergeneric field of circulation ideologized as a public. "The attribution of agency to publics works in most cases because of the direct transposition from private reading acts to the sovereignty of opinion. All of the verbs for public agency are verbs for private reading, transposed upward to the aggregate of readers. Readers may scrutinize, ask, reject, opine, decide, judge, etc. Publics can do exactly these things. And nothing else. Publics, unlike mobs or crowds, remain incapable of any activity that cannot be expressed through such a verb. Activities of reading that do not fit the ideology of reading as silent, private, replicable decoding, curling up, mumbling, fantasizing, gesticulating, ventriloquizing, writing marginalia, etc. also find no counterparts in public agency." Thus where the modern imaginary of the public sphere is the background of literate practice, this hierarchy of faculties will acquire a certain inevitable force.

18. Andrew Ford, *The Origins of Criticism: Literary Culture and Poetic Authority in Classical Greece* (Princeton: Princeton University Press, 2002), 266.

19. Ford, *Origins*, p. 22. Ford makes similar points throughout his study, as for example p. 155: "what might be called an increasing 'textualization' of song through the fifth century abetted the formal study of its 'inner' properties."

20. Ford, *Origins*, p. 251.

21. Adler and Van Doren, *How to Read a Book*, p. 95.

22. See Patrick Collinson, "The Coherence of the Text: How it Hangeth Together: The Bible in Reformation England," in *The Bible, the*

Reformation and the Church, ed. W. P. Stephens (Sheffield: Sheffield Academic Press, 1995), 84–108.

23. Peter Stallybrass, "Books and Scrolls: Navigating the Bible," in Jennifer Andersen and Elizabeth Sauer, eds., *Books and Readers in Early Modern England* (Philadelphia: University of Pennsylvania Press, 2002), 42–79, quotation at p. 47.
24. On the transmission and impact of this early work of Spinoza's, see Jonathan Israel, *Radical Enlightenment: Philosophy and the Making of Modernity 1650–1750* (Oxford: Oxford University Press, 2002).
25. Baruch Spinoza, *Theological-Political Treatise,* trans. Samuel Shirley (Indianapolis: Hackett, 2001), 87.
26. Mary Rowlandson, *The Sovereignty and Goodness of God* (1682), in Myra Jehlen and Michael Warner, eds., *The English Literatures of America, 1500–1800* (New York: Routledge, 1997), p. 357.
27. Charles Hambrick-Stowe, *The Practice of Piety: Puritan Devotional Disciplines in Seventeenth-Century New England* (Chapel Hill: University of North Carolina Press, 1982), 159. Further information on the hermeneutic context can be found in Lisa M. Gordis, *Opening Scripture: Bible Reading and Interpretive Authority in Puritan New England* (Chicago: University of Chicago Press, 2003), though unfortunately Gordis does not mention Rowlandson and does not raise the larger questions posed here. A very instructive piece of scholarship is the chapter by David D. Hall titled "Readers and Writers in Early New England," in *A History of the Book in America, Volume One: The Colonial Book in the Atlantic World,* ed. Hugh Amory and David D. Hall (Cambridge: Cambridge University Press, 2000), 117–51, as well as pp. 377–410 in the same work.
28. The most ingenious such reading is Mitchell Breitweiser, *American Puritanism and the Defense of Mourning: Religion, Grief, and Ethnology in Mary White Rowlandson's Captivity Narrative* (Madison: University of Wisconsin Press, 1990).
29. For the most part; see such notable exceptions as Paul Griffiths, *Religious Reading: The Place of Reading in the Practice of Religion* (New York: Oxford University Press, 1999), a useful book though marred by its polemicizing dismissal of critical reading as "consumerist."
30. The relation between critical reading and modern social imaginaries is an enormous problem to which I can only gesture here; for an explanation of how the partly unconscious grasp of the social is linked to ideas of an order of mutual benefit, see Charles Taylor's *Modern Social Imaginaries* (Durham: Duke University Press, forthcoming).
31. This is arguably true in Spinoza's case even though the text was published anonymously; it immediately sparked an attempt to identify its author.
32. This argument is advanced partly in his *What Is Ancient Philosophy?* trans. Michael Chase (Cambridge, MA: Harvard University Press, 2002), and also in *Philosophy as a Way of Life: Spiritual Exercises from Socrates to Foucault.* ed. Pierre Hadot and Arnold I. Davidson. trans. Michael Chase (NY: Blackwell, 1995).
33. Bernard Williams, *Shame and Necessity* (Berkeley: University of California Press, 1993), 158–59.

2

Reading as Self-Annihilation

Amy Hollywood

Beloved, what will beguines
and religious people say
When they hear the excellence
of your divine song?
Beguines, priests, clerks, and preachers,
Augustinians, and Carmelites,
And the Friars Minor will say that I err,
Because I write of the being
Of purified Love/the one purified by Love.
I do not work to save their Reason,
Who makes them say this to me. (*Mirouer,* Ch. 122, p. 344)

For Germany, the *criticism of religion* has been largely completed; and
the criticism of religion is the premise of all criticism.

—Karl Marx, "Contribution to the Critique of Hegel's
Philosophy of Right: Introduction"

Critical Reading

When I first read Michael Warner's proposal that scholars begin to consider the nature and importance of "uncritical reading," I immediately
began to wonder what "critical reading" was and the extent to which it
differed across contemporary disciplines (however fraught these
boundaries, first established by Kant in *The Conflict of the Faculties*,
have become). My presumption is that our conceptions of what

constitutes uncritical reading depend on what we understand critical
reading to be and I'm not sure that what's considered critical reading
in one discipline might not occupy the site of that presumed to be
uncritical within another. On the other hand, it might be that certain
broad conceptions of reason as the source of criticism are so hegemonic within the academy as to render invisible other possible modes of
reading (which might themselves, I'll suggest, be critical, although in
not yet—or no longer—recognizable ways.)

The first English uses of the words critical and criticism occur in the
seventeenth and eighteenth centuries and seem primarily to refer to the
evaluation of literary and artistic works.[1] This usage is related to the earlier (and ongoing) development of textual criticism—the attempt to
determine the "complete" and "correct" text of a given, at first almost
always classical, work through comprehensive study of the original language and careful collection and comparison of manuscripts (and later
also of printed editions). Textual criticism is also pertinent for religious
studies; the later Middle Ages and Reformation witnessed the desire to
render the Biblical text uniform, stable, and correct in the face of proliferating manuscript versions, both liturgical and extraliturgical, and the
rise of vernacular translations.[2] Scholars increasingly applied the methods developed by the humanists for establishing the texts of classical literature to the Bible (although always with the understanding that as the
word of God, the Bible differed fundamentally from classical literature).[3]

The term "criticism" takes on new nuances within religious studies
in the eighteenth century, most pointedly with Hermann Samuel
Reimarus (1694–1768) and G. E. Lessing (1729–81). Reimarus's
work, first published in fragmentary form by Lessing, is routinely
taken to be the point of origin for critical readings of the Bible.[4]
Critical here refers to the ability to see and name contradictions
between and within texts (not that earlier readers didn't see these contradictions, but they always sought to explain them in light of the purported unity of scripture and had allegorical modes of interpretation
available to help in this task), to test the claims of scripture against
those of reason (understood in various ways over the course of the next
two hundred years), and to think historically about the nature of the
biblical text and its claims (and, of course, conceptions of history will
also change).[5] The trajectory of what will become the historical-critical

method of biblical study reaches a high point—or nadir, depending on your perspective—in 1835 with the publication of David Friedrich Strauss's *The Life of Jesus,* in which Strauss undermines claims for the historicity of Jesus and for the accuracy of the accounts of Jesus' life and death found within the New Testament. Strauss's work was one of those Marx had in mind when he announced that in Germany, the criticism of religion was largely complete and the stage now nearly set for social, political, and economic critique and transformation. Yet Strauss himself made no such claims for his work. Rather, Strauss argued that the criticism of the historical picture of Jesus on which previous Protestant theologies too often depended was the necessary prelude to establishing the correct dogmatic account of Christianity. True faith, according to Strauss, does not require, but is in fact hindered by, a grounding in history.[6]

The quest for the historical Jesus, of course, was not rendered obsolete by Strauss's attack, but instead became the center of the historical study of the Bible (at least of the New Testament). Theologically inclined biblical scholars and biblically-focused Christian theologians still argue about the extent to which the historical Jesus is required by or is an impediment to faith; yet most Christians ignore these debates and quietly assume that the historical nature of Jesus' life and mission is fundamental to their belief. Despite mainstream biblical scholarship's ultimate rejection of Strauss's and other critics' more radical claims (few today question Jesus' existence—questioned by some followers of Strauss—or the New Testament's account of the broad outlines of his mission and many accept a core group of New Testament texts as genuine sayings of Jesus—although which texts is still the subject of acrimonious and no doubt ultimately undecidable debate) and despite the significant advances beyond, supplements to, and refinements of the historical-critical method in terms of form and redaction criticism, comparative religious studies, and literary approaches to the Bible, the historical-critical method continues to pose a challenge to many Christian believers.

Although we can easily see what is being criticized within biblical scholarship—the reliability of scripture itself—the particular force of the term critical still remains opaque.[7] This opacity is a result, I think, of the changing conceptions of reason and history with which biblical critics operate. Reimarus was a deist and shared with men like John

Locke and David Hume the conviction that all of our beliefs should be subject to reason, understood in generally empirical terms. Although some religious belief—that in a creator God, for example—might survive such a critique, much of the specificity of Christianity and other "revealed religions" does not. For most Protestants, the only basis for adhering to claims about Jesus' miracle working or his resurrection, for example, is the authority of the source from whence we know of these events—sacred scripture or the Christian Bible. (And of course, scripture's authority is derived from the Bible, a bit of circularity not lost on its critics.) Hence Reimarus's turn to the Bible and to a criticism of the Bible grounded in his understanding of what it is rational to believe and of what we can hold as historically possible (history now itself constrained by human reason). As more sophisticated accounts of history emerge and the understanding of reason itself becomes historicized (most definitively, perhaps, with Hegel, thereby setting the stage for reason's critique of itself in Marx, Nietzsche, and Freud), the relationship between the rational and the historical becomes more complex. Yet within biblical studies the understanding of historiography as guided by reason—quite broadly defined[8]—remains firm.

Friedrich Schleiermacher, who died in 1834, the year before Strauss's *Life of Jesus* appeared, was the first to insist on philosophical and theological grounds that the forms of criticism applied to classical texts are (or should be) the same as those applied to the Bible.[9] He also arguably responds to Strauss and other radical critics of the Bible (in the case of Strauss, before the fact). Schleiermacher claims that what is essential in the New Testament is less the historical accuracy of the picture of Jesus presented within it than the accounts provided by these texts of how Jesus' followers and early believers apprehended him. Hence Schleiermacher, at least in theory, will have no difficulty dealing with the contradictions between the four gospel accounts, ascribing them to the different modes of religious apprehension found among the four authors.[10]

With Schleiermacher, religious experience—*sui generis*, according to Schleiermacher, but arguably a kind of aesthetic experience—becomes a mediating term between historical criticism and theology.[11] This move has been central to the nineteenth- and twentieth-century mainstream liberal Protestant response to the challenges posed by historical-critical biblical scholarship as well as to religious studies as an academic discipline. Although Schleiermacher, against the background and in response to the arguments of Kant's first two critiques, argues that religion is something other than either reason or morality, that it is a mode of receptivity to the divine prior to and/or beyond the split between subject and object necessary to rational knowledge and morality, at the same time he allows reason to be determinative of the limits within which the divine can be experienced. Seeking both to reconcile reason and faith and to safeguard faith from the critical incursions of reason, Schleiermacher remains committed to forms of critical thought dependent on reasoned accounts of what we can know and how we can and should act. What is critical in religious reading, then, or in the reading of religious texts, remains that which is guided by reason. Although religious experience may transform human beings' apprehension of the world and the divine, it does so in ways always compatible with reason. There is little sense that religious experience might give rise to forms of understanding or consciousness on the basis of which reason itself might be judged.[12]

With Marguerite Porete, to whom I'll devote most of the rest of my discussion, we are, quite obviously, in a different world. Written in the closing years of the thirteenth and opening years of the fourteenth century, Porete's *The Mirror of Simple and Annihilated Souls and Those Who Remain Only in the Will and Desire of Love* is an allegorical dialogue in which Love, Soul, Reason and a host of less prominent interlocutors provide an account of the free, simple, and annihilated soul. Love, avatar of the divine, is the primary authority, although Soul—who shifts throughout the dialogue between an encumbered and an unencumbered state, is also a source of information about the gap between the two conditions. Reason is the foil; the dimwitted audience to Love's and the Soul's high-flown dialogue who constantly asks them please to explain themselves. As I will show in what follows, ultimately Reason must die if the Soul is to apprehend and become one with divine Love. In the process, what Porete calls the Understanding of Divine Love emerges, an understanding that guides those now possessed of two eyes to abandon one-eyed Reason and in the process to learn to read both the Bible and Porete's book. Through Love, then, comes a higher mode of understanding, thereby complicating the apparent dichotomy between Reason and Love that governs the *Mirror* (and arguably this paper). I want to stay with the main lines of Porete's allegory here, deploying it for my own allegorical purposes, yet we should keep in mind that the apparent dichotomy between reason and love (or reason and the passions, reason and emotion, etc.) is never quite so simple as this allegorizing mode suggests. At any rate, from the standpoint of divine Love, the Soul and Love criticize Reason, her adherents (who include what Porete refers to as Holy Church the Little, as opposed to Holy Church the Great), and their limitations. Reason, despite her claims to critical power (and despite Porete's caricature of Reason's limitations, her pretension to critical power looms both within the text and on its peripheries), is unable to afford true insight because she is always blind to the double meanings that run throughout Love's discourse (which includes, once again, the Bible and Porete's own book).

Despite the apparent modernity of the critical reading practices to which modern scholars of religion adhere, then, the debate between reason and faith on which accounts of critical reading rest (at least within religious studies) has a long prehistory, one in which the terms are often slightly different and their valuation radically so.[13] Behind my desire to expose the variety of competing practices of critical reading visible within and around a single medieval text lies a concern to raise questions about what we now consider critical reading to be. We often presume that to read religiously is to read *uncritically,* yet for Porete, the insight gained through the annihilation of reason, will, and desire gives rise to powerful critiques of critical reason itself. Insofar as criticism is grounded in the character Reason, it is dead. Yet at the same time, Porete implies that Love is a more apt site from which to read critically. She is not alone. The later Middle Ages witnessed many powerful critiques of church and society by men and women who claimed to be possessed by or unified with the Holy Spirit. Porete is simply one of the most explicit in associating the institutional church with reason and in arguing for another, invisible Church (Holy Church the Great) governed by divine Love.

In *Serving the Word: Literalism in America from the Pulpit to the Bench,* anthropologist Vincent Crapanzano refers to "our own particular chivalry toward belief and faith."[14] Yet many if not most intellectuals presume, like Marx, that the criticism (read here rational destruction, although again grounded in claims to critical engagement) of religion is the necessary preliminary to any political, social, and economic transformation of society. Where chivalry is evident, I think it is due to the lack of seriousness with which religion is often taken. The Christian fundamentalists about whom Crapanzano writes seem to criticize contemporary culture from a perspective other than that of reason. As long as fundamentalist or evangelical Christians are perceived as powerless and irrational, secular Americans don't much care about their critiques. (When they are perceived as powerful, on the other hand, fundamentalist Christians inspire great fear.) Secular or liberal Christian Americans, or Americans of other faith traditions, can refuse to engage with fundamentalist Christians at least in part because the former claim that fundamentalist Christians refuse to engage rationally with the world around them. Thus Crapanzano argues that fundamentalists deny the possibility of genuine dialogue with those who disagree with them (thereby shifting his central emphasis from the issue of literalism to that of engagement. It remains an open question to what extent literalism necessitates a refusal to engage with outsiders.)

Yet I can't help wondering, prompted as you will see by Porete, whether there are things about which the critical, generally skeptical reason that governs much modern scholarship and intellectual life refuses to speak. Do fundamentalist Christians refuse dialogue, or are they responding to a prior refusal on the part of the world around them? At the very least, the current world situation suggests that the potentially silencing chivalry of secular intellectualism is no longer adequate. Students of religion are perhaps most inescapably confronted with the problem. As scholars, primarily within the secular academy, we are committed to at least some conception of reason. Yet because we purport to read, interpret, and explain religious texts and practices, we are ultimately forced to confront the limitations of reason as a source of critique. Is it possible to remain open to both critical impulses? Or do we need, at the very least provisionally, to allow other modes of apparently uncritical reading—modes I'll argue are often, in fact, themselves critical, albeit in different ways—to challenge what we conceive critical reading to be?

Reading the Mirror of Simple Souls

The earliest witness we have to Marguerite Porete's life and book is the anonymously authored continuation of the *Chronicon* of William of Nangis, written at Saint-Denis shortly after Porete's death on June 1, 1310.

> Around the Feast of the Pentecost it happened in Paris that a certain pseudo-woman of Hainault named Marguerite Porete published a book that according to the judgment of all the theologians who diligently examined it contained many errors and heresies. Among these were "that the soul annihilated in the love of the Creator may and should grant to nature whatever it wishes or desires, without reprehension or remorse of conscience." This is manifestly consonant with heresy. She would not renounce this book or the errors contained in it and stubbornly withstood for a year or more the sentence of heresy pronounced against her by the inquisitor (since, although sufficiently warned before him, she chose not to appear in court), but remained tenaciously obdurate in her malice to the end. She was therefore finally exposed before the clergy and populace, who were called together on the advice of experts at the common Place de Grève, and was handed over to the secular court. The provost of Paris immediately took her into his power and had her executed by fire on the following day. She showed many noble and devout signs of penance in her passing, by which many people were moved piously and tearfully to pity her, as those who saw may testify.[15]

We know nothing about Porete beyond what we find in her book (that's very little), the trial documents, and contemporary chronicles. She is referred to as a beguine often enough to make that attribution convincing to most historians. Moreover, the fact that she traveled throughout the Southern Low Countries and Northern France with her book corroborates these reports, for the beguines' semi-religious life style, in which one devoted oneself to religion without taking formal vows or submitting to strict enclosure (as did most nuns and canonesses), would have facilitated her travel.

The *Chronicon* of Nangis, the later *Grand chroniques de France,* and most importantly the trial records found among the document collections of William of Nogaret and William of Plaisans allow scholars to reconstruct the probable chronology and details of Porete's trial and condemnation. Most important for our purposes is that, following standard contemporary procedures, suspect passages were taken from the *Mirror* and submitted for evaluation by a panel of prominent theologians. The theologians did not see the book as a whole, but only these selected passages. Special care was taken with Porete's case, perhaps because she had submitted the book to three theologians, each of whom had approved of it. One of these men, Godfrey of Fontaines, was a master of theology and would have been known to at least some of Porete's judges. The approbation appended to the first Latin translation of the *Mirror* claims that Godfrey said the book described divine practice, but it also reports that he warned against the dangers the book might pose to those unversed in the religious life. Working against these approbations, however, is the fact, also made known in the trial documents, that Porete's book (or perhaps an earlier version of it) had been condemned by Guy of Colmieu, bishop of Cambrai sometime before 1305 (the year of his death). Guy burned the book before Porete and warned her that she would be judged as relapsed and handed over to secular authorities if she disseminated further the teachings contained within it. Porete ignored Guy of Colmieu, admitting to authorities on two occasions that she still possessed the book and that she had sent copies of the book, or one similar to it, to many people.

When the Paris inquisitor condemned Porete to death he also ordered that all copies of her book be burned with her on the Place de Grève. For over six centuries, it was assumed that the book had been effectively destroyed in 1310 and that no copies survived. In 1946, however, Romana Guarnieri announced that she had discovered Porete's book in an anonymous French text (*Le Mirouer des simples ames anienties et qui seulement demourent en vouloir et désir d'amour*).[16] She based her claim on the near identity between the three condemned passages cited in the trial documents and the chronicle of Nangis and portions of the *Mirror*. The attestation is unquestioned,[17] scholarly debate centering on how to read the *Mirror* now that it's known to be Porete's work. Despite the *Mirror's* condemnation, surviving manuscript evidence shows that it was copied and translated many times during the Middle Ages. About fourteen manuscripts survive, in French,[18] Latin, Middle English, and Italian.[19] There is also evidence of a Flemish translation, although a manuscript has not been found.[20] The available evidence, then, shows that the *Mirror* continued to be read, translated, and copied at least until the fifteenth century, albeit anonymously.[21]

As I hope to discuss elsewhere at greater length, the *Mirror* and its manuscripts offer multiple possibilities for the analysis of medieval reading practices.[22] As I've said, central for me here is how Love, the Soul, and the Author who caused the book to be written (another occasional interlocutor within the dialogue) demand that the *Mirror* be read and the ways in which Porete prefigures, through Reason, the modes of misreading in which her critics will engage. (Although it should be noted that the *Mirror* more often speaks of auditors than of readers, pointing to the possible specificity of the interpretative communities to which it was addressed in ways with which a longer version of this paper will have to deal.) The crucial issue for me here is what it would mean to read in the way the *Mirror* demands, what stops Porete's inquisitors from reading in this way, and what might hinder the modern reader. If, as I will show, Love and the Soul demand the annihilation of reason, will, and affection as the necessary prerequisite to two-eyed reading, does a space remain for critical reading as generally understood? Given Love's and the Soul's outspoken criticism of Holy Church the Little, of actives, contemplatives, clerics, and members of the religious orders, it seems instead that critical reading has been transformed—arguably even made possible—by the debates between Love, Reason, and the Soul enacted within the *Mirror*.

The Annihilation of Reason, Will, and Desire

As I've suggested, Reason's role in the dialogue is precisely that of the one-eyed reader, unable to understand the words of Love without intensive glossing (and even then, Reason often remains unable to understand Love's and the Soul's seemingly contradictory accounts of the simple soul).[23] This tendency toward contradiction can be seen already in Love's first description of the free and annihilated soul, which takes the form of nine points:

> [*Love*]. For there is another life, which we call the peace of charity in the annihilated life. Of this life, says Love, we wish to speak, in asking where one could find

1. a soul
2. who is saved by faith without works
3. who is only in love
4. who does nothing for God
5. who leaves nothing for God to do
6. to whom nothing can be taught
7. from whom nothing can be taken
8. or given
9. and who has no will.[24]

In the following chapters—and in a sense throughout the book as a whole—Love and the Soul, prompted by Reason, comment on this initial description.[25] Understanding, moreover, is hierarchically graded, with different glosses required for "contemplatives and actives" (Chapters 11–12) and for "ordinary people" (Chapter 13). Throughout, Reason cries out in pained incomprehension ("For God's sake, Love, what can this mean?" is a continual refrain here and throughout the book), only to receive in reply further paradoxical analogies and images to which she responds with shock and horror.

So to Reason's questions about how the soul can both take nothing and have nothing taken from her, Love replies with extended dialectical discussions about the nothingness of the soul. When the soul falls into her own nothingness, she becomes God who is all.

> *Love.*—It is fitting, says Love, that this Soul should be conformable to the deity, for she is transformed into God, says Love, through whom she has retained her true form, which is confirmed and given to her without beginning from one alone who has always loved her by his goodness.
> *Soul.*—Oh, Love, says this Soul, the meaning of what is said makes me nothing, and the nothingness of this alone has placed me into an abyss, below less than nothing without measure. And the knowledge of my nothingness, says the Soul, has given me the all, and the nothingness of this all, says the Soul, has taken litany and prayer from me, so that I pray for nothing. (Ch. 51, 150)

Holy Church the Little whose practices (particularly after the Fourth Lateran Council in 1215) center on litanies, fasting, prayers, and the sacraments asks, "What do you then do, sweetest lady and mistress over us?" The Soul, now free and unencumbered, replies;

> I rest wholly in peace . . . alone and nothing and entirely in the gra-
> ciousness of the single goodness of God, without stirring myself, not with
> one single wish, whatever riches he has in him. This is the end of my
> work, says this soul, always to wish for nothing. For so long as I wish for
> nothing, says this Soul, I am alone with him without myself, and entire-
> ly set free, and when I wish for anything, she says, I am with myself, and
> thus I have lost my freedom. But when I wish for nothing, and I have lost
> everything beyond my will, then I have need of nothing; being free is my
> support (*maintien*). I want nothing from no-one. (Ch. 51, 151–52)[26]

There the free soul "lives and remains and was and will be without any being" (Ch. 52), "where she was before she was" (Ch. 81, 89, 91, 111, 134).

At the center of these oft-repeated characterizations of the simple, free soul lies a distinction between those souls who will and desire and perform, even the things of God, and those souls who have passed beyond external and internal works to complete freedom. The first are members of Holy Church the Little, whereas the second make up the invisible community of Holy Church the Great. Porete will eventually lay out a complex hierarchical scheme in which there are two deaths— to nature and to the spirit—and seven modes of being culminating in the beatific vision available only after the death of the body. Most cru-cial, however, remains the move from stage four (that of the lost and bewildered souls who remain tied to the virtues, love, will, affection, and reason) to stages five and six (in which, dead to the spirit, will, and reason, the soul is completely free). This central distinction and the changing role of the virtues as the soul moves from an encumbered to an unencumbered state (later described as from stage four to stage five) appears early in the *Mirror* and is, not surprisingly, the subject of two of the three condemned passages known to us.[27]

Explaining how the free soul is saved by faith without works, the dialogue shows the Soul taking leave of the Virtues:

> Virtues, I take leave of you forever,
> I will have a heart most open and gay;

Your service is too constant, you know well.
One time I placed my heart in you, without any disservice,
You know that I was entirely abandoned to you;
I was thus a slave to you; now I am free. (Ch. 6, 24)

The Soul goes on to explain, however, that she is no longer subservient to the Virtues because they now freely serve her. She has left the dominion of Reason, the Virtues, and law to enter that of Love. Since Love is mistress of the Virtues, so the Soul now has dominion over them as well.

Elucidating her purpose to a scandalized and perplexed Reason, Love explains that she wishes to free souls from their suffering servitude to works, asceticism, and the cycle of ecstasy and alienation so common among the religious women among whom Porete lived and worked.

> *Love.*—When Love dwells in them, the Virtues serve them without any contradiction and without the work of such souls. Oh, without doubt, Reason . . . such souls who have become free have known for many days what Dominion usually does. And to the one who would ask them what was the greatest torment that a creature could suffer, they would say that it would be to dwell in Love and to be in obedience to the Virtues. For it is necessary to give to the Virtues all that they ask, whatever the cost to Nature. For it is thus that the Virtues demand honor and goods, heart and body and life. It is to be expected that such souls leave all things, and still the Virtues say to this Soul, who has given all to them, retaining nothing to comfort Nature, that the just one is saved by great pain. And thus this exhausted Soul who still serves the Virtues says that she would be assaulted by Fear, and torn in hell until the judgment day, and after that she would be saved. (Ch. 8, 28–30)

To live in Love, subject to the absolute nature of Love's desire, and yet still to remain subservient to Reason and the Virtues is torture, for the Soul can never do all that it might for Love. The greater her love for God, the more glaring her faults and omissions; the greater her ecstasy in the divine embrace of Love, the more unbearable Love's absence. In this frenzy, the Soul recognizes her nothingness; in recognizing she is nothing, she sacrifices herself to Love and becomes united with her. The annihilated Soul no longer requires to give or to receive; hence "poverty or tribulation, masses or sermons, fasting or prayers" are all one to her and she is free to give "to Nature all that is necessary to it without any remorse." (These are two of the passages condemned at Paris.) This will not lead to sin, however, for the Soul is so transformed into divine Love that everything she requires is absolutely innocent.

These double meanings, as Love calls them—Virtue as both master and servant or the Soul as both nothing and all—are impossible for Reason to grasp. (Porete here foresees the inability of her inquisitors to read her book.) Reason, for Porete, apprehends the divine in terms of univocal meanings and fixed exchanges. Porete is unusual in that she condemns not only "ordinary people"—those who attempt to follow Christ's commands and participate in his sacraments as promulgated by scripture and the Catholic church—but also religious people— those nuns, monks, clerics, and beguines who have devoted their lives to the fulfillment of the apostolic way. For Porete, "actives and contemplatives" also belong to Holy Church the Little, governed by Reason, as long as they believe that through their prayers, fasts, vigils, and even their extraordinary experiences of divine Love, they can attain salvation. They are, according to Porete, "merchants" rather than "noble" and "free." The Soul must instead recognize her absolute nothingness in the face of divine Love in order to become unencumbered. (And I hesitate to equate freedom with salvation given that Porete insists the former takes precedence over the latter.)

Love, finally, has no desire to placate Reason (and Holy Church the Little, which is governed by her), but seeks instead to destroy her. Reason's death is enacted twice within the *Mirror*. After her first death, Love asks what Reason would ask, if she were alive, in order to render the book comprehensible to those not yet annihilated in Love (Chapters 87–88). Eventually Reason returns to ask the questions herself, demonstrating the centrality of her role within the book. The second and more dramatic death occurs toward the end of the book and precipitates its close. Here the Soul engages in a process of meditation that leads to the death of reason, will, and affection. She seems here to dramatize a moment she wishes the reader, through a similar meditative practice, to follow.[28]

Then in my meditation I considered how it would be if he might ask
me how I would fare if I knew that he could be better pleased that I
should love another better than him. At this my mind failed me, and I
did not know how to answer, nor what to will nor what to deny; but
I answered that I would ponder it.

And then he asked me how I would fare if it could be that he could love
another better than me. And at this my mind failed me, and I knew not
what to answer, or will or deny.

Yet again, he asked me what I would do and how I would fare if it could
be that he would will that another love me better than he. And in the
same way, my mind failed, and I did not know what to answer, any
more than before, but again I said that I would ponder it.

Reason here arrives at its limits, unable even to think that which Love
proposes. The final transformation of the Soul demands the annihilation of all creatureliness, including love itself insofar as it is created and
human. In confronting these imagined demands, then, the Soul kills
her reason, as seen above, and ultimately also her will and desire.

If I have the same as you have, with the creation that you have given
me, and thus I am equal to you except in this, that I might be able to
exchange my will for another—which you would not do—therefore
you would will these three things that have been so grievous for me to
bear and swear. . . . And thus, lord, my will is killed in saying this. And
thus my will is martyred, and my love is martyred: you have guided
them to martyrdom. To think about them leads to disaster. My heart
formerly always thought about living by love through the desire of a
good will. Now these two things are dead in me, I who have departed
from my infancy. (Ch. 131, 384–88)

In this movement beyond human love and the human will, the necessity for works, either external or spiritual, comes to an end. As the Soul
loses herself in Love, Love works in and through her.

From what we know of Porete's trials, her critics, like Reason, were
unable to see with two eyes and to accept the double meaning of her

words. The method of decontextualizing passages itself precludes two-eyed readings, which depends on shifts of perspective facilitated by the movement of the text. For her inquisitors, the virtues are the mistresses of the soul rather than the soul's servant, and the switch in perspectives that enables Porete to make both claims, each suitable to a different mode of being, escapes her Inquisitors. Or does it? Two issues are crucial here. First, although Porete is not guilty of the antinomianism with which she seems to have been charged—Porete does not hold that the free soul can give to nature anything contrary to the law, but rather that the law is so internalized that she can give to nature anything it wants and all that it wants will be licit—Porete does clearly argue that the free soul no longer needs the mediation of the Church, its laws, and sacraments, in order to attain innocence and freedom. Although one must move *through* the laws of the church, the dictates of the church's reason, and the mediation of its sacraments in order to attain annihilation, the final freedom of the soul depends on surpassing them. This her inquisitors seemed to intuit, even if they were unable or unwilling to name the full force of her challenge to ecclesiastical authority.[29] They are unable to conceive of reason outside of those forms embodied by the institution of the Church itself.

Second, we know that Porete refused to respond to the charges made against her. Her younger contemporary, the Dominican preacher and scholar Eckhart, also charged with disseminating teachings dangerous to good Christians, did respond to his critics and in language that might easily have been used by Porete. He claims that while the statements pulled out for censure were subject to heretical readings, they were also capable of being read in an orthodox way. In other words, he asked his critics to read with two eyes and hence to see the perspective from which his words were true. The commission charged to review the list of twenty-eight articles taken from Eckhart's work finally decided that were heretical "as stated" (*prout verba sonant*), suggesting that they could only hear with one ear. As Michael Sargent argues, Eckhart's critics were radical literalists and their reasoned criticism of his work rests on a literalist hermeneutics (or anti-hermeneutics, if you will) in which words simply mean what they say.[30] If it sounds dangerous, it *is* dangerous. And as good literalists, Eckhart's critics would have been much more palatable to historical-critical scholarship than Eckhart, with his wild allegorizing, for much of the force of the criticism of religion and of religious texts rests on a deeply literalist set of presumptions. If today we find the literalist interpretation of the Bible stultifying and uncritical, it is important to remember its roots in a radical and *reasoned* critique of allegory.

Silence and/as Engagement

Porete's silence in the face of her inquisitors sparks radically different responses in modern readers. Some admire the firmness of her resolve, while others see her as intransigent and willfully self-sacrificing in the face of an authority that could—and would—kill her. We might assume that her refusal to speak involves an implicit claim that she has surpassed dialogue.[31] Just as with the death of Reason, the will, and affections, the *Mirror* itself must end, with the author apologizing for a prolixity engendered by an uncomprehending Reason and assuring her auditors that those who attain the state of simplicity and freedom recognize each other without words, so perhaps Porete believed herself to have attained annihilation and so to stand in a place from which she could no longer speak to Reason's minions. Yet despite repeated warnings and censures, Porete continued to disseminate her book and presumably to add to it, further attempting to explain to "ordinary people" and to "actives and contemplatives" governed by Reason the wonders of divine Love, which lay just beyond the latter's grasp, and to enact before them a process of transformation they might effectively mime.[32] To read the *Mirror* well, Porete suggests, is to follow the Soul depicted within it in her transformation to freedom, to give up Reason's one-eyed readings in favor of the double-words and double-perspectives of the Understanding of divine Love. Seen from this angle, Porete's silence speaks to her sense of her *interlocutors'* refusal to engage with her. Pulling decontextualized sentences out of her book so destroys its movement as to render it unrecognizable. It is her readers, then, who are incapable of dialogue.

Where does this leave me as a scholar of religious studies? What would it mean for me to read in the way Porete's text demands, to annihilate myself before the power of divine Love? How can I critically engage with a text whose critical force rests on the abdication of

reason—at least according to one understanding of reason, an understanding that would certainly include the forms of historical interpretation that still pass for critical in much religious studies scholarship?
Is it possible to explore, confront, even engage in a dialogue with that
which is on the edges of or beyond reason?[33] Although my reading of
the *Mirror* may be two-eyed compared to that of Porete's inquisitors,
without the annihilation of reason and of the self, how adequate an
understanding of the *Mirror* can I ever plausibly claim to have? Most
importantly, how can I allow—and when might I claim successfully to
have allowed—alternative conceptions of rationality, or conceptions of
criticism not grounded in rationality, to challenge my own assumptions about critical reading? Given that my subjectivity is in part
shaped by critical reading and thinking as formative practices, what
level of self-annihilation would be required for me really to read Porete?
What is challenged by Porete that I don't want to let go of?

These are questions to which I only have partial and still tentative
answers. What I most want to take from this allegorizing of Porete—
itself a dangerous enterprise—is that there are situations in which what
looks like another's refusal to engage with us in fact covers over our
own refusal to engage with her. In other words, when we turn to the
contemporary world and those communities or individuals who seem
to refuse forms of rationality premised on engagement and debate, we
need to ask what is entailed by our demands for engagement and how
these demands annul central premises of the other's position. One presumption I generally refuse to give up—what I hold on to in the face
of Porete, for example—is the power of constant skeptical questioning
and critical reflection. My oddly intertwined conceptions of reason, of
scholarship, and of democracy depend on the high value I place on
criticism as a form of engagement in which I allow my assumptions to
be changed by powerful counter-arguments. Yet the one assumption I
don't allow to come into question is that of the value of critical, rationally grounded engagement itself. What would it mean to give oneself
over—even provisionally—to a form of life in which criticism is
grounded in the divine, in tradition, authority, or community (just to
name some of the obvious possibilities)? I can't begin to argue for the
value of my own commitments without at least attempting to hear and
understand those of my interlocutor—without assuming that she

might have good grounds for her commitments, even if those commitments contradict my own.[34]

Porete, then, demands a different, more radical form of engagement—one in which my most treasured presumptions are questioned. But she's been dead for seven hundred years and the challenge she poses is therefore both complicated (hence this paper's need for greater historical specificity in its account of Porete on Love, Reason, and reading) and attenuated by distance. The world is full of others—living others—who challenge me more immediately, and to whose challenge I must respond with a willingness to hear what is truly different in their beliefs, their words, and their actions, even if those differences call into question the things I most deeply hold and am. The force of this injunction rests, paradoxically, in my own values. Porete's allegiance to Love leads her to annihilate love. Perhaps my allegiance to rational critique demands a similar annihilation of rational criticism—even, insofar as my subjectivity is tied up with my self-conception and practice as rational—self-annihilation. Here I follow Porete, even if not quite in the way she intended.

Notes

1. "Critical," and "Criticism," *Oxford English Dictionary* (Oxford: Oxford University Press, 1971).
2. Why and when multiple versions become seen as a problem is a pertinent question. Earlier theologians, preachers, and ecclesiasts recognized the diversity without viewing it as a major problem.
3. Reformation scholars are generally credited with the return to the original languages of scripture, but the impetus, if not the ability, was there long before Luther and Melancthon. The 1311 Council of Vienne called for chairs of Greek and Hebrew at the major universities. Lack of qualified teachers was presumably responsible for the failure to implement the plan. See Beryl Smalley, "The Bible in the Medieval Schools," in *The Cambridge History of the Bible: The West from the Fathers to the Reformation,* ed., G. W. H. Lampe (Cambridge: Cambridge University Press, 1969): 218–219.
4. See *Reimarus: Fragments,* ed. C. H. Talbert, trans. R. S. Fraser (Philadelphia: Fortress Press, 1970). For one influential account by an important Protestant theologian, see Hans W. Frei, *The Eclipse of Biblical Narrative: A Study in Eighteenth and Nineteenth Century Hermeneutics* (New Haven: Yale University Press, 1974), pp. 113–16. For a more recent summary account, this time by biblical scholars, see Robert Morgan with John Barton, *Biblical Interpretation* (Oxford: Oxford University Press, 1988): 52–57.

5. On divergent conceptions of history within early modern exegesis, see Debora Kuller Shuger, *The Renaissance Bible: Scholarship, Sacrifice, and Subjectivity* (Berkeley: University of California Press, 1994), esp. pp. 11–53.

6. See David Friedrich Strauss, *The Life of Jesus Critically Examined,* trans. George Eliot (Philadelphia: Fortress Press, 1972); Frei, *Eclipse,* pp. 233–44; and Morgan with Barton, *Biblical Interpretation,* pp. 44–52.

7. A number of questions arise at this point about the historical contingency of Western conceptions of critique in the face of the historical claims and historical dubiety of much of the Bible. Would the term "criticism" carry such destructive resonance in the Western academy if the Hebrew and Christian Bibles had been more "reliable" documents? To what extent does this "unreliability" depend on the peculiarly historical claims made by these documents and the traditions that arise from them? Or is it a feature of reason to attack, such that *any* document of faith would have been found wanting? And might it be that criticism, understood as *engagement,* necessarily comes into conflict with religious texts, understood as providing an all-encompassing, unsurpassable, and central outlook on existence? This is the account of religion recently provided by Paul Griffiths in his perceptive—albeit highly polemical—account of religious reading, but one with which many scholars of religion and religious people would contend. See Paul Griffiths, *Religious Reading: The Place of Reading in the Practice of Religion* (Oxford: Oxford University Press, 1999).

8. I take this broad definition of rational discourses to include those that 1) follow the rules of logic and correct argumentation (informal logic); 2) adhere to developing rules of evidence and/or; 3) have a plausibility grounded, for most historians and biblical scholars, in a kind of rough empiricism.

9. See, for example, Friedrich Schleiermacher, *Hermeneutics and Criticism and Other Writings,* trans. and ed. Andrew Bowie (Cambridge: Cambridge University Press, 1998).

10. See Friedrich Schleiermacher, *The Life of Jesus,* ed. and intro. Jack C. Verheyden, trans. S. Maclean Gilmour (Philadelphia: Fortress Press, 1975). Despite these claims, Schleiermacher's *The Life of Jesus* argues that one of these accounts—that of John—marks a superior apprehension of Christ. Of course, if all we can apprehend of the object of religious experience comes through our own experience or the accounts of others, it is not clear on what basis Schleiermacher judges one account superior to another. Is it closer to his own? This seems a mere personal preference. Does it more fully capture what is merely alluded to in other accounts but crucial to them? But on what basis does one determine which features are primary and secondary, given that no one account can be taken as more objectively true than another? These questions raise the issue of what kind of judgments religious judgements are. They seem closer, perhaps, to aesthetic judgments than to historical or epistemological ones, yet what does this imply about aesthetic judgments?

11. For this argument, see Morgan with Barton, *Biblical Interpretation.*

12. See especially Friedrich Schleiermacher, *On Religion: Speeches to its Cultured Despisers,* trans. Richard Crouter (Cambridge: Cambridge University Press, 1988), esp. pp. 96–140. For the centrality of Schleiermacher's account of experience to the modern study of religion, see Wayne Proudfoot, *Religious Experience* (Berkeley: University of California Press, 1985), esp. pp. 1–40.

13. Biblical scholars, it should perhaps be noted, find antecedents to their practices only in those early Christian and medieval interpreters who eschew allegory—two-eyed reading in Porete's terms—for literal and historical interpretation. Most famous among these are the fourth- and fifth-century Antiochenes and the twelfth-century Augustinian canons of St. Victor in Paris, in particular the great scholar of Hebrew, Andrew of St. Victor. See Beryl Smalley, *The Study of the Bible in the Middle Ages* (Notre Dame: University of Notre Dame Press, 1964), esp. pp. 83–195.

14. Vincent Crapanzano, *Serving the Word: Literalism in America from the Pulpit to the Bench* (New York: The New Press, 2000): 329. For a nuanced reading of fundamentalist modes of interpretation and speech, see Susan Friend Harding, *The Book of Jerry Falwell: Fundamentalist Language and Politics* (Princeton: Princeton University Press, 2000).

15. Paul Verdeyen, "The procès d'Inquisition contre Marguerite Porete et Guiard de Cressonessart (1309–1310)," *Revue d'histoire ecclésiastique* 81 (1986): 88–89; Paul Fredericq, ed., *Corpus documentorum inquisitionis haereticae pravitatis neerlandicae,* 2 vols. (Ghent: The Hague, 1888 and 1906), vol. 1, p. 160. The translation, slightly modified, is from Michael G. Sargent, "The Annihilation of Marguerite Porete," *Viator* 28 (1997): 253.

16. The announcement was first made in the *Osservatore Romano* (June 16, 1946). The article is reprinted in Romana Guarnieri, "Il movimento del Libero Spirito," *Archivio Italiano per la storia della pietà* 4 (1965): 661–63.

17. For literature confirming Guarnieri's discovery, see Robert Lerner, *The Heresy of the Free Spirit in the Later Middle Ages* (Notre Dame: University of Notre Dame Press, 1972): 73.

18. Of the three French manuscripts believed to have survived into modern times, only one is available for scholarly study (the Chantilly manuscript, Musée Condé MS F.xiv.26). Of the other two, one disappeared on route between the municipal library of Bourges and the Bibliothèque Nationale in Paris. The other was reported to be in the possession of a French-speaking community in Canada, who would not grant access to scholars. Some now consider this claim to be a hoax. See Sargent, "Annihilation," p. 260. Evidence points to a fifteenth-century date for the manuscript and for its language, suggesting it is a translation from Porete's thirteenth-century French dialect (presumably Picard, the dialectic of the French-speaking Southern Low Countries).

19. The *Mirror* was translated into Latin probably in the fourteenth century (five complete manuscripts and a number of fragments survive), twice into Italian (one survives in a single manuscript, the other in

three), and once into English in the early-fifteenth century (three manuscripts survive, all associated during the fifteenth century with the
Carthusian houses around London). The English translator (M.N.)
added a preface and fifteen explanatory glosses. This English translation
was then translated into Latin at the end of the fifteenth century by
Richard Methley of Mount Grace Charterhouse, who added his own
glosses to the text. The 1984 *Corpus Christianorum* edition brings
together Guarnieri's version of the Chantilly manuscript with Paul
Verdeyen's critical edition of the first Latin translation. Marilyn Dorion
has edited the Middle English *Mirror,* whose glosses have been edited
and translated by Edmund Colledge and Romana Guarinieri. Colledge
also edited, together with James Walsh, Methley's glossed Latin translation but it has yet to appear in print. See Romana Gaurnieri and Paul
Verdeyen, ed., *Le Mirouer des simples ames anienties et qui seulement
demourent en vouloir et desir d'amour,* in *Corpus Christianorum:
Continuatio Mediaevalis,* Vol. 69 (Turnhout: Brepols, 1986); Marilyn
Dorion, ed., *"The Mirror of Simple Souls*: A Middle English
Translation,"* Archivio Italiano per la Storia della Pièta* 5 (1968):
242–355; and Edmund Colledge and Romana Guarnieri, "The Glosses
of 'M.N.' and Richard Methley to 'the Mirror of Simple Souls',"
Archivio Italiano per la storia della pietà 5 (1968): 357–82.

20. Walter Simons provides evidence that there may also have been a
Flemish translation of the *Mirror,* although no manuscripts are known
to survive. See Walter Simons, *Cities of Ladies: Beguine Communities in
the Medieval Low Countries, 1200–1565* (Philadelphia: University of
Pennsylvania Press, 2001), p. 137.

21. Although I know of no evidence for the *Mirror* being excerpted in the
mystical compendia that begin to appear in the fifteenth and sixteenth
centuries, these manuscripts and manuscript collections are only beginning to be carefully studied. Further research may yield new results.
The manuscript lost at the Bibliotheque Nationale is particularly tanta-
lizing, as it was a collection of mystical and religious manuscripts like
those so important to the dissemination of Mechthild of Magdeburg's
Flowing Light of the Godhead. For the dissemination of this key beguine
text, see Sara Poor, *Mechthild of Magdeburg and Her Book: Gender and
The Making of Textual Authority* (Philadelphia: University of
Pennsylvania Press, 2004).

22. For recent work in English on the centrality of understanding medieval
textual, reading, and hearing practices within the context of a manuscript culture, and the methodological implications of this understanding, see John Dagenais, *The Ethics of Reading in Manuscript Culture:
Glossing the Libro de buen amor* (Princeton: Princeton University Press,
1994); and Andrew Taylor, *Textual Situations: Three Medieval
Manuscripts and Their Readers* (Philadelphia: University of Pennsylvania
Press, 2002). This work is an extension of much earlier work on reading, writing, and manuscript culture, important among them Brian
Stock's call for an understanding of medieval reading communities.
See Brian Stock, *The Implications of Literacy: Written Language and*

Models of Interpretation in the Eleventh and Twelfth Centuries (Princeton: Princeton University Press, 1983).

Although I'll only be able to focus on two interpretative levels, let me outline the multiple ways in which the manuscript traditions might be approached in order to suggest the complexity attendant on the study of medieval reading practices. First, *The Mirror of Simple Souls* engages in textual and biblical interpretation, from the Prologue (which recasts a story from the medieval Alexander legend) through the final chapters (devoted to biblical texts). Second, the central interlocutors within the *Mirror*'s allegorical dialogue, Love, Soul, and Reason, repeatedly offer instructions and/or provide models for how the text itself should be read. Third, the first Latin translation includes an approbation of the text by three theologians. Although brief, the text is suggestive for the ways in which learned men both condoned and warned against the dangers of the *Mirror*. Fourth, the trial documents record, at least partially, the way in which the *Mirror* was read by those who condemned the book. Fifth, the translations themselves all warrant careful study in order to understand the dynamics of medieval translation as a mode of reading. Sixth, two of these translations include glosses by the translators (included in all of the surviving manuscripts of these translations). Although the Chantilly manuscript, the three manuscripts that contain the Middle English translation, and Richard Methley's Latin have been extensively described and studied, all the available manuscripts should be reconsidered in light of contemporary interest in manuscripts and their transmission. With what other texts was the *Mirror* bound? Are there other readerly markings that can be uncovered? What, if anything, can we discern about the owners and readers of the manuscript? Finally, there is testimony from at least one other early reader. Marguerite of Navarre's 1547 poem, *Prisons,* includes over a hundred lines praising the *Mirror* and its author (who Marguerite knew to be a woman although we cannot know if she knew her to be Marguerite Porete). On this last issue, see J. Dagens, "Le 'Miroir des simples ames' et Marguerite des Navarre," *La Mystique Rhénane,* Colloque de Strasbourg, 16–19 mai 1961 (Paris: Universitaires de France, 1963); and Suzanne Kocher, "Marguerite de Navarre's Portrait of Marguerite Porete: A Renaissance Queen Constructs a Medieval Women Mystic," *Medieval Feminist Newsletter* 26 (1998): 17–23.

23. The *Mirror* continually refers to those who will hear it being read, suggesting a performance context or reading out loud within religious communities.

24. Guarnieri and Verdeyen, *Mirouer,* Ch. 5, pp. 18–20. Further references will be parenthetical within the text. All translations are my own unless otherwise noted.

25. My suspicion is that Porete wrote the book in pieces, piling on new analogies, images, textual readings, and paradoxes in ever new efforts to get across her understanding of the free and simple soul.

26. For this reading of *maintien,* see Margaret Porette, *The Mirror of Simple Souls,* trans. Edmund Colledge, J. C. Marler, and Judith Grant (Notre Dame: University of Notre Dame Press, 1999): 71, n. 2.

27. The claim that "a soul annihilated in the love of the Creator could, and should, grant to nature all that it desires" and that "the soul neither desires nor despises poverty, tribulation, masses, sermons, fasts, or prayers and gives to nature, without remorse, all that it asks." Fredericq, 1, 76–77. For the condemnation seen within the context of the fourth Lateran Council (1215), see Kent Emery, Jr., "Foreword: Margaret Porette and Her Book," in Colledge, Marler, and Grant, trans., Mirror, pp. xvii–xviii.

28. Porete draws here, as elsewhere in the text, on meditative traditions within late medieval Christian spirituality. Whereas most meditations on Christ's love are meant to provoke and augment the affections and desire, however, Porete here uses these techniques against themselves in order to destroy reason, will, and affection. For some reflections on these meditative traditions and their relationship to contemporary theory and practice, see Amy Hollywood, *Sensible Ecstasy: Mysticism, Sexual Difference, and the Demands of History* (Chicago: University of Chicago Press, 2002): 69–79.

29. As Caroline Walker Bynum, Dyan Elliott, Walter Simons and others show, in the thirteenth century the clergy's sole control over the sacraments and the centrality of the sacraments to Christian life are relatively new. See Caroline Walker Bynum, *Jesus as Mother: Studies in the Spirituality of the High Middle Ages* (Berkeley: University of California Press, 1982), 247–62; and Dyan Elliott, *Fallen Bodies: Pollution, Sexuality, and Demonology in the Middle Ages* (Philadelphia: University of Pennsylvania Press, 1999). For splits among the clergy on these issues, particular with regard to lay and women's piety, see Simons, *City of Ladies,* pp. 118–37; and Hollywood, *Sensible Ecstasy,* pp. 241–57.

30. It is perhaps worthy of note that modern critical reading of the Bible begins with an emphasis on the literal and historical meaning of the text not unlike that embraced today by many fundamentalist Christians.

31. As I suggested earlier in the paper, I think that this is the real issue for Crapanzano in his engagement with the literalism of Christian fundamentalists. He suggests that literalism may lead to particular problems with engagement, although without fully endorsing the claim. Porete's case can be used both for and against that thesis.

32. Porete's conceptions of reading and hearing might usefully be explored within the larger context of medieval conceptions of reading. Very suggestive in this light, although dealing with a different historical moment, is Adrian Johns's account of the physiology of reading in the seventeenth-century. See Adrian Johns, *The Nature of the Book: Print and Knowledge in the Making* (Chicago: University of Chicago Press, 1998): 380–443.

33. My thanks to Jonathan Crewe for helping me articulate and refine these questions.

34. Saba Mahmood helped me articulate this point, one in line with much of her own recent work on the anthropology of religion and gender in contemporary Islam. See Saba Mahmood, "Feminist Theory,

Embodiment, and the Docile Agent: Some Reflections on the Egyptian Islamic Revival," *Cultural Anthropology* 16 (2001): 202–36; Saba Mahmood, "Rehearsed Spontaneity and the Conventionality of Ritual: Disciplines of *ṣalāt*," *American Ethnologist* 28 (2001): 827–53; and Saba Mahmood and Charles Hirschkind, "Feminism, the Taliban, and Politics of Counter-Insurgency," *Anthropological Quarterly* 75 (Spring 2002): 339–54.

3

"Thou art a scholar, speak to it, Horatio"

Uncritical Reading and Johnsonian Romance

Helen Deutsch

The ghost of the writer most likely to be designated the father of English literary criticism looms at the crossroads of critical and uncritical reading. He personifies a vision and names an age of eighteenth-century English letters. Resolutely embodied, staunchly eccentric, Samuel Johnson haunts his critics to this day. His dominion has recently come under siege: a recent MLA panel wondered "Whatever Happened to the Age of Johnson?," while the concurrent offering at the American Society of Eighteenth Century Studies more provocatively asked "Is There Room in Samuel Johnson for the New Eighteenth Century?" For an older guard of eighteenth-century scholars, the figure of Johnson evokes nostalgia for an earlier mode of professing literature before literary criticism became too professional. In his practical concern that literature enable us "better to enjoy life or better to endure it,"[1] Johnson brought a collective audience to life in the newly imagined form of "the common reader." This fictional figure, to whom Johnson so often deferred in crises of judgment, summons the author's image in a communal mirror, solitary yet befriended through the thriving medium of print. I am curious about how Johnson, even or especially in our postmodern moment, still haunts the profession of English letters not as a great writer, but as a "great man, writing."[2] However we as critics might try to demystify this vision of Johnson, to turn back to the printed page and away from the human image, his ghost still beckons.

In a volume reprinted throughout the first half of the twentieth century on *Dr. Johnson & His Circle* for the *Home University Library of*

Modern Knowledge,[3] only the second in the series (after Shakespeare) to focus on a single author, the literary critic John Bailey in a chapter titled "A National Institution" praised Johnson as "the embodiment of the essential features of the English character" (8–9). Distinguished for "a sort of central sanity . . . which Englishmen like to think of as a thing peculiarly English" (109–110), Bailey's Johnson lacks "genius" but possesses something better, "something broadly and fundamentally human . . . which appeals to all and especially to the plain man" (11). "We never think of the typical Englishman being like Shakespeare or Milton," he writes, but thanks to Johnson's very typicality, that "quiet and downright quality which Englishmen are apt to think the peculiar birthright of the people of this island," "we can all imagine that under other conditions, and with an added store of brains and character, we might each have been Doctor Johnson" (9–10). Johnson, in other words belongs not to the literary critic but to the common reader.

As this example of two hundred years of Johnsonian worship attests, Johnson has never fully died. He exists on the border between the dead and the living, a divide significantly figured by Bailey as separating singular genius from common humanity, literary masterpiece from representative man. At the root of the *unheimlich* (as Freud reminds us) is the familiarity of home—and the Home University Library. "More intimately known to posterity than other men are known to their contemporaries," as Thomas Macaulay put it, Johnson's national genius, his ghost, is as proximate, as reassuringly present, as the stone he kicked in Boswell's *Life* to refute Berkeley thus.

In his infamous 1831 review of J. W. Croker's edition of Boswell's *Life of Johnson,* the biography most responsible for bringing Johnson's ghost into being, Macaulay takes a most uncritical view of the phantom through the lens of communal nostalgia:

> As we close [Boswell's book] the clubroom is before us, and the table on which stands the omelet for Nugent, and the lemons for Johnson. There are assembled those heads which live forever on the canvas of Reynolds. There are the spectacles of Burke and the tall thin form of Langton, the courtly sneer of Beauclerk and the beaming smile of Garrick, Gibbon tapping his snuff-box and Sir Joshua with his trumpet in his ear. In the foreground is that strange figure which is as familiar to us as the figures

of those among whom we have been brought up, the gigantic body, the huge massy face, seamed with the scars of disease, the brown coat, the black worsted stockings, the grey wig with the scorched foretop, the dirty hands, the nails bitten and pared to the quick. We see the eyes and mouth moving with convulsive twitches; we see the heavy form rolling; we hear it puffing; and then comes the 'Why, sir!' and the 'What then, sir!' and the 'No, sir;' and the 'You don't see your way through the question, sir!'"[4]

By evoking the memory of a figure from the national past, "as familiar to us as those among whom we have been brought up," Macaulay transforms the reading community into children viewing the world of adults, replacing the reader's critical distance with admiration. Untainted by academic prejudice, this nostalgia for a literary childhood renders the author as comforting as an eccentric uncle, a nursery companion.

Yet this image (as is also true of childhood perception) has its darker side. Macaulay's tableau of Johnson is a still-life reanimated as caricature. The metonymic details—omelets, lemons, spectacles, sneers, smiles—move from the inhuman to the human as if animated toys, as the bodies of the members of Johnson's famous club come into focus and to life. Dominating the perspective is the Great Man himself, a monumental form marked by disease, adorned with condensed anecdote (the scorched wig borrowed from Hester Thrale's account of the disastrous results of Johnson's reading in bed by candlelight), and propelled, in an uncanny blurring of animate and inanimate, by a series of compulsions. Twitches, rollings, puffings, and habitual sayings turn his uncontrolled body and conversational mannerisms into the sort of automaton that would have been at home in Freud's essay.[5] Devoted readers over the centuries have given this monstrously loveable creature a human voice and face. He can leave even the most rigorous of critics speechless.

*****

In his famous essay "The Double Tradition of Dr. Johnson," Bertrand H. Bronson charts the endurance of Johnson's ghost in excess of his texts in order to exorcise the author's spirit in the service of clear-eyed critical vision. "After his death there springs up the eidolon of an author," Bronson begins by claiming, "and it is of this ever-changing surrogate, not of the original, that we inevitably form our judgments, and that by so judging we further change."[6] Literary tradition, he argues, is thus "double": Bronson therefore proposes to pay unconventional attention not to "the operative power of tradition which we denominate influence," to the realm of texts, but to "something more akin to transmitted recollection, to a song or ballad" (156), namely the popular folk tradition in which Johnson "exists for us also like a character in one of our older novels, and on the same level of objectivity and familiarity" (157).

By analyzing this eidolon, Bronson implies, we can escape its subtle influence, an influence that operates at an uncritical level and in the realm of unconscious knowledge, of "recollection" and "familiarity." Bronson devotes the bulk of his essay to charting the work of "devoted specialists" in eighteenth-century literature whose labors have succeeded (thanks, he claims, to a decline in the critical currency of both Romantic individualism and isolated naturalistic detail) in successfully reforming the Johnsonian imago. These critical efforts have revived Johnson's conservatism and orthodoxy, not in his familiar fixed image, but as a creative energy "that vibrates like a taut wire" (170). But despite such academic success, Bronson concludes, "it appears likely that the folk-image still persists on a far higher level of culture than the specialist would ever dream possible" (173). As if to rehearse the futility of his own critical efforts to remake Johnson's ghost in the image of his texts, Bronson concludes by invoking the uncanny connection between printed text and authorial eidolon in the form of another famous ghost:

But how can we sufficiently admire the vitality of this folk-image? It captures the imagination of generation after generation; it takes possession of some minds to such an extent that they spend years reading about Johnson and his circle, and even publish their own books on him, and all the while before them looms the same imago, unabashed and incorrigible. It is a humbling spectacle and a chastening one to the specialist. Each of us brings his burnt offering to the altar of truth, and the figure we invoke becomes momentarily visible, obscurely forming and reforming in the smoke above us, never the same. But the folk-image moves irresistibly onward, almost unaffected by our puny efforts to arrest or divert it.

We do it wrong, being so majestical,
To offer it the show of violence;
For it is, as the air, invulnerable,
And our vain blows malicious mockery. (176)

Bronson refers to the play that haunts his own evocation of the Johnsonian eidolon, *Hamlet,* I. 1.145–8, as he summons the armored ghost of Hamlet's father, the same ghost evoked by Boswell at the founding moment of and in the *Life* of his and Johnson's first meeting. *Hamlet* begins, so this allusion reminds us, with a dramatic refutation of scholarly doubt. Horatio dismisses the guardsman Marcellus' report of an apparition as "fantasy," only to be confronted with ocular proof in the form of the ghost himself, on stage, in full armor. "Thou art a scholar, speak to it, Horatio" (I.1.42), Marcellus demands. But Horatio is paralyzed by his learning. "Harrow[ed] by fear and wonder" (I.1.44), caught between an enlightened skepticism that had doubted the ghost's existence, and the overwhelming evidence of his own eyes, he trembles and looks pale, his questions and commands rebuffed. The ghost responds neither to the scholar's words nor the soldier's assault. It disappears, summoned by the crowing of the cock to its unknown "confine," perhaps its temporary hell. It speaks only to its son and heir in whom it will live on, who will perform his bidding, rescue him from purgatory.

Johnson's ghost strikes Bronson, skeptical but awestruck like Horatio, with a similar involuntary admiration. Like the ghost of old Hamlet, Johnson's spirit will not speak to skeptical critics, but only to true believers, "generation after generation" who, as Boswell put it, "strongly impregnated by Johnsonian aether,"[7] perpetuate an image that dwarfs the literary efforts of "specialists." The labors of the critic, sacrificed at the altar of truth, produce only changeable figures as ephemeral as smoke. Substantive as stone, Johnson's gigantic ghost stalks away, untouched by time or "puny" critics, inspiring instead popular books by those "possessed" by its powers and thus with the desire to reproduce it in print.

The ghost of old Hamlet haunts Johnsonian biographers, critics and parodists alike. By summoning Shakespeare's words to echo past his own, Bronson concludes his essay suspended, like Horatio, between lay belief and learned doubt. Johnson's ghost, like that of Hamlet's father, refuses to rest. Whether vengeful or victimized, his spirit leaves the reader disarmed, prey—as was Johnson himself—to superstition.[8] Through his own tragic and impenetrable doubt—a doubt at once anti-Enlightenment in its Puritan religiosity, and post-Enlightenment in its almost existential confrontation with the possibility of annihilation—the figure of Johnson transforms the symbolic remains of Christianity into a vehicle of community through the preservation and consumption of the author in print. The paradigmatic critic of English letters inspires uncritical reading at its spiritual height.

*****

> What I read now elevated my mind wonderfully. I know not if I can explain what I have felt, but I think the high test of great writing is when we do not consider the writer, and say, "Here Mr. Johnson has done nobly"; but when what we read does so fill and expand our mind that the writer is admired by us instantaneously as a being directly impressing us as the soul of that writing, so that for a while we forget his personality, and, by a reflex operation, perceive that it is Mr. Johnson who is speaking to us. I feel quite well what I have now written. I wish I could make it clear in words.
>
> —James Boswell[9]

In his certainty that he *feels* the truth of his response to Johnson's text, and in his inability to express that feeling in words, James Boswell, in his journal entry for March 17, 1775, sounds more like (what indeed he was) an ardent amateur, or to our professorial ears a besotted student grappling with the need for a clearly articulated thesis, than a literary critic. Perhaps Johnson's ghost endures because it allows, indeed demands, this return to a pre-professional and pleasurable certainty, a return that is a retreat from critical distance and doubt. Rendering even the living Johnson a disembodied spirit, smitten by the power of his text, Boswell, that literary fan of epic proportions, enacts uncritical reading as sublime communion, a submission to the text that "impresses" the reader with the author's speaking voice. Resonating with Horatio's "wonder" at things undreamt of by his critical philosophy, Boswell's surrender to a text brought to ghostly life enacts a devotion that transcends the love of literature. Not Horatio but self-anointed Hamlet, Boswell is inspired by an encounter with literature experienced as connection to the author. He enacts uncritical reading as author love, helping to inspire two centuries worth of Johnsonians to remember their ghostly father.

Boswell's textual epiphany starts with his frisson of uncritical and self-congratulatory pride in private familiarity with the man behind the celebrity. Reading excerpts in the newspaper of "Mr. Johnson's new pamphlet, *Taxation no Tyranny*," he is "new struck with admiration of [Johnson's] powers."[10] He thus re-appraises Johnson's familiar public style in the context of intimate association, a context that lends him glory: "I was proud, and even wondered that the writer of this was my friendly correspondent." Pride by association with Johnson's printed prowess leads (in a manner typical of the Boswell of the journals) to personal fantasy: "I thought that he who thinks well of my abilities might recommend me to the Sovereign and get me highly advanced, and how should I delight to add riches and honour to my family in a Tory reign, by the recommendation of Mr. Samuel Johnson" (80). This is intellectual height turned to social climbing.

Yet from the petty glories and mercenary fantasies of particular acquaintance with a famous writer rises the pinnacle of intellectual elevation of the passage that follows. Here the author is absorbed completely into the text, becoming "a being directly impressing us as the soul of that writing," his personality and person forgotten, the word replacing the flesh. "Impress" here paradoxically contains a hint of physicality, as if the writing makes a literal mark upon the receptive reader, who has become warm wax to the imprint of the spiritual "being" the text bodies forth. This readerly rapture can be felt "quite well," but transcends words to become a transparent experience of extraliterary communion. Feats of style, the province of proper critical evaluation from a distance, are forgotten: a living voice is "speaking to us." Boswell's selfish "I" thus is effaced, by force of recognition, into the "we" of literary community.

This is one pole of Johnsonian communion—the couplet pair to the authorial corpse that will cast its shadow over the writing of Boswell's *Life*, a corpse that is never fully forgotten and to which this essay will return.[11] This corpse has become an enduring object of scientific scrutiny, dissected by the surgeons, its interior cataloged, preserved, and published in contemporary newspapers and subsequent generations of medical texts. While the Johnsonian medical community scrutinizes the burden and mystery of Johnson's materiality, the Johnsonian literary community combats the loneliness of mortality, and of the critic's mortal work.[12]

The uncritical reading that Boswell exemplifies thus effaces the text in the service of the author "himself." Boswell struggles to describe a "reflex operation" of knowing and not knowing that results, uncannily, in recognition of the author as a kindred spirit. Such devout disavowal inverts the proper critical approach to the text. But it also exposes the critic's attention to the text as itself a form of fetishism—a fruitless substitution of the word for the living writer. From the Johnsonian perspective, critics disavow the vital power of the author's presence in the text by embracing the dead letter.

In a striking counterexample to Johnsonian uncritical communion, Eric O. Clarke has traced the critical industry that arose from textual editing of Shelley's literary corpus to the original worship of his corpse. In Clarke's history of Shelley love, the author's queer body gives way to the flawed text in need of editorial correction; the worship of Shelley's corpse is sublimated into the fetishization of his texts in scholarly editing.

> The fetishist believes that what an object represents "lives" in that object, yet the very fact that it must be re-presented by a substitute object implicitly acknowledges the original's absence. This contradictory attitude approximates the fantasy involved in recreating the presence of an author through imagining a fully present intention organizing an authoritative text.

Despite its queer particularity, Shelley's case still seems more familiar to us in its replacement of loving devotion to the author's body with scholarly attention to the text. Johnsonian worship, by contrast, operates by a disavowal not (as Clarke has claimed in Shelley's case) of the text's flaws, but of the text itself. For Johnsonians, neither the author's mortal body nor his book is sufficient. Texts must remain imperfect and incomplete, open to "life" and the living author. Johnson "himself," rather than Shelley's governing intention in the text, becomes the fetish.[13] The magnificent scholarly achievement of the Yale edition of Johnson's *Works* notwithstanding, Johnsonians must devote themselves, whether in commendation or refutation, to the endlessly proliferating and eternally present-tense genre of the anecdote, extratextual supplement on the margins and footnotes of scholarly editions. The pressing question for the study of Johnson becomes not a decision on a textual variant, but rather a confrontation with the form that summons up the here and now of the embodied speaking voice, the form that, as epitomized by Boswell's *Life,* demands communion and response.[14]

In her recent study of marginalia, H. J. Jackson has traced such communion book by book. Boswell's *Life of Johnson* plays a unique role in her study because of her inability to generalize about the history of its marginalia; what endures is its status over centuries of lively individual response as "a book that has been taken for a man."[15] So effectively does Boswell animate Johnson, speaking in published writing, private letters, and dramatic scenes of conversation, that readers are compelled in their own notes to talk back. At the intersection of private and public modes of discourse, having only personal idiosyncrasy in common, generations of readers have responded directly on the pages of his *Life* to a dead man reanimated by living speech. Leigh Hunt, for example, recounts his own experience of melancholy in response to Boswell's account of Johnson's youthful suffering—"I had it myself at the age of 21, not with irritation & fretfulness, but pure gloom & ultra-thoughtfulness. . . . During both my illnesses, the mystery of the universe sorely perplexed me; but I had not one melancholy thought on religion" (169–70). In a Harvard copy of an 1887 scholarly edition, one reader highlights Johnson's remark, "A man may have a strong reason not to drink wine; and that may be greater than the pleasure," noting "see Aristotle Eth. Nich. Book I." Another retorts, "You don't have to brag about taking Phil. A. You aren't Samuel Johnson. L.S.K." (172). In the case of the great critic, so this snarky exchange shows us, uncritical reverence prevails.

*****

There are some authors who exhaust themselves in the effort to endow posterity, and distil all their virtue in a book. Yet their masterpieces have something inhuman about them, like those jewelled idols, the work of men's hands, which are worshipped by the sacrifice of man's flesh and

blood. There is more of comfort and dignity in the view of literature to which Johnson has given large utterance: 'Books without the knowledge of life are useless; for what should books teach but the art of living?'
—Walter Raleigh[16]

I have begun to uncover the ways in which the peculiarly uncritical worship of Johnson's ghost exposes the traditional critical reverence for the literary text as a form of fetishism. My epigraph from the Johnsonian Walter Raleigh takes this claim one step further. If, as Bertrand Bronson discovered to his own chagrin, the sacrifice of critical labor to the altar of truth results in Johnson's case only in airy phantoms, the sacrifice of authors to the altar of art involves a bloodier and equally useless tribute. Literature in this passage is a man-made god who demands the "flesh and blood" of the author himself. The finished work of art is a "jewelled idol" masquerading as a living deity. Johnsonians prefer the stolid humanity of the author's ghost to the arid perfection of a masterpiece. Rejecting the love of literature for its own sake as pagan fetishism, they reenact Christian communion with the author himself. In the case of Johnson such communion can take the form of private marginalia or civic ritual. Whether individual or communal, the love of Johnson disavows literary labor and with it, human mortality. Nowhere has this been better exemplified than in Johnson's birthplace, Lichfield.

Every September in the English city of Lichfield, a name that means "field of the dead," the town's polite society gathers to celebrate the birthday of their most famous native, eighteenth-century man of letters and moral philosopher Samuel Johnson. At the Johnson Society Annual Supper, celebrants enjoy a hearty British repast fit for their Rabelaisian hero: haunches, saddles, or joints of meat (2000 was the first time since the Society was founded in 1910 that a vegetarian option was offered), followed by apple pie and cream, ale, cheese, punch, and the smoking of long clay "churchwarden pipes," handed round by a servant dressed in full eighteenth-century livery. Formal toasts punctuate the proceedings in traditional order: the Queen (proposed by the Mayor of Lichfield), followed by "The Immortal Memory of Dr. Samuel Johnson," proposed by the President of the Society, followed by five minutes of silence.

On the morning before the annual Johnsonian feast, a different sort of ceremony takes place. Civic community supplants the dinner's exclusivity as town dignitaries including the Mayor and Mayoress, the Sheriff, the Alderman and Councillors, the Dean and Canon of Lichfield join the Senior boys of Johnson's old school who form the Cathedral Choir, along with members of the Johnson Society and the general public in the market square. Ascending a ladder, the Mayor adorns Johnson's statue with a laurel wreath (stored during the rest of the year at the base of Johnson's bust in Lichfield cathedral). "From a platform erected on the steps of the Birthplace—an innovation which was much appreciated," the Cathedral Choir sings "with their customary charm, the 'anthem' and appropriate hymns."[17] Choirboys receive a special token from the Mayor in memory of their participation.

The singing of the Johnson Anthem combines literary with religious memory in a living evocation of the author's death. Set to music by Arthur B. Platt in 1909 for the bicentenary birthday celebration, the text, taken from Johnson's last prayer, composed on December 5, 1784, eight days before his death "previous to his receiving the Sacrament of the Lord's Supper," reads as follows:

> Almighty and most merciful Father grant that my hope and confidence may be in Jesus' merits and Thy mercy. [semichorus]: Confirm my faith, establish my hope, enlarge my charity, Pardon my offences, and re-ceive me at my death to everlasting happiness for the sake of Jesus Christ.[18]

The entire prayer, first published in Arthur Strahan's 1785 edition of Johnson's *Prayers and Meditations,* and on sale at the Johnson Birthplace Museum as a calligraphed text superimposed on James Barry's portrait of an elderly Johnson, reads thus:

> Almighty and Most Merciful Father I am now, as to human eyes it seems, about to commemorate, for the last time, the death of Thy Son Jesus Christ our Saviour and Redeemer. Grant, O Lord, that my whole hope and confidence may be in His merits, and Thy mercy; enforce and accept my imperfect repentance; make this commemoration available to the confirmation of my faith, the establishment of my hope, and the enlargement of my charity; and make the death of Thy Son Jesus Christ effectual to my redemption. Have mercy upon me, and pardon the multitude of my offences. Bless my friends; have mercy upon all men.

Support me, by the Grace of Thy Holy Spirit, in the days of weakness, and at the hour of death, and receive me, at my death, to everlasting happiness, for the sake of Jesus Christ. Amen.[19]

Platt's anthem omits Johnson's evocation of the perspective of "human eyes." Since Johnson's death was a public spectacle recorded by many, this reminder of an uncertain worldly gaze might self-consciously evoke the particular witnesses of his final communion. More abstractly, Johnson destabilizes his personal confrontation with mortality, in all its "seeming," by addressing disembodied divine omniscience. To frame the uncertain view from "human eyes" is to ascend, obliquely and ironically, to the possibility of the god's eye view that a poem like Johnson's *Vanity of Human Wishes* initially summons in its figure of all-encompassing "Observation" and ultimately prays for in the form of "Celestial Wisdom." In the context of Johnson's life and work, even this simple prayer shows, conventional devotion is existentially fraught with contradiction and paradox. Impending death can never be known, is always a "seeming," both because the time of one's end is known only to God, and because death, or so Johnson hopes and fears, is only corporeal, a prelude to everlasting happiness or everlasting punishment. To identify with Johnson at this unedited moment would be unbearable, because at this instant of imminent death—the founding moment of Johnsonian memory—hope and fear are indistinguishable and unending. "Where then shall Hope and Fear their Objects find?" the speaker of the *Vanity* finally and desperately asks (343). In the context of a poem glutted with personified agents and devoid of human control, this query is both grammatical and existential. The questions that follow haunt Johnson's life and work:

> Must dull Suspence corrupt the stagnant Mind?
> Must helpless Man, in Ignorance sedate,
> Roll darkling down the Torrent of his Fate? (344–346)[20]

Rather than answer, the poem commands silence. "Enquirer, cease," interrupts an anonymous voice. We never learn that speaker's identity, nor are we told whether the "petitions" to heaven for sanity, obedience, patience, and resignation the voice prescribes will be granted.

Platt also omits the original text's self-abnegating references to "imperfect repentance," and the "multitude of my offenses." Like the voices in the *Vanity,* these too are double: at once typically pious (only truly repentant Christians could receive the Eucharist) and, in Johnson's case, personally fraught reminders of his notoriously excessive fear of death and the threat of death's eternally painful aftermath. This particular Christian humility borders on an almost Calvinist conviction of guilt disturbing to the comfortable belief of an Anglican establishment.[21]

The tranquil and eminently didactic death of Joseph Addison, recorded by Edward Young twenty-five years earlier in his *Conjectures on Original Composition,* was much more to the public taste.

> Forcibly grasping [his stepson's] hand, he [Addison] softly said, "See in what peace a Christian can die." He spoke with difficulty and soon expired. Thro' Grace divine, how great is man? Thro' divine Mercy, how stingless death? Who would not thus expire?[22]

"By undrawing the long-closed curtain of his death-bed," Young turns the author of the popular Roman tragedy *Cato* into the exemplary Christian actor "of a part, which the great master of the drama has appointed us to perform to-morrow" (889). Death puts all upon the stage while distinguishing the earlier master of print culture as a truly moral genius whose virtue sets his performance apart: "have I not showed you," Young asks, "a stranger in him whom you knew so well? Is not this of your favorite author,—*Nota major imago?* VIRG. [a greater image than the well-known one (*Aeneid,* II, 773)].[23] His compositions are but a noble preface; the grand work is his death." The "grand work," not written word but live animation of authorial likeness, imago, or ghost, transfixes an audience who, it is implied, violates the privacy of the dying man, drawing the bed-curtains to reveal a stage. The performance that ensues is that of an author, an invisible "spectator" previously known through his texts alone, whom death renders a "stranger" authored by another.[24]

Young domesticates the unsettlingly uncanny transformation of familiar to stranger in his revelation of the author-turned-actor by offering unequivocal evidence of Addison's Christian virtue and salvation.

Despite the title of his essay, Young admits, his ultimate goal went
beyond mere literary criticism. His "chief inducement for writing at all"
was to bring to light this particular author's final hours.

> For this is the *monumental marble* there mentioned [at the beginning of
> the text], to which I promised to conduct you; this is the sepulchral
> lamp, the long-hidden lustre of our accomplished countryman, who
> now rises, as from his tomb, to receive the regard so greatly due to the
> dignity of his death; a death to be distinguished by tears of joy; a death
> which angels beheld with delight. (889)

The image of the "monumental marble" in a "wide Pleasure-
Garden" evoked to describe Young's "somewhat licentious" and digres-
sive text at its outset becomes the open tomb of a resurrected Addison.
The prying light of Young's curiosity submerges itself in the self-illu-
minating "sepulchral lamp" of his hero's own "long-hidden lustre," as
Addison takes his final bow to long overdue death-bed applause.

As the ambiguities and controversy generated by Johnson's fear of
death in general and last prayer in particular indicate,[25] the later
author's tortured life and ambiguous death make such a polite rewriting of Christ's resurrection impossible. Addison's tomb is reassuringly
empty—Johnson's corpse endures. Even in the composition of a prayer
familiar enough to become a popular commodity, Johnson both invites
and undermines the easy exemplarity that facilitates collective identification. As they sing, the innocent choirboys and the proud town offi-
cials perpetually repeat, inhabit, and disavow the ambivalent and
irreducibly singular moment of imminent death. Their mass commemoration violates solitude and erases aberrant fear, evoking and
assuaging both in the creation of a uniquely literary kind of secular
saint, to whose words they must always return since mere words are
never sufficient.[26]

From the death of Addison to the life and afterlife of Johnson, the
author in eighteenth-century England becomes an increasingly ambiguous object of religious curiosity. For this monumental man of letters and
mass-moralist in a burgeoning print culture, literary talents are inex-
orably linked to an aberrant doubt monumentalized at the moment of
incomplete self-reckoning.[27] Ventriloquizing their countryman at his

final communion praying for hope and redemption, the good people of Lichfield pray for a confirmation of faith—not in literature but rather in the author himself—that will render an uncertain end one of everlasting happiness. They render the moment of impending doom—the hero's most solitary and dangerous, the biographers' most elusive—one of collective desire. They remember Johnson at the moment of death while willing him back to life.

*****

Let's return for a moment to those five minutes of silence at the Johnson supper—a long time to impose on guests at the social event of the Lichfield season. What does that silence signify? Ritualized silence, a counterpoint to the ritual singing of the Johnson hymn, marks Lichfield's participation in collective Johnsonian memory, while bringing that memory to its limit in an encounter with death.

At Samuel Johnson's old haunt, the Cock Tavern, Fleet Street, London, the club of belle-lettrists, journalists, statesmen and scholars founded in his name in 1884 "exactly one hundred years from Dr. Johnson's death," met quarterly for supper and a paper presented by one of the members. Lionel Johnson's poem, "At the Cheshire Cheese," surely one of the most dramatic of such presentations, conjures the great man from the dead in the form of an eminently clubbable ghost to grace the "Brethren's" proceedings. The fantasy ends with a return to reality and that same silent affirmation of melancholy community:

> If only it might be! . . . But, long as we may,
> We shall ne'er hear that laughter, *Gargantuan* and gay,
> Go pealing down *Fleet Street* and rolling away.
> In silence we drink to the silent, who rests
> In the warmth of the love of his true lovers' breasts.[28]

Death haunts this idyll of a literary Last Supper. Summoned and silenced by collective reverie, that Gargantuan laughter resounds (in a moment the poet must have had in mind) in Boswell's *Life of Johnson* "in peals so loud, that in the silence of the night his voice seemed to resound from Temple-bar to Fleet-ditch." Ironically, the subject in Boswell's anecdote that reduced Johnson "almost [to] a convulsion" of hilarity was news of a friend having made his will.

He now laughed immoderately, without any reason that we could perceive . . . called him the *testator*, and added, 'I dare say, he thinks he has done a mighty thing. He won't stay till he gets home to his seat in the country, to produce this wonderful deed: he'll call up the landlord of the first inn on the road; and, after a suitable preface upon mortality and the uncertainty of life, will tell him that he should not delay making his will; and here, Sir, will he say, is my will, which I have just made, with the assistance of one of the ablest lawyers in the kingdom; and he will read it to him (laughing all the time). He believes he has made this will; but he did not make it: you, Chambers, made it for him. I trust you have had more conscience than to make him say, "being of sound understanding;" ha, ha, ha! I hope he has left me a legacy. I'd have his will turned into verse, like a ballad.'

In this playful manner did he run on, exulting in his own pleasantry, which certainly was not such as might be expected from the authour of *The Rambler*, but which is here preserved, that my readers may be acquainted with even the slightest occasional characteristics of so eminent a man.[29]

Johnson's epic and spectral mirth, echoing down Fleet Street in the clubmen's ears over a hundred years later, mocks the futility of individual authorial attempts to assert the self beyond the grave. In his efforts to transform Johnson into a Christian exemplar, Boswell edits out his own raucous participation in the joke when he transforms his original 1773 journal entry into this episode in the 1791 *Life*.[30] In the process he creates a collective defined by their puzzled yet faithful gaze at an embattled hero whose confrontation with death at once invites and resists identification.

Their gaze seems to animate the dead. Johnson's ghostly laughter at the futility of personal wills haunts Johnsonians from Boswell to the present as they bring their hero back to life by collective will. This uncanny resurrection divides the psychic labor of Johnsonian mourning between the medical and literary professions, beginning with the emergence—and initial divergence—of those professions as distinct and respectable collectivities during the eighteenth century. The division of devotional territory between immortal spirit and mortal flesh began at the moment of Johnson's autopsy and endures to this day as the author's twitchy, inimitably voluble anecdotal ghost haunts critics, biographers, and teachers of literature, while medical writers who puzzle over his dissected corpse grant his contribution to anatomical science the unique honor of an indelibly individual name, labeling images of his organs in medical textbooks as if they were personal relics.

Two centuries later a disavowed corporeality has come to mark Samuel Johnson as ruler of English literature and representative of Englishness. He is both a monument who names an age and an eighteenth-century canon, and an uncannily familiar character (in Macaulay's phrase) "more intimately known to posterity than other men are known to their contemporaries," more beloved by many readers for his pungent sayings, anecdotal exploits, physical oddities, and medical history than for his works.[31] Perhaps more than any other English writer, Johnson makes it clear that rumors of the death of the author have been greatly exaggerated.

Inspiring both spiritual communion and moral outrage, literary Johnsonians have preserved their hero in anecdotal detail, just as medical Johnsonians have preserved his corpse in parts. Both have turned uncritical reading into author love, and thus into a kind of national secular religion based on the necessary insufficiency and self-transcending power of the printed text. Johnsonian communities vary across time and place—the festivity of the self-styled "Brethren" of the *fin-de-siècle* Johnson Club; the nostalgic Oxbridge camaraderie of early twentieth-century British critics such as Walter Raleigh and R. W. Chapman; the gentlemanly curiosity of the Royal College of Surgeons dining out at their annual London meeting on details from the manuscript of Johnson's autopsy; the professional historicism of American scholars of eighteenth-century England who found in Johnson and Boswell both a scholarly treasure trove and corporeal supplement to the text-based disembodiment of the New Criticism; the politeness of the Lichfield citizenry listening to Dame Beryl Bainbridge deliver an after-dinner lecture depicting Johnson's nervous breakdown; the sociability of the guests—amateurs and academics alike—of the wealthy Los Angeles lawyer and literary collector who hosts the annual cocktail party of the Johnson Society of Southern California in his Beverly Hills mansion.[32] Yet each of these groups shares a desire to transcend time, place, and above all, mortality, turning the individual communion of reading (that which the critic must murder to dissect), into a communal conversation with the author's spirit.

In their haunted disavowal of Johnson's mortality, and in their reinternment of Johnson in their individual breasts, Johnson's devotees both confront and avoid the double nature, material and immortal, of Johnson's body. In a literary version of the cult of the saints, Johnsonians accomplish Christian miracles, joining, in Peter Brown's phrase, "Heaven and Earth at the grave of a dead human being."[33] Just as the graves of saints provided physical sites for new forms of community that crossed social bounds, contaminating (from the pagan perspective) the "public life of the living city" with the corrupt bodies and relics of the dead, so the initial rage for published anecdotes that immortalized Johnson in intimate detail brought the dead back into uncanny contact with the living.[34]

Object of longing and fantasy, Johnson thus endures (anti-Boswellian critical efforts notwithstanding) not in the dead letter but in romance's eternal present.[35] While such resurrection evokes the romantic trope of bringing the dead to life, Johnsonian tradition also evokes the genre of romance in its blurring of the borders of history and fiction, and of secular and religious realms of meaning. From this perspective, a text like Boswell's *Life,* which in the view of many critics achieves *both* objective truth and aesthetic integrity through its impregnation with Johnsonian aether, resonates with Northrop Frye's definition of Romance as "secular scripture."[36]

In a series of lectures provocatively titled "Fiction as History," the classicist G. W. Bowersock argues that the popular genre of prose romance emerged in late antiquity as the pagan response—sometimes parodic, always imaginative—to the "miraculous narratives, both oral and written, of the early Christians."[37] Petronius in his *Satyricon,* to name one powerful example, rewrites the New Testament (in particular the Last Supper) as a brutally literalized, cannibalistic legacy.[38] Like Hamlet in the graveyard, Johnsonians contemplate their Yorick's skull in anecdotal form, with the same Shakespearean mixture of humor and pathos, scatological comedy and devout tragedy that eighteenth-century readers deplored in Shakespeare's play. Melancholic comedy and tragedy inhere in Boswell's staging and staged disavowal in the *Life* of Johnson's grim laughter at the thought of life after death. In the critical response that ensues, some of it defending a less commercial and grossly material form of Johnsonian reverence, some of it denouncing the Johnsonian phenomenon altogether, we can hear tonal echoes of satiric pagan responses to Christianity, Protestant attacks on the Catholic mass, and early modern skeptical interrogations of Western religious belief (for example, Montaigne and Swift).[39] The Johnsonian devotion of Boswell, Thrale and other anecdotal collectors, in short, inspires and contributes to a late-Enlightenment rewriting of the pagan confrontation with the corporeal nature of Christian faith.

Over their mugs of ale at the Cheshire Cheese, churchwarden pipes at the Lichfield town hall, or glasses of wine at the Dorothy Chandler Pavilion, Johnsonians thus raise, however distantly, however decorously, what Stephen Greenblatt, in a series of essays on the eucharistic controversies that dominated thought on the nature of linguistic signs in the early modern period, has recently termed "the problem of the leftover." More a problem of matter than the words that transform it, more the province of literature than theology, the Eucharist's material remainder joins the holy sacrament to human waste, Christ's immortality to mortal filth. Speaking of the Protestant reinterpretation of the sacrament as metaphorical, Greenblatt describes "an uneasy meeting: the conjunction of gross physicality and pure abstracted spirituality, of Body and Word, of corruptible flesh and invulnerable ghost, of rotting corpse and majestical ruler. We have another name for this meeting when it assumed an apparently secular form: we call it *The Tragedy of Hamlet*."[40] We could also call it Johnsonian Romance. In the originating anecdotal explosion that followed his death, to which I now turn, ghost and corpse are fused; to summon the former is to evoke the latter as the literary marketplace becomes both violated graveyard and haunted purgatory.[41]

*****

To a sophisticated audience of eighteenth-century men and women of letters, the ancestors of today's professional literary critics, the desire Johnson inspired for intimate communion through published anecdote was nothing less than a profanation of both the author's corpse and the reader's humanity. The common reader's love of Johnson, in their view, took the abstraction of critical "taste" too literally, rendering it abjectly ephemeral. In an uncanny inversion of the tradition of satiric depictions of the Christian Eucharist as cannibalism, the unprecedented demand for Johnsonian anecdote in the years following his death was denigrated as literary consumption at its most savage. As one reviewer of Thrale's *Anecdotes* put it, "An orthodox tartar may possess a certain degree of veneration for the *Dalai Lama,* without either worshipping or eating his excrements."[42]

The primitive idolatry that made Johnsonian worship a print phenomenon is brought closer to home in "a curious letter from a medical gentleman" appended to a superlatively odd anonymous satiric 1787 pamphlet aptly entitled *More Last Words of Doctor Johnson* (if Johnsonians believe in collective silence, this parody of Johnson speaks beyond the grave). This medical Johnsonian is also a man of letters, who "while busied in the sublimest physical researches, . . . ha[s] not thought it beneath [him] to inspect the water-closets of the learned." With a relentlessly materialist vision worthy of Swift's hack in *Tale of a Tub,* our author boasts that he is driven by "that curiosity which looks into the *bottom* of things, and which must of course be *fundamentally* learned."[43] Recognizing a kindred spirit in the "rank"-minded "dirty fellow" and Johnsonian biographer Sir John Hawkins, this literary acolyte plunders the spoils of the "house of office" (outhouse), "an house which has afforded me the greatest literary knowledge; not more from diving with no unhallowed hands into its sacred merdicular abyss, than from perusing the various inscriptions on its walls and windows" (33–4). There resides the stuff of Johnsonian anecdote, which is also, quite literally, shit. With all the scrutiny, at once scientific and devotional, given to the material remains of saints or sovereigns,[44] our author demonstrates his proficiency in a language of excrement that bears visible links to varieties of learning and literary styles:

Thus profound and erudite authors generally emit long and sturdy ones, somewhat in the shape of ninepins; and these are either perfect or broken as their compositions are regular or unequal, and rugged or smooth according to the asperity or courtliness of their style. Johnson's, which was large, but to appearance evacuated with great labour, was surrounded with protuberances, like a cucumber or a pomegranate; so was Swift's. Pope's was extremely uniform and elegant in its structure, with some appearance, indeed, of internal roughness; but Shenstone's was as polished, as delicate, and as mournful, as a roll of the most elegant black sealing-wax. (32–3)

Here we have, courtesy of one of its first satirists, the ultimate Johnsonian fetishism in which the author's elusive ghost is reduced to his leavings. The "great labor" of art, disavowed by Johnsonians, as my epigraph from Raleigh epitomizes, in favor of the author himself, returns in the gift of his shit, stand-in and relict of both the authorial body and its work. Critical pleasure and instinctual repulsion, refined aestheticism and gross corporeality, meld in this excremental catalog of authorial devotion (and it should be noted here that our author bases his cloacal experiments as much on taste as on sight). In this parodic treatment of the traffic in anecdotes that John Wolcot termed "Johnso-mania," the written word is transformed through contact with human filth into the very flesh it seeks to transcend. Johnsonian worship, from this skeptical perspective, inverts the sacrament, transforming the tainted text into the remains of the author "himself." Such materialist logic is reminiscent of the excremental world of Pope's *Dunciad,* while summoning up a language of resurrection, communion, and material ingestion that is parodically and suggestively eucharistic.

Speaking of Hawkins' scandalous biography, our satirist mixes classical philosophy with a smutty dismantling of the body's wholeness at the Resurrection when he recollects the "prediction of some philosophers. . . viz. *That all things which now owe their shape to mixture and alteration shall return to their first state*; for, in the houses-of-office of my friends and acquaintance, I generally see leaves of Sir John's book deposited on the shelves as offerings to Cloacina" (30). The letter culminates with the speaker's voyeuristic enjoyment (through a telescope) of the "extremely sublime" sight of Johnson defecating, his subsequent theft of the manuscript with which the great man has wiped his posterior, his presentation of the page to Boswell, its apprehension by the cook who uses it to wrap a joint of meat for dinner, and the "providential discov[ery]" of the "*literary morceau*" "by a young lady's being seen to lay something like skin on the side of her plate, that she had attempted to chew in vain."

The taste Miss___ observed was rather strong in her mouth; but the cook persisted in saying that both the taste and colour arose from the gravy of the meat....we *tasted* it all round, and it felt to the palate much more bitter than gravy. Mr. Boswell was enraged, dismissed his cook at a moment's warning, and scarcely spoke a word during the remainder of the day. Thus was a day's pleasure destroyed by the ignorance of a cook, whose folly deprived us of that pure gratification which we should have received from the perusal of what had perhaps never yet been printed, and what from the Doctor's posteriors might have been handed down to his posterity! (53–4)

Johnson's aphoristic conversation, his sayings, and in this case his ephemera, are literalized here as his "droppings."[45] Rather than read the great man's immortal words, his misguided fans, in their rage for private matter, ingest his excrement in futile attempts at communion with celebrity.

This aggressively excremental satire exposes the abject dimension of uncritical reading: from eighteenth-century posteriors to twentieth-century posterity, Johnson's corporeality has been both desired and disavowed. The author's ghost, resonating so powerfully in contemporary imaginations with the eucharistic "host," is (to play on J. Hillis Miller's etymological ponderings in his classic essay "The Critic as Host") at once host and guest, stranger and friend, of matter and beyond it, at once a vehicle for the immortality of "pure" intellectual community and that immortality's fleshly, filthy remainder.[46]

In a discussion (indebted to Miller) of the Johnson industry that emerged and proliferated in both serious and satiric modes after the great man's death, Donna Heiland has termed Johnson a "body god." Boswell's "anatomization" and "dissemination across England" of both Johnson's body of work and physical body are culturally analogous, she argues, to "the Dionysian ritual of *sparagmos*—in which a sacrificial body often identified with the god is torn to pieces, and then consumed, in the separate ritual of *omophagia*—as well as [to] the Christian counterpart to these two rituals, the celebration of the Eucharist."[47] We might also speculate that this stalwartly British version of eucharistic practice conflates (along the lines of the Anglican fusion of institutional and individual bonds in the administration of the sacrament) the ritual of Jewish Passover, with its affirmation of family and national ties, with the Christian annihilation of those ties in the service of individual membership in universal community.[48]

For contemporaries who saw such consumption as more profane than sacred, the resultant miracle was not Boswell's claim to have

"Johnsonized the land," but rather a seemingly endless process of commodification that turned the host into cheap print. One reviewer, after acknowledging what he called "Hawkins' 'entré,'" noted that Mr. Boswell's 'gleanings' and Mrs. Piozzi's 'gatherings' were about to come forth. 'The Doctor's bones must be acknowledged to be the bones of a giant, or there would be poor picking, after their having furnished *Caledonian Haggis,* and a dish of *Italian Macaroni,* besides slices innumerable cut off *from the body* [by] Magazine mongers, anecdote merchants and rhyme stringers.'"[49] "Poor DR. JOHNSON," another surfeited reviewer complained, "has been served up to us in every shape—We have had him boiled to a rag, *roasted, fricassed,* and now we are to have him scraped into a sermon on his wife's death."[50] In George Colman's 1786 "Posthumous work of S. Johnson," the author's ghost terrorizes Grub Street, reproaching his first biographer Thomas Tyers:

> Enough! The Spectre cried; Enough!
> No more of your fugacious stuff,
>   Trite Anecdotes and Stories;
> Rude Martyrs of SAM. JOHNSON's name,
> You rob him of his honest fame,
>   And tarnish all his glories.
> First in the futile tribe is seen
> TOM TYERS in the Magazine,
>   That teazer of Apollo!
> With goose-quill he, like desperate knife,
> Slices, as Vauxhall beef, my life,
>   And calls the town to swallow.[51]

At once surgeon and priest, Tyers cuts up a hero transformed into that most British of dishes, roast beef, and feeds him to the nation.[52]

The particular stakes of this struggle over embodiment have been erased over time as it has been successfully won. In contrast to the relatively disembodied figure of Shakespeare, the character of Johnson seems to gain its power to transcend local boundaries the more English and embodied it remains, the more vividly it can be summoned from the past to speak not through its texts as character-creating author but in characteristic style.[53] The Johnsonian monument, remembered as long as the

English language endures, is built with embodied trifles, displayed in literal and anecdotal parts, and haunted by its material remainder.

*****

While medical Johnsonians still puzzle over the records and relics of a corpse shadowed by an ineluctable particularity, literary Johnsonians continue to be preoccupied by authorial remains in the form of the anecdote, the genre that defeats narrative time and narrative closure, that as Joel Fineman put it, "as the narration of a single event . . . uniquely refers to the real."[54] Whether Johnsonian dissection is anecdotal or anatomical, its motive is best encapsulated by a particular anecdote about the making of anecdotes and the fragmentary "real" to which they refer. This anecdote's fascinating afterlife explicitly thematizes the vexed dynamic of Johnsonian curiosity and its object's self-conscious resistance. Boswell boasts,

> I won a small bet from Lady Diana Beauclerk, by asking [Johnson] as to one of his particularities, which her Ladyship laid I durst not do. It seems he had been frequently observed at the Club to put into his pocket the Seville oranges, after he had squeezed the juice of them into the drink which he made for himself. Beauclerk and Garrick talked of it to me, and seemed to think that he had a strange unwillingness to be discovered. We could not divine what he did with them; and this was the bold question to be put. I saw on his table the spoils of the preceding night, some fresh peels nicely scraped and cut into pieces. "O, Sir, (said I,) I now partly see what you do with the squeezed oranges which you put into your pocket at the Club." JOHNSON. "I have a great love for them." BOSWELL. "And pray, Sir, what do you do with them? You scrape them, it seems, very neatly, and what next?" JOHNSON. "Nay, Sir, you shall know their fate no further." BOSWELL. "Then the world must be left in the dark. It must be said (assuming a mock solemnity,) he scraped them, and let them dry, but what he did with them next, he never could be prevailed upon to tell." JOHNSON. "Nay, Sir, you should say it more emphatically:—he could not be prevailed upon, even by his dearest friends, to tell." 1 April, 1775.[55]

"You shall know their fate no farther." In this remarkable scene, biographer and subject self-consciously ironize the inexplicable and not wholly inedible remains of orange peel as figures for their collaboration on the *Life*. Relics, metonymic fragments of consumption and of the *Life* itself (in the manner of the incorruptible corpses of saints?)[56], the orange peels turn fragrant waste into the stuff of mystery and posterity's communal speculation. In their resolute "thingness," and their indeterminate end, they evoke Johnson's afterlife along with his corpse. They are literature's leftovers: not the triumphant proof of Addison's open tomb that makes his texts extraneous but rather the author's irreducible bones. At this paradigmatically self-referential moment, we are reminded that the *Life* was constructed as both monument and tomb: Boswell's text is haunted throughout by the ghost it endeavors to put to rest, by the undeniable fact and irresolvable mystery of its hero's death. "It is my design," Boswell wrote in a private letter, "in writing the Life of that Great and Good Man, to put as it were into a Mausoleum all the precious remains that I can gather."[57]

The orange peels have in fact endured, as Boswell and Johnson intended they should.[58] The young Samuel Beckett, deeply depressed and recovering from an unhappy love affair, took special note of this anecdote in his research for an unfinished play on Johnson (the first he attempted) called *Human Wishes*. (He also transcribed the autopsy report and many pages detailing Johnson's bodily ills). Orange peels festoon Beryl Bainbridge's curious recent novel, *According to Queeney*, an account of Johnson's relationship with Hester Thrale as seen through her daughter's eyes, which begins with an account of the autopsy.[59] In an early poem by James Merrill, "The Flint Eye," the orange peels are the ultimate memento mori, recollected by a "matriarch with eyes like arrowheads" as she sits beneath an "orange noon":

> Ah, Dr. Johnson kept the peels, she said,
> In his coat-pocket till they withered quite.
> The rinds of noon like orange-rinds had blown
>
> Out of her lap across the bright, dazed grass,
> Lay shriveling flat upon a scorched perspective,
> As though her gaze imperial had expressed
> No wish to fix them or, since all flesh is grass,

Fix poets, gross eccentrics who exist
High in the shallowest stratum of the past.

These learned gentlemen are frivolous soil,
She said, that one plows up for relics—skulls
And pottery.[60]

From the "scorched perspective" of the timeless "imperial gaze" of the
poem's heroine, at once fossil herself and anti-collector, the orange peels
remain un-"fixed," trivial, scattered upon the scorched grass. Shriveling
in the sun, linked by syntax and the leveling truism that reduces flesh to
grass in the mode of *The Vanity of Human Wishes,*[61] they stand in for the
bodies of dead poets, "gross eccentrics who exist/High in the shallowest
stratum of the past." Those poets and their followers, critical and uncritical alike, indulge in archaeological digs in just such "frivolous soil," in
search of "relics—skulls/and pottery," possessed by a need to defeat such
truisms and "fix" the passage of time. At once sophisticated and primitive, like the "amber heads" that hang from the woman's "tribal ears,"
the authorial remnants they glean from not-so-ancient history are an
attempt to defeat death, or at least to objectify it. Withered flesh, the
orange peels remind us of the carapace the soul leaves behind. Dr.
Johnson kept the peels just as Johnsonians keep his corpse. Their
ploughing up for relics is an ongoing autopsy, an excavation, at once literal and metaphorical, of an interior world, a world of the spirit, otherwise closed to them and always eluding their grasp.

In their writing of "The Gospel According to Dr. Johnson," and in
their summoning of his living ghost from a scrutinized corpse,
Johnsonians create a secular will—their own Testament—based on a
Christian paradox, that of the immortal spirit of Literature dwelling in
the author's mortal body. Ritually ventriloquizing his idol in "The
Gospel According to Dr. Johnson" (1892), the politician and man of
letters Augustine Birrell shows us how Johnsonians are made:

Death is a terrible thing to face. The man who says he is not afraid of it
lies. . . . The future is dark. I should like more evidence of the immortality of the soul. There is great solace in talk. . . . Let us constitute ourselves a club, stretch out our legs and talk. . . . Sir, let us talk, not as men

who mock at fate, not with coarse speech or foul tongue, but with a manly mixture of the gloom that admits the inevitable, and the merriment that observes the incongruous. Thus talking we shall learn to love one another, not sentimentally but essentially.[62]

To worship Johnson is to reverence and to conjure what a prominent Johnsonian has more recently called "some opening to life that texts do not close off."[63] If the love of art is pagan barbarity, the setting up of "jewelled idols, the work of men's hands, which are worshipped by the sacrifice of man's flesh and blood," then the love of authors is the work of the spirit. For scholarly Johnsonians, even (or perhaps especially) Johnson's own texts transcend their material status as objects, their artifice, in order to take on the human face of their author.[64] Johnsonian morality rejects art's painful evidence of authorial labor as human sacrifice, substituting instead, through a sacramental logic, a profoundly uncritical experience of reading that produces individual revelations of communion and community. "The writing," as our modern Johnsonian puts it, "erases itself to diffuse through the reader."[65] Like the Anglican version of the Eucharist, such reading consumes symbolically, through an act of faith, one man's singular materiality; it remembers an individual life and death that cannot be repeated yet must always be imitated ("what should books teach but the art of living?").[66] And like the Anglican sacrament, such reading emphasizes the transforming power of individual *reception* of the host over the nature of its substance. What counts in both cases is the creation of a collective body of believers through individual incorporation of an embodied example. In the case of Johnson, we might call that body the profession—once imagined as personal calling and gentlemanly conversation—of English letters. Its materiality—cast off as corpse, excrement, the peel of an orange, the print on the page—remains; its spirit endures. If we are scholars, it demands our speech.

*****

[W]hen he was about nine years old, having got the play of Hamlet in his hand, and reading it quietly in his father's kitchen, he kept on steadily enough, until coming to the Ghost scene, he suddenly hurried up the stairs to the street door that he might see people about him.

—Hester Thrale[67]

On the Cathedral Square in Lichfield, the house where Johnson was
born and spent his childhood has been renovated as the Samuel
Johnson Birthplace Museum. The front of the house was restored in
1989 to its original status as a bookstore. It was here that the young
Johnson, a masculine Eve in search of an apple, stumbled upon a volume of Petrarch and acquired a secret taste for romance that stayed
with him all his life. The other rooms are used as galleries. Some
display Johnsonian artifacts—Elizabeth Johnson's wedding ring,
Samuel's shoe buckles, ivory writing tablets, a favorite China saucer
Johnson nicknamed "Tetty" after his wife and used daily after her
death. The museum is scattered with appeals to children—Johnson's
cat Hodge introduces himself as "one of Dr. Johnson's favorite cats,"
and exhorts children to find the five cats hiding in the house; another
flier, a page from a coloring book, challenges them to design stylish
wigs for Boswell and Johnson; an elaborate electronic device festooned
with portraits of Johnson bears a label reading "can you return the dictionary to Dr. Johnson without making a sound?" This house is haunted by a friendly ghost, the Samuel Johnson described by Macaulay as a
childhood familiar, a Johnson glimpsed from the nostalgically posses-
sive perspective of the miniature.[68]

Unlike other tastefully empty author's houses, including the
Johnson museum in London, the Lichfield museum is rather tackily
embodied. Several rooms recreate tableaux from the hero's life. In one
scene a department store mannequin dressed as Johnson's father pre-
sides over a reproduction of a bookseller's workroom. The educational
fliers nearby pinpoint the display as one of general historical interest,
useful for teachers taking school children on tours. Another tableau,
rendering the details of an eighteenth-century kitchen, recreates a
Johnsonian anecdote that inadvertently imbricates the viewer in a less
distanced form of curiosity, engaging not historical interest but literary
imagination. It portrays, aptly enough for our purposes, a scene of
uncritical reading.

A young Sam Johnson (a boy mannequin with a mop of visibly arti-
ficial dark hair) dressed in a nightshirt sits before the fire with a book.
The flier describing the scene reads as follows:

> "He that peruses Shakespeare, looks around alarmed, and starts to
> find himself alone."

The tableau depicts the famous incident, which took place in this room when Samuel Johnson was about nine years old.

> "Having got the play of Hamlet in his hand and reading it quietly in his father's kitchen, he kept on steadily enough, till he came to the ghost scene, he suddenly hurried upstairs to the street door that he might see people about him."

> Because of the lack of warmth in his family Johnson must have found a source of comfort in reading the books he discovered in his father's shop. As well as Shakespeare we know that he found a volume of Petrarch, the Renaissance poet and philosopher, and a book on Scotland, which he recalled when he made his own Scottish tour. He also became an avid reader of tales of chivalry & romance. (SJ Birthplace Museum Flier, Panel 1, The Kitchen)

Immortalized in awkward effigy is an exemplary scene of Johnsonian reading: a transcendence of time, enabled by literature, fixed in "this room," the very room in which the author-as-reader once sat. This tableau's paradoxical embodiment of a private moment of imagination demands the viewer's act of faith in things not seen. Driven by a lack of familial warmth to imaginary companionship, the kitchen fire, and *Hamlet,* the impressionable young Johnson sees a ghost; in the tableau's aftermath he rushes to the street in order to verify his place in reality and history, to erase the terror of the supernatural world of his reading that has momentarily supplanted the real world. He abandons the play and its dreadful encounter with a dead father to "see people about him."

That ghost, the flier reminds us, still haunts the adult Johnson's criticism of Shakespeare; his individual experience of the scene from *Hamlet* comes to epitomize the universal response of the common reader of Shakespeare in general who "starts to find himself alone." In the flier's quotation from the *Preface to Shakespeare,* Johnson has erased fear, his youthful dash to the street, his need to see people about him. The common reader fills that need. And so, as we gaze at the kitchen, do we: standing before the clumsy surrogate of the young Johnson who is rapt before a ghostly vision, we provide the living companionship of "people about him," becoming reassuring flesh and blood counterparts to the play's ghostly world.

Literature, so this tableau shows, perpetually confounds the dead with the living; by disarming us of our critical distance it threatens to substitute one for the other. *Hamlet,* in particular, is set in motion by the obligations of the living to the restless dead, whose sin leaves their fate unconcluded. "Remember me," the ghost demands. A ghost himself, Johnson is remembered in this scene in the act of terrified encounter with his own future image.

In her reading of *Hamlet* in *Shakespeare's Ghostwriters,* Marjorie Garber meditates on Shakespeare himself (who was known for his stage portrayal of the ghost in *Hamlet*) as the ultimate ghost, the ultimate absent presence, of the father/author, of history, and of writing itself.[69] While Garber can build a compelling psychoanalytic/deconstructive reading of the author's ghostly presence by focusing on the disembodied figure of Shakespeare, the character of Johnson, more beloved by Johnsonians precisely because he is neither Shakespeare nor Milton, gains universality the more particularly and locally embodied it remains. The reading mannequin reminds us of the real corpse beneath this author's ghostly figure. Like the orange peel, it at once blocks and solicits our identification. In a secular version of religious communion, Johnsonians build their monument to the author, and with it their professional and national identities, in the disfigured shape of a flawed mortal body. They reinvent their ghost as a benign father, intent not on revenge but on self-perpetuation through companionable common reading. We cannot help but recognize him—his fate is our own. Our hero of reading's romance, he allows us to know that fate no further.

Notes

My special thanks go to Claudia Johnson for her ongoing support and inspiration. She solicited this essay and found it an ideal audience. I am grateful to Rick Barney, Lorna Clymer, Page duBois, Jayne Lewis, Michael Meranze, Vivian Sobchack and Julia Stern for their insights into various drafts of this essay. My enduring thanks go to Jane Gallop for her invaluable editorial contributions.

1. Samuel Johnson, Review of Soame Jenyns' *A Free Enquiry into the Nature and Origin of Evil* (1757), in Donald Greene, ed., *The Oxford Authors: Samuel Johnson* (Oxford: Oxford University Press, 1984), 536.
2. Michael Joyce, *Samuel Johnson* (London: Longman's, 1955), vi.
3. John Bailey, *Dr. Johnson and His Circle, The Home University Library of Modern Knowledge* 64 (Oxford: Oxford University Press, 1913), rev. L.F. Powell, 1945.

4. Thomas Babington, Lord Macaulay, "Samuel Johnson" (1831), in *Critical and Historical Essays,* ed. Hugh Trevor Roper (New York: McGraw Hill, 1965), 115.

5. For the ambiguities of agency posed by Johnson's tics see my "The Author as Monster: The Case of Dr. Johnson," in Helen Deutsch and Felicity Nussbaum, eds., *"Defects": Engendering the Modern Body* (University of Michigan Press, 2000), 177–209.

6. Bertrand H. Bronson, "The Double Tradition of Dr. Johnson," in *Johnson Agonistes and Other Essays* (Berkeley: University of California Press, 1965), 156–176.

7. James Boswell, *Life of Johnson,* ed. R. W. Chapman (Oxford: Oxford University Press, 1980), 297.

8. Joseph Roach's reading of the socially liminal yet culturally representative figure of the actor Thomas Betterton in chapter 3 of *Cities of the Dead: Circum-Atlantic Performance* (New York: Columbia University Press, 1996), whose performance of Hamlet in particular served to immortalize him as national mediator between the living and the dead, and Kevin Hart's consideration in his first chapter of the "life in death" state of Johnson as a monument aware of his representative status before he died to commemorate it in *Samuel Johnson and the Culture of Property* (Cambridge: Cambridge University Press, 1999), both underline my analysis of Johnson's ghost. Roach's brilliant analysis of Betterton's funeral and its dissemination in print epitomizes his investigation of the "cultural use of marginal identities to imagine a new kind of community" (17). While Roach does not discuss the figure of the author (whose self-made status, as Johnson's case exemplified and as I have discussed elsewhere, made him a kind of social monster), I see striking homologies between the author and the actor, both marginal and central to British culture and its production, both inspiring communal bonds of love. For a suggestive treatment of *Hamlet* that deals specifically with theater as the post-Reformation residual and liminal space of departed souls, see Stephen Greenblatt, *Hamlet in Purgatory* (Princeton: Princeton University Press, 2001).

9. Frederick A. Pottle and Charles Ryskamp, eds., *Boswell: The Ominous Years 1774–1776* (New York: McGraw Hill, 1963), 80.

10. Boswell would later attempt to distance Johnson from this anti-American pamphlet in the *Life.* See 590–91.

11. Interestingly the flesh resurfaces almost immediately in the journal entry: Boswell's merging with Johnson's spirit is followed by a meditation on the desirability of polygamy and its permissibility for monarchs ancient and modern.

12. For more on the convergence of literary and medical Johnsonians at the event of the autopsy, see Helen Deutsch, "Dr. Johnson's Autopsy," *The Eighteenth Century: Theory and Interpretation* 40.2 (Summer 1999), 113–127.

13. Eric O. Clarke, "Shelley's Heart: Sexual Politics and Cultural Value," *Yale Journal of Criticism* 8 (1995), 199. This difference is not unrelated to the differing sexual politics of Shelley love and Johnson love. In Clarke's account, Shelley love becomes too queer as definitions of masculinity

change over the course of the nineteenth century. Thus the fetishization of the text allows the poet's readers, like Freud's fetishizer of a jock strap, to have their homoerotic cake and deny it too. For the Johnsonian "Brethren," the manly love of an unthreatening and desexualized father is much less dangerous.

14. See Hart, for an analysis of the G. B. Hill and L. F. Powell magisterial 1934 edition of Boswell's *Life* as "an annotated scripture for eighteenth-century literary scholars," a microcosm of the period that "devalues Johnson in favor of his age" (88).

15. H. J. Jackson, *Marginalia: Readers Writing in Books* (New Haven: Yale University Press, 2001), 165. Frustrated by her inability to find an intellectual pattern of response to the *Life,* Jackson concludes "Boswell's readers were looking for help with their own lives and were most struck by those places in which there was something at stake for them personally" (178).

16. Walter Raleigh, *Six Essays on Johnson* (Oxford: Clarendon Press, 1910), 31. Raleigh first delivered this as the Leslie Stephen Lecture in the Senate House, Cambridge, 1907.

17. *Transactions of the Johnson Society* (Lichfield, 1949–50), 12–13. Johnson's birthplace, a house and bookshop on the Lichfield Market Square, was purchased by the city of Lichfield in 1887 and turned into a museum in 1901.

18. Boswell, *Life,* 1391–2; Arthur Murphy, *Essay on Johnson's Life and Genius* (1792), in Hill, *Miscellanies,* 1, 356.

19. This prayer has been the source of controversy among Johnson scholars, who have debated whether or not it documents a "late conversion" to evangelical Christianity. While the consensus seems to be that Johnson remained a high-Church Anglican to the end, it is generally agreed that he did experience a marked "turn" (in the literal sense of conversion) toward repentance and grace during the last months of his life. What interests me about such narratives of Johnson's religious life is that, whatever their differences, all are structured as romances of quest and Christian resolution that the conflicting endings to his story refuse to grant. For one of many examples, see Charles E. Pierce, Jr., *The Religious Life of Samuel Johnson* (Hamden, CT: Archon Books, 1983).

20. *Samuel Johnson: The Complete English Poems,* ed. J.D. Fleeman (New Haven: Yale University Press, 1982), 91–2.

21. For a guide to the multiple and conflicting accounts of Johnson's death motivated by differing attitudes toward his fear of death, see Paul J. Korshin, "Johnson's Last Days: Some Facts and Problems," in Paul J. Korshin, ed., *Johnson After Two Hundred Years* (Philadelphia: University of Pennsylvania Press, 1986), 55–76. Johnson would have understood the Anglican sacrament of the Eucharist as meant to provide "spiritual nourishment," and "medicine that provided to the soul needed grace." Most important in Johnson's case, the Eucharist "gave assurance of the resurrection to eternal life, calming fears concerning one's eternal state" [Robert D. Cornwall, *Visible and Apostolic: The Constitution of the Church in High Church Anglican and Non-Juror Thought* (Newark: University of Delaware Press, 1993)], 139.

22. Edward Young, *Conjectures on Original Composition* (1759), in Geoffrey Tillotson, ed., *Eighteenth-Century English Literature* (New York: Harcourt, Brace & World, Inc., 1969), 888.

23. The context of the line is intriguing. Aeneas, about to kill Helen of Troy in retribution for the damages of the war, recognizes his mother Venus, revealed to him for the first time as immortal.

24. Addison's persona of disembodied *Spectator* comes to mind here, as if Young's project were to provide a supplement to such elusiveness by displaying the author at the moment of death.

25. For the controversy provoked by the publication of the *Prayers and Meditations,* a text that revealed, among other things, Johnson's unorthodox and superstitious belief in Purgatory, see Maurice J. Quinlan, "The Reaction to Dr. Johnson's *Prayers and Meditations,*" *The Journal of English and Germanic Philology* 52.2 (April 1953), 125–39.

26. The Transactions of the Johnson Society of Lichfield for 1988 contain an essay by the Bishop of Oxford proposing Johnson as an Anglican saint, complete with a drafted commemoration service. See Hart, 66–67. Such canonization (underwriting the literary canon as a religious one) was ironically proposed in *The St. James Chronicle* soon after Johnson's death under the heading of DEIFICATION. Undated clipping, Samuel Lysons' Book of Cuttings, Columbia University Rare Book Library.

27. In this regard, Johnson's embattled Christian death was often compared to the peaceful death of the skeptic David Hume (Boswell went to witness the latter). See, for example, Rev. William Agutter, A.M., *On the Difference between the Deaths of the Righteous and the Wicked, Illustrated in the Instance of DR. SAMUEL JOHNSON, and DAVID HUME, Esq. A Sermon, Preached before the University of Oxford at St. Mary's Church on Sunday, July 23, 1786* (London, 1800). In his defense of Johnson's fearful death, Agutter addresses the failure of exemplarity by exposing it as inherently theatrical. See also Michael Ignatieff, *The Needs of Strangers* (New York: Viking, 1985); Stephen Miller, *Three Deaths and Enlightenment Thought: Hume, Johnson, Marat* (Lewisburg, PA: Bucknell University Press, 2001). For Johnson's life-long obsession with the parable of the talents (Matthew XXV 14-30) and the punishment of the "unprofitable servant," see Boswell, *Life*, 1400; Johnson, *Rambler* 77; and "Verses on the Death of Dr. Robert Levet," whose "single talent" was "well employed" (28).

28. Lionel Johnson, "At the Cheshire Cheese," in George Whale and John Sargeaunt, eds., *Johnson Club Papers by Various Hands* (London: T. Fisher Unwin, 1899), 276.

29. Boswell, *Life*, (May–July 1773), 548–9.

30. Greg Clingham, *James Boswell: The Life of Johnson* (Cambridge: Cambridge University Press, 1992), 59–60. Clingham notes in addition that Boswell's partly uncomprehending novelistic "hyperbole" in this passage "moves away from burlesque towards nightmare" (54).

31. Macaulay, "Samuel Johnson," 115.

32. I am indebted here to Claudia Johnson's ongoing work on the history and multiplicity of meanings of Jane Austen as "cultural fetish." Many

of the early twentieth-century British Janeites Johnson analyzes, "committed to club rather than domestic society," to a queer form of literary reproduction rather than the heterosexual imperative, and to a love of tangential detail rather than the teleology of plot, were also Johnsonians. Some of the same queer impulses toward male community outside of domesticity linked to a common nostalgia for a past Britain fuel the love of Johnson. He seems to be her male counterpart, living a single literary life (the queerness of his household almost a parody of domesticity) free from both the novel genre and the tyranny of the novel's plot. Claudia Johnson, "Austen Cults and Cultures," in Edward Copeland and Juliet McMaster, eds., *The Cambridge Companion to Jane Austen* (Cambridge: Cambridge University Press, 1997), 212, 216. For a history of Johnson as cultural monument with an emphasis on that monument's status as public property, see Hart.

33. Peter Brown, *The Cult of the Saints: Its Rise and Function in Latin Christianity* (Chicago: University of Chicago Press, 1981), 1. Brown's book reminds us of how radically alien, even monstrous, the worship of the bodies of saints seemed to pagan minds in late antiquity. Rendering bodily resurrection (previously unimaginable to the sophisticated pagan imagination and conceivable only in the distant future to Jews and early Christians) literally commonplace, the saint crossed the seemingly immutable boundaries of the late-antique universe, "between those beings who had been touched by the taint of human death and those who had not," between mortal heroes and immortal gods, between dead matter and living soul. The saint, in short, permanently altered the pagan "familiar map of the relations between the human and the divine, the dead and the living" (5). On pagan ideas of the afterlife and an argument about the treatment of Christianity in pagan romance to which I am much indebted, see G. W. Bowersock, *Fiction as History: Nero to Julian* (Berkeley: University of California Press, 1994).

34. On the new physical proximity of the dead in the Christian cult of the saints, see Brown, 4–5. Joseph Roach discusses the emergent eighteenth-century practice of segregation of the dead from the living as symptomatic of complex problems of empire's memory, denial, surrogation, and fetishization. The print frenzy that immortalized Johnson before and (especially) after his death demonstrates beyond doubt that the eighteenth-century world of print is also an uncanny world that brings the dead, at once marginal and representative back into contact with the living.

35. Boswell's foremost critic is the Johnsonian Donald Greene, who played the Puritan text-based counterpart to Boswell's Anglican mode of author-worship. See in particular his "The Logia of Samuel Johnson," in Paul J. Korshin, ed., *The Age of Johnson: A Scholarly Annual* 3 (New York: AMS Press, 1990), 1–33, which models its dissection of the "truth" of Boswell's *Life* upon the philological study of scripture. The *Life*'s status as Johnsonian bible is paradoxically bolstered by this attack. See also Greene's vituperative, "The World's Worst Biography," *The American Scholar* 62.3 (Summer 1993), 365–82.

36. Northrop Frye, *The Secular Scripture: A Study of the Structure of Romance* (Cambridge, MA: Harvard University Press, 1976). On questions of truth and fiction in Boswell's *Life* as mediated by Johnson's character and animated presence, see Fredric V. Bogel, "Did You Once See Johnson Plain?: Reflections on Boswell's *Life* and the State of Eighteenth-Century Studies," and Ralph Rader, "Literary Form in Factual Narrative: The Example of Boswell's *Johnson*," in John A. Vance, ed., *Boswell's Life of Johnson: New Questions, New Answers* (Athens: University of Georgia Press, 1985), 73–93 and 25–52; Clingham, *Boswell: Life of Johnson*; William C. Dowling, *Language and Logos in Boswell's* Life of Johnson (Princeton: Princeton University Press, 1981), particularly on "perspective as moral choice" (158–9).

37. "Fiction became antiquity's most eloquent expression of the nexus between polytheism and scripture" (Bowersock, 141).

38. For a contemporary reference to Petronius that attempts to justify Johnson's autopsy, see Thomas Tyers, "A Biographical Sketch of Dr. Johnson," in *The Early Biographies of Samuel Johnson,* eds. O M Brack, Jr. and Robert E. Kelley (Iowa City: University of Iowa Press, 1974), 62. The *Satyricon* reached the height of its popularity in Europe in the eighteenth century.

39. See for example, George Hoffmann, "Anatomy of the Mass: Montaigne's 'Cannibals'," *PMLA* 117.2, 207–221.

40. Stephen Greenblatt, "Remnants of the Sacred in Early Modern England," in *Subject and Object in Renaissance Culture,* eds. Margreta de Grazia, Maureen Quilligan, and Peter Stalleybrass (Cambridge: Cambridge University Press, 1996), 342, 344. See also Greenblatt's "The Mousetrap," in Catherine Gallagher and Stephen Greenblatt, *Practicing New Historicism* (Chicago: University of Chicago Press, 2000), 136–62.

41. "It may be said, the death of Dr. Johnson kept the public mind in agitation beyond all former example. No literary character ever excited so much attention" [Arthur Murphy, *Essay on Johnson's Life and Genius* (1792), in Hill, *Miscellanies*, 1, 356].

42. *English Review* VI (April 1786): 259. The article begins: "The love of anecdote is one of the most prevailing passions, or rather appetites, of the present age" (254).

43. Francis, barber [pseudonym], *More last Words of Dr. Johnson: consisting of important and valuable anecdotes, and a curious letter from a medical gentleman: now published, for the first time, from the doctor's manuscripts, with some original and interesting stories of a private nature, relative to that great man: to which are added several singular and unaccountable facts relative to his biographical executor, formerly chairman of the quarter sessions* (London, 1787), 29. The pseudonym alludes to Johnson's black ward and servant, the West Indian-born Francis Barber, whom Johnson educated, and, scandalously, made his executor. For a reading of Swift's materialism in *Tale of a Tub* that resonates with my thinking on the double nature of Johnson's corpse, see James Noggle, *The Skeptical Sublime* (Oxford: Oxford University Press, 2001), 71–96.

44. In a longer version of this essay I would discuss this pamphlet in relation to the concurrent public and medical obsession with the bodily leavings of the intermittently mad George III on the one hand, and the published autopsy of George II, who died on the commode, on the other. Also germane is the medical gentleman's recording of scientific experiments involving the application of authorial feces to his skull—apparently, this made him smarter. This seems to me to be a secular literary/medical version of the magical power of saints' relics.

45. I owe this phrase to Robert Griffin, personal communication.

46. J. Hillis Miller, "The Critic as Host," in Harold Bloom et al., *Deconstruction and Criticism* (New York: Seabury Press, 1979), 220–21.

47. Donna Heiland, "Remembering the Hero in Boswell's *Life of Johnson*," in Greg Clingham, ed., *New Light on Boswell: Critical and Historical Essays on the Occasion of the Bicentenary of* The Life of Johnson (Cambridge: Cambridge University Press, 1991), 199–200.

48. Gillian Feeley-Harnik, *The Lord's Table: Eucharist and Passover in Early Christianity* (Philadelphia: University of Pennsylvania Press, 1981), chap. 5. In this regard, it is worth noting that Anglican theology emphasized the ecclesiastical nature of the Eucharist, its meaning as collective body of the English church.

49. Unidentified newspaper clipping, Quoted by Mary Hyde, *The Impossible Friendship* (Cambridge MA: Harvard University Press, 1972), 80.

50. *Morning Post,* 12 March, 1788, qtd. in Robert E. Kelley and O. M. Brack, Jr., *Samuel Johnson's Early Biographers* (Iowa City: University of Iowa Press, 1971), 11.

51. John Wilson Croker, ed., *Johnsoniana; or, Supplement to Boswell* (London, 1836), 476.

52. During Johnson's own lifetime such cannibalistic discourse articulated a struggle for a representative national body and language. Consider a Glasgow paper's response to the author's visit to the Isle of Skye, quoted toward the end of Boswell's *Tour to the Hebrides*:

> We are well assured that Dr. Johnson is confined by tempestuous weather to the isle of Skye. . . Such a philosopher, detained on an almost barren island, resembles a whale left upon the strand. The latter will be welcome to everybody, on account of his oil, his bone, &c. and the other will charm his companions, and the rude inhabitants, with his superior knowledge and wisdom, calm resignation, and unbounded benevolence. (R. W. Chapman ed., James Boswell, *Journal of a Tour to the Hebrides* [Oxford: Oxford University Press, 1924, rep. 1979,], 392).

Likening the "consumption of Johnson's conversation to corporeal decimation," this passage in Orrin N. C. Wang's reading also evokes "an anxiousness that it be Scotland's citizens who first and foremost make off with the benefits of [union] with England" (80). Johnson's conversation and intellect provide a feast of cultural capital figured here as the rewards of national community. "The Politics of Aphasia in Boswell's *Journal of a Tour to the Hebrides*," *Criticism* 36.1 (Winter 1994): 73–100.

53. It's important to remember however that the eighteenth century was the first era that saw fit to embody Shakespeare in his own anthropomorphic monument, while founding a Shakespeare industry that rivaled Johnson's in its author worship. Shakespeare's disembodiedness served him better in later periods since it allowed him to translate empire through print in a way that Johnson's resolutely corporeal ghost could not. I am indebted to Coppelia Kahn's work in progress for this point, as well as a reminder from Jennifer Davidson. For Shakespeare's monumentalization see Michael Dobson, *The Making of the National Poet: Shakespeare, Adaptation, and Authorship, 1660–1769* (Oxford: Clarendon Press, 1992).

54. Joel Fineman, "The History of the Anecdote: Fiction and Fiction," in H. Aram Veeser, ed., *The New Historicism* (New York, 1989), 56.

55. Boswell, *Life,* 602–03. My thanks to Jerome Christensen for pointing out the connection between autopsy and orange peel.

56. Thanks to Julia Stern for this suggestion.

57. James Boswell to Joseph Walker, in Marshall Waingrow, ed., *The Correspondence and other Papers of James Boswell Relating to the Making of* The Life of Johnson (New York: McGraw-Hill, 1966), 96. "When people today choose Boswell as a guide to Johnson, they pick up his biography little realizing it is a sepulchre" (Hart, 32).

58. They are preserved in a literary reliquary that I will be examining in more detail over the course of the book of which this essay is a part.

59. Beckett's *Human Wishes,* as well as the notebooks in which he researched the play, are discussed by Ruby Cohn in *Just Play: Beckett's Theater* (Princeton: Princeton University Press, 1980), 143–62. Cohn also prints the fragment itself in an appendix (295–305). The orange peel reference, my own discovery, appears in notebook 1, pp. 2–3. Beryl Bainbridge, *According to Queeney* (New York: Carroll & Graf, 2001). It will be worth considering why both modern and post-modern authors chose to focus on "Johnson in love" by telling the story of Johnson's unrequited relationship with Hester Thrale, and why Beckett ultimately shifts his gaze to Johnson alone at the moment of death.

60. James Merrill, *First Poems* (New York: Alfred A. Knopf, 1951), 8. I am indebted to Wayne Gochenour for calling this text to my attention. My thanks to Stephen Yenser for his help with this poem, and for his reminder that Merrill returned to "Oranges" in one of the last poems of his career.

61. And possibly in an evocation of Whitman, who himself imagined bodily communion through his book? (Thanks to Julia Stern for initiating this connection).

62. Augustine Birrell, *Self-Selected Essays: A Second Series* (London: Thomas Nelson and Sons, 1916?), 86–87.

63. "The contradiction between life and writing where the modern critic ends is the point at which Johnson begins, the problem he sets out to solve. And if Johnson cannot be said to have solved that problem once and for all, neither can it be said that modern theories of intertextuality have proved very satisfactory at accounting for Johnson. We need some opening to life that texts do not close off" (Lawrence Lipking,

"Johnson and the Meaning of Life," in James Engell, ed., *Johnson and His Age, Harvard English Studies* 12 [Cambridge, MA: Harvard University Press, 1984], 19).

64. The name of this trope is prosopopeia. I discuss its relevance to Johnsonian reading, and to Paul de Man's particular definition of the trope in "Autobiography as De-Facement" (in *The Rhetoric of Romanticism* [New York: Columbia University Press, 1984], 67–81) in another section of the book of which this essay is a part. Also drawing on de Man, and outlining Johnson's own eucharistic disavowal of schol-arly knowledge in the service of creating a "common reader" is an essay to which I am greatly indebted and discuss at length elsewhere, Neil Hertz's "Dr. Johnson's Forgetfulness, Descartes' Piece of Wax," *Eighteenth-Century Life* 16 (November 1992), 167–81.

65. Lipking suggestively continues, "Hence Johnson becomes the container and thing contained: simultaneously a mode of thinking and the object of that thought, an example of something and the something it exem-plifies, an instance of life and the life that gives it meaning" ("Johnson and the Meaning of Life," 23). In his serious contemplation of Johnson's moral project, Lipking's evocation of the author rehearses (however unconsciously) a structural symbolism that is profoundly Christian.

66. From a Protestant perspective, to repeat the sacrifice of the crucifixion would be sacrilege; from the pagan perspective, to sacrifice a god rather than to a god was the ultimate barbarity. See William R. Crockett, *Eucharist: Symbol of Transformation* (New York: Pueblo Publishing Co., 1989), 128–63 for a good summation of Reformation thinking on the Eucharist.

   In a parallel vein, Anglican doctrine held saints to be exemplary but not divine—models for imitation rather than worship. The translation of Johnson into the category of secular saint works well when we consider the ways in which the Protestant transformation of the saint also dis-avows a history of hagiographic embodiment (commemorated in Johnson's case by the preservation of his corpse by medical writers). See Paul Elmer More and Frank Leslie Cross, eds., *Anglicanism: The Thought and Practice of the Church of England, Illustrated from the Religious Literature of the Seventeenth Century* (London: Society for Promoting Christian Knowledge, 1935), 524–40.

67. Hester Thrale, *Anecdotes of Samuel Johnson,* in Hill, *Miscellanies,* 1, 158.

68. I am indebted in my thinking on miniaturization and collection to Susan Stewart's *On Longing: Narratives of the Miniature, the Gigantic, the Souvenir* (Baltimore: Johns Hopkins University Press, 1984).

69. Marjorie Garber, *Shakespeare's Ghostwriters: Literature as Uncanny Causality* (New York: Methuen, 1987), 124–76.

4

Argument and Ethos

Amanda Anderson

An insistence on the subjective, psychological, or irreducibly human elements of ostensibly impersonal or objective theories informs much of contemporary scholarship in the humanities. Yet at the same time a key dimension of subjectivity in the tradition of ethics and in the practical criticism of many literary genres—character or ethos—has suffered a kind of exile from theoretical work in the field of literary and cultural studies. Indeed, the theoretical terms of art used to denote subjective experience in contemporary literary and cultural studies—identity, hybridity, performativity, disidentification, embodiment—simply fail to capture key features of character and ethos. To be sure, characterological terms appear with a kind of regularity across many debates in theory; at the least, they form part of the adjectival and adverbial arsenal that enlivens any richly descriptive analytical critique. We have become accustomed to hearing pragmatists called smug, or rationalists depicted as defensive and uptight. The hermeneut of suspicion is paranoid; the p.c. brigade oppressively pious. But in part because of established disciplinary protocols, such ascriptions often seem not to be an integral part of the formal argument; indeed, it typically remains unclear, when they appear, whether they are gratuitous or crucially significant, descriptive flourish or evaluative death blow. On the one hand, as terms of critique, such statements seem to dismiss without examining, to imply deficient psychology rather than misguided argument. On the other hand, such judgments are assumed to matter, to need saying, to carry some vital explanatory force. And indeed, appeals to character appear not only at moments of negative judgment; theorists sometimes feel impelled to flesh out their accounts through appeal to characterological enactment. What the critic of pragmatism sees as smugness, for example, the practitioner occasionally elaborates as an admirable characterological achievement. In the case of Richard Rorty's "ironist" or Barbara Herrnstein Smith's "postmodern skeptic," in fact, a properly casual and unbothered relation to the post-foundational world is offered up precisely as exemplary character.[1]

As the example of pragmatism shows, the concept of character is not always fated to outright exile, though it is salient that both Rorty and Smith work across the fields of philosophy and literature. Within the philosophical field more generally, the concepts of character and ethos have enjoyed something of a resurgence, not only within the subfield of "virtue ethics," but also across a range of writings in political philosophy that might be seen as affiliated with this larger development.[2] Yet even as there are multiple lines of influence extending from political philosophy to literary studies, the concepts of character and ethos have tended to undergo strange transformations and suppressions in the literary field, despite widespread claims of a "turn to ethics."[3] It is worth exploring when and how such transformations and suppressions occur, especially given the persistent refusal to avow categories of thought that nonetheless make themselves felt with such persistence.

The odd status of character and ethos in contemporary literary and cultural studies in some ways might be viewed as the effect of a more general skepticism toward the self-authorizing subject. But as concepts allied above all with habitual practice and self-cultivation, character and ethos need not evoke or consolidate mystified notions of autonomy or individuality. Indeed, these concepts might be seen as fully pertinent to a theoretical field obsessively occupied with naming and delineating the subjective effects and potentialities of its more general, transsubjective claims. The subjective forms that currently prevail in literary and cultural studies—identity, hybridity, performativity, and so on—all imagine various ways in which one might enact, own, or modify one's relation to the impersonal determinants of individual identity. As such, they involve a high level of attentiveness to the experiential and practical dimensions of theory. But these understandings of subjective experience typically do not assign importance to, or even recognize, characterological concepts or rhetoric, stressing instead forms of self-understanding that revolve around sociological, ascribed understandings of group identity: gender, race, class, nationality, sexuality.

Certainly ethical language may be employed to suggest better or worse ways of dealing with the dynamics of identity and with others. But the notion that those practices that constitute our various intellectual and political spheres, whether actively cultivated or less reflectively routinized, carry ethical significance in part because they tend to become inscribed as character and ethos, seems incompatible with the popular notion that dramas of identity are staged as a performance or subversion of multiple and variously experienced social identities. The latter framework for understanding selfhood and practice equates inscribed or fixed identities with hegemonic force, while it imagines subversion as a practice that negates identity rather than builds anything like character, which in its eyes would be an anachronistic, ideological term associated with individualism and moralism.

The present essay proposes to examine what at first blush might look like the strongest counter-example that could be drawn from the theoretical field influencing literary and cultural studies: the later work of Foucault, which very much foregrounds an ethos of self-cultivation. My analysis will comprise two parts. First, I will argue that the appeal to ethos in Foucault's late work—and more importantly in the reception of that work by the Anglo-American academy—actually functions to cloud the ways that character and ethos might redress the underdeveloped normative and practical dimensions of much current theory. The prominence accorded to ethos by many of Foucault's admiring commentators has taken place within a specific polemical field: it has been introduced as a key element in the response to charges of normative incoherence leveled by Habermas and like-minded critics. Consequently, a misleading and unfortunate opposition between ethos and rational argument has become entrenched. To pursue and amplify this claim, I will in the final portion of the essay turn to Habermas's writings, including his critique of Foucault, so as to show where we might begin more fully to acknowledge the role played by ethos in Habermas's own theories. While I shall identify the ways that Habermas himself plays into the tendency to oppose reason and ethos, I will try to tease out the important and overlooked ways in which he also relies upon ethos in his own conceptions of intellectual attitude and democratic practice. This particular strand of his work suggests compelling ways in which reason and ethos might be configured dialectically, rather than oppositionally. More generally, by exploring the category of ethos in the work of both thinkers, this essay hopes to illuminate the ways in which the analysis of intellectual fields of debate might be advanced by a fuller acknowledgment of the insistent presence of ideals of character and ethos in our practical philosophies.

My yoking of the terms *character* and *ethos* requires preliminary comment, especially insofar as the term *ethos* does enjoy some privilege in certain dimensions of current theory, and insofar as it functions prominently in the Foucaultian literature, whereas *character* tends not to appear at all. As I will show, the term *ethos* can allow for pronounced mystification: as a term that can loosely mean habit, custom, practice, or manner, *ethos* often allows one to assign honorific status or moral resonance without seeming to specify virtue or value in any bald, vulgar way. Precisely because ethos cannot be reduced to the explicitness of a rule or code, it is open to slippery usage, and seems especially useful to theorists who seek to avoid direct avowal of norms and principles yet nonetheless want to affirm their commitment to practical ethics and politics. On the Foucault side of the Foucault/Habermas literature, as I will show, it functions in this way.

In this essay, I will favor the word *ethos* over *character*, not only because *ethos* is the operative word in the Foucault literature I'm examining, but also because across the Foucault/Habermas debate, the term tends to cover both individual and collective understandings of practice, thereby making a distinction between individual character and collective ethos less necessary. But I introduce the terms as a pair in this prefatory discussion so as to amplify the cluster of meanings and the complex genealogy I mean to invoke. To some extent, by using the terms together I mean to evoke the Aristotelian conception of ethos *as* character, which stresses the elements of self-cultivation and confirmed habit that can be said to shape and define any successfully realized ethical practice. But I also intend for the modern-day gap between the terms to allow each to perform a useful connotative correction on the other. It is not simply that the solidity of the term *character* helps to give shape to the otherwise simply positive yet somewhat indeterminate *ethos*. In its designation of cultivated ethical practices that have become settled and that can inform collective as well as individual practice, *ethos* serves as an important corrective to the individualist focus of *character*.

There are objections that might be raised against foregrounding the term *character* at all, I realize. Not least is the sense that it can be taken to announce, or at least entail, an alliance with the political right in contemporary U.S. culture. The conservative rhetoric of character persistently peddles the view that the solution to larger social and political problems lies within the (potentially heroic) individual, rather than in larger forms of restructuring that result from political projects, institutional changes, and the systemic analyses that make them possible. For many who would opt to avoid the term, *character* is fatally shadowed by its long ideological history in the service of mystified notions of distinction, nobility, and worthiness. Such a concern motivates the critiques of republican virtue by Habermas and Rawls, who precisely want to avoid heroic and elitist implications in their proceduralist theories.

The criticism of character and virtue is pertinent and should promote vigilance in the usage of the word. But it is also the case that the history of the term is not limited to its ideological uses by governing classes: there is another tradition that allies notions of character and self-crafting to the progressive projects of liberalism and socialism. Moreover, if one simply cedes terms such as *character* and *virtue* to the right, one pays a considerable political price, especially insofar as such terms appear to resonate so powerfully with such considerable segments of the population. Beyond such political concerns, there is the more basic issue of how integral the concept of self-cultivation is to *any* practical philosophy. If, as my analyses suggest, some version of the characterological haunts all forms of contemporary practical philosophy, then the character issue, broadly conceived, is not simply to be evaded or rejected. A more direct avowal of ideals of character and ethos, in my view, will extend our resources for talking about ethics and politics, at the same time correcting for some of the more narrow understandings of the "personal" and of "identity."

I

If we take even a modest historical perspective on the genealogy of characterological thought, it becomes clear that the narrowing of the "personal" to exclude or at least significantly downplay characterological dimensions is a rather distinctive feature of contemporary literary and cultural studies. In nineteenth-century European thought, for example, character functioned in large measure as the site where threateningly impersonal practices might be given meaningful enactment, might take form as embodied virtue. As I have argued elsewhere, part of what defines the peculiarly Victorian response to the disenchantments of modernity is the attempt to imagine the methods of modern science, critical reason, and cosmopolitan detachment in terms of exemplary or heroic characterology: in this way, what we might call early antifoundationalism was underwritten by ethos, and thereby imbued with value, achieved or earned through practices that could successfully take on a human face.[4] Prominent examples include Arnoldian disinterestedness; those forms of "moralized objectivity" in scientific practice charted by historian of science Lorraine Daston; and the imbrication of character-formation and epistemological advance in the thought of John Stuart Mill, where the quality of a particular truth takes its coloring from the dialogical process by which it was attained. For Mill, truth held in the absence of such a process may be accidentally true, but the individual who holds it will not own it properly and, as a consequence, will fail to attain to the epistemological virtue that safeguards intellectual practice as well as the characters of its practitioners.

What has become, one might well ask, of this inter-articulation of method and ethos that so defined the precarious modernity of the nineteenth-century, where the manner of enactment was seen to legitimate or effectively moralize those practices constructed on the scaffolding of the post-Kantian dispensation? One can certainly trace how the emphasis on manner—initially fused with the impersonal methods of modern aesthetic and disciplinary practice—breaks away from the yoke of its service to variously defined transsubjective or objective projects. The glorification of the subjective in Wilde, the will to power and the heroic characterology of Nietzsche (becoming who one is), the more general aggrandizement of the individual in early modernism. But what happens to the dialectic of subjectivity and impersonality in the major paradigmatic transformations of the twentieth century—throughout the complex development of modernism, in the movement from modernism to post-modernism, or in the line of development from structuralism to post-structuralism to cultural studies?

Foucault merits reconsideration in the context of this large question because his own trajectory—his famous turn somewhere between volume I and volume II of the *History of Sexuality*—dramatizes the dialectic I refer to, and his work as a whole, taking into account the distance it travels from its structuralist beginnings, helps to focus the paradigmatic shifts referred to above as well. But I in no way intend a comprehensive discussion of Foucault; I am interested rather in approaching his work, and his famous so-called debate with Habermas, from an oblique angle, one which brings the submerged or at least underexplored category of ethos to light.

I refer to this as a "so-called debate" to highlight two points. First, and most basically, although both thinkers discussed each other's work on various occasions, there was never any formal debate between Foucault and Habermas.[5] A conference scheduled for Berkeley in November 1984, which promised a fruitful exchange, never took place due to the untimely death of Foucault.[6] Second, and more importantly, from within the context of literary and cultural studies, what has since the early to mid-nineteen eighties passed as an understanding of the differences between Habermas and Foucault has often served to foreclose rather than foster debate. Indeed, what occurred in this arena would better be described as a bloodless coup on the part of the Foucaultians. In the years which saw routine contrasts between the two thinkers, a time when Foucault's work was pervasively influencing the literary field, Habermas was more often glancingly invoked than seriously discussed, typically serving to exemplify or condense a rationalist or utopian position that could help negatively to define the favored Foucaultian approach. His position was caricatured, as was his complex relation to the Frankfurt School: he was alleged to be simply on the side of Reason and Enlightenment, a promulgator of the deluded and dangerous belief that communication has the capacity to be "transparent." The complexity of Habermas's systems-theory was left to the side, as was his careful differentiation between forms of reason and his insistence that enlightenment is an unfinished project. To be sure, the historical argument about the public sphere fared better. There are several reasons why this was the case: it was seen as more acceptably historical in nature; it was amenable to being treated separately from the rest of his theory; and it was productively revised to accommodate more plurality and contestation than the original theory seemed to house.[7] The critiques here were immanent, in the interest of retaining an extremely serviceable concept, whereas the theory of communicative action and the discourse ethics seemed to require outright rejection insofar as they were seen to be irretrievably marred by transcendental, developmental, universalist, and utopian assumptions. Leaving aside the more capacious uses of the public sphere work, however, in general the name Habermas was used economically to signify any number of denigrated practices, from the mere distastefulness of rationalist modes to the inevitable oppressiveness of normative thinking to the dangers of a totalized Reason seeking to disavow its drive to power.[8]

I pause to make this point because I want to stress at the outset that this analysis returns to Foucault/Habermas material in order to explore the particular way in which an appeal to ethos functioned within it during its late stages. I am not returning to the "debate" in its original form, when it focused centrally on the question of the relation between power and communication. But the history is salient insofar as habitual contrasts between the two thinkers retain a hold over the discursive community, occluding the specific issues I wish to bring to the fore and prompting resistance to the attempt to give Habermas a fuller hearing. As it did in the earliest days of the "debate," the name "Habermas" often continues to provoke a knowing weariness in the literary field, one which defines a certain consensus about what Habermas signifies—plodding style, an embarrassing optimism of the intellect, and dangerous complicity with the Enlightenment. This entrenched view is all the more striking in view of the fact that Habermas's work has developed in complex and historically sensitive ways, and continues to hold the potential for productive dialogue with literary and cultural studies, particularly in the arena of cosmopolitanism.[9] In any event, I want to stress at the outset that to the extent that I do reinvoke the terms and texts of the original debate, it is to shift and reframe them, so as to acknowledge the polemical contours of the Foucault/Habermas literature as a founding instance of key elements in our current habits of argumentation. This claim requires rethinking what has been at stake in the reception of the Foucaultian turn, and returning to a late stage in the debate with Habermas, one very much invested in the implications of the Foucaultian turn, as a key moment where ethos played an utterly central—if consistently misrecognized—role.[10]

Foucault's "turn" constitutes a movement away from the monistic theory of power dominating *Discipline and Punish* and the *History of Sexuality Volume I*, toward an art of living—what he variously calls "practices of the self" or an "aesthetics of existence." As such, it shares affinities with those elaborations of subjective enactment or practice that were formed in reaction, as I earlier noted, to the impersonality of structuralist and poststructuralist paradigms of thought. Deliberately myopic, restricting its gaze to the middle distance at best, Foucault's aesthetics of existence affirms agency by circumscribing its venue, like those modest Dickensian endings, where the glare of omniscience is relinquished and the perspective descends to meld with the participant's view. Highly individualized, the aesthetics of existence also imagines itself as an achievement of certain forms of ethical practice; it carries an echo of the Nietzschean ideal of self-becoming; in this it is distinct from those poststructuralist forms of individual enactment that focus the self's relation to self predominantly within the terms of sociologically ascribed identities: gender, race, class, nationality. It is in this sense that Foucault's "aesthetics of existence" constitutes a theoretical event that could be said to reintroduce the exiled categories of ethos and character.

Yet, as a rule-proving exception, the Foucaultian turn to ethos also manages to emphasize the constraints of the defining intellectual terrain, in a symptomatic and even exacerbating way. This is above all the case to the extent that Foucault is seen, as a thinker, to instantiate a certain philosophic ethos. Partly with Foucault's own help and reflective endorsement, the dramatization of Foucault as enacting a model of intellectual practice parallels and draws energy from the late Foucault, where ethos becomes important conceptually across a range of classical topics, culminating in his last course at the Collège de France on the *parrhesiast*, or the philosopher as truth teller.[11] The topical attention to ethos in the later Foucault is construed as continuous with his more encompassing *style* of negative critique, what Paul Bové has described, at least in part, as "ironic integrity."[12] Beyond the methodological investment in genealogical detachment, a provocative posture of deliberate evasion and negation is certainly intermittently in evidence throughout the interviews, which are themselves often treated as privileged moments by those commentators who are invested in what we might call "the ethos-bearing Foucault." Most readers of Foucault's work are familiar with the form of response that acts as a refusal of the very terms of the question, a refusal of certain characterizations of his thought, and, it might even be said, a kind of studied refusal to engage the terms that shape debate. Thus Foucault will act bemused in the face of terms like postmodernity—"What are we calling postmodernity? I'm not up to date"—or emphasize the inapplicability of any labels to him or his work—"It's true that I prefer not to identify myself and that I'm amused by the diversity of the ways I've been judged and classified."[13] This tendency toward refusal of terms is allied, by Foucault's admiring commentators, with exemplary ethos, associated to varying degrees with rhetoric, style, dialogue, and artful disruption, and placed in ennobling contrast to the constraints of rationality, doctrine, and formal argument. In fact, in some sense—and this is displayed most strikingly in the so-called debate with Habermas—the aversion to formal argument in Foucault becomes, for many of his admiring commentators, ethos-defining.[14]

This approach to Foucault encompasses those scholars in both the literary and philosophical fields who are particularly concerned to defend him against rationalist and political critique, with Habermas as the central but not only opponent. In his foreword to Deleuze's book on Foucault, for example, Bové advocates an attention to style over and against "position," faulting the philosopher Charles Taylor for imagining that paraphrase is adequate to Foucault, and charging that the literary critic Fredric Jameson makes hermeneutic demands that similarly miss the prevailing significance of style. Critical of thinkers who base their readings of Foucault on predetermined philosophical or political criteria, Bové makes appeal to sensibility, style, and ironic negation, placing Foucault in a line of thinkers that includes Socrates, Montaigne, and Nietzsche. Among political theorists, both William Connolly and Richard Bernstein present Foucault as a canny rhetorical strategist aiming to play upon and thwart our presuppositions, to disrupt and dislodge our comfortable ways of thinking—in this view he deliberately eschews formal coherence in argument, which would only reinforce our settled habits.[15] Both of these critics see Foucault's project as the enactment of an ethos that cannot be reduced to doctrine or theory. Assumed here is also Foucault's commitment to a tutelary,

Socratic mode that schools the reader in negative critique, that prompts the reader to "critique" as an attitude of questioning. As with Foucault's own characterization of the philosopher as one who cares about the care of others, these readings position Foucault's philosophic ethos as simultaneously an ethical and intellectual model.[16]

The context for these defenses of Foucault are the charges of incoherence and self-contradiction that have been leveled against his work, and that are associated above all with Habermas's critique. The argument that Foucault is self-refuting is based on the claim that Foucault cannot really account for his account: if critique is itself a form of power then it cannot be used coherently to criticize power. This argument rests on a prior assumption of the existence of communicative reason itself, one which challenges Foucault's own refusal to distinguish communicative reason sufficiently from instrumental or disciplinary reason.[17] For Habermas, there are assumptions entailed in the very act of rational argumentation, assumptions about possibilities for rational critique, and it constitutes a performative contradiction to deny those assumptions at the level of theory, when the very act of communicating the theory must presuppose them. The reason this is a performative contradiction and not simply a contradiction is because the contradiction is not internal or locatable at the level of the theory but instead a result of the incoherent gap between the very nature of human communication and the content of the theory proffered. In some sense, then, while Habermas is insisting on rational criteria, he is also insisting, more deeply and existentially, on the unlivability of Foucault's theory, in the same manner that theorists like Cavell speak to the unlivability of skepticism. I point to this aspect of Habermas's critique to provide context for the appeal to ethos in the defenses of Foucault, which proposes an art of living based on conditions Habermas fundamentally contests, and to lay the groundwork for a later discussion of Habermas's own views on practice, enactment, and ethos. For the purposes of the present discussion, what is central to note is that the significance invested in the notion of ethos is conditioned, and ultimately limited, by the terms of the Habermasian critique: the investment in ethos is cast above all as a refusal of the insistence on rational coherence, and often justifies itself in these terms. The forms of restless and negative critique that the genealogist manifests, it is stressed, are themselves a *practice*. To try to force them into a rationalist framework is wrongheaded not only because the genealogist is engaged in a critique of rationality, but also because such a criticism fails to recognize the way in which negative critique is inseparable from its manner of enactment: it is not a performative contradiction but rather a form of critique dependent upon its performance as a refusal of the logic of contradiction.[18]

One of Foucault's own statements about Habermas illuminates this dynamic and indicates the extent to which ethos specifically challenges rational argument. This statement occurs in the 1984 interview, "The Ethic of Care for the Self as a Practice of Freedom." In response to a question about how games of truth might become, in certain societal conditions, relatively independent of structures of power, Foucault replies,

> This is indeed an important problem; I imagine you are thinking a little about Habermas when you say that. I am quite interested in what Habermas is doing. I know that he does not at all agree with what I say—I for my part tend to be a little more in agreement with what he says. But there is something which always causes me a problem: it is when he assigns such an important place to relations of communication and, above all, a function that I would call "utopian".[19]

Of especial interest here is Foucault's assertion that while Habermas does not agree at all with what he says, he (Foucault) is a little more in agreement with what Habermas says. This is a provocative and complicated utterance. First and most strikingly, it refuses the strictures of logic, insisting that ethos—attitude or stance—is utterly crucial to determining the relation of one person's thought to another. By essentially saying, "I am a little more in agreement with him than he is with me," rather than, "I think we are more in agreement than he acknowledges," Foucault implies that there is no external perspective from which one might adjudicate their differences or agreements, precisely because one essential element of agreement stems from the attitude of the thinker toward the other's work. Second, this utterance constitutes a pause in which Foucault congratulates himself upon his own good manner. Foucault is capacious enough to see through to and acknowledge an affinity or coincidence between Habermas and himself, while Habermas has fully rejected Foucault's views: Foucault displays higher communicative delicacy than the theorist of communicative action. By extension, there is the suggestion that Habermas is rigidly defending his position against those who do not conform utterly to its governing principles and claims. There is the suggestion, in other words, that Habermas is ethos-challenged. This dimension of Foucault's comment is continuous with much stronger remarks he makes elsewhere about his dislike of polemic:

> The polemicist. . . proceeds encased in privileges that he possesses in advance and will never agree to question. On principle, he possesses rights authorizing him to wage war and making that struggle a just undertaking; the person he confronts is not a partner in the search for truth but an adversary, an enemy who is wrong, who is harmful, and whose very existence constitutes a threat. For him, then, the game consists not of recognizing this person as a subject having the right to speak but of abolishing him, as interlocutor, from any possible dialogue.[20]

What interests me here is a certain inversion or doubling back that occurs, in both the statement on Habermas and the mini-diatribe against polemic: the thinkers who are most wedded to reason and to strong versions of argument are revealed to be ungenerous and even violent in relation to those they oppose, so much so that they discredit the purity of their arguments. Formal or strong argument is itself necessarily an ethos, and a not very appealing one at that. So is Foucault a little more in agreement with Habermas than Habermas is with him? How exactly can he be, when there is no agreement without attunement, and attunement here is demonstrated to be the element that divides them?

We might call the appeal to ethos, on the part of Foucault and his admiring commentators, an attempt to evade or trump the moves of the rationalist. Above all, this move opposes a valorized ethos to reason, exacerbating an inverse tendency in Habermas and his followers. But there are further criticisms that can be lodged against this appeal to ethos, especially as it appears in the secondary literature. It disavows its own polemical status in imagining itself beyond or to the side of polemic. And it relies very heavily upon the charismatic force of Foucault as a figure, in its positioning of his statements in interviews—whether evasive or revisionist—as somehow oracular. Thus, critics of Foucault are wrong because Foucault's own accounts of what he was always up to constitute the last word on the matter. For example, Michael Kelly, offering a synopsis and commentary on Foucault in his interesting anthology, *Critique and Power: Recasting the Foucault/Habermas Debate*, takes as his starting point for a response to the Habermasian critique Foucault's statements in the interview "Critical Theory/Intellectual History," because, in his view, it offers Foucault's "most complete account of his intellectual development from *Madness and Civilization* to the *History of Sexuality*."[21] But an approach that credits Foucault's own assertions about the guiding questions of his work, assertions clearly tilted toward his most recent interests and orientations, is highly questionable methodologically. Foucault was a famous self-revisionist, going so far as to disavow or rewrite some of his already published works: this seems a tendency to be analyzed, not simply accorded hermeneutic privilege.[22] Kelly's statement is strange also because such questionable methodology sits right next to more traditional ones in his analysis, as when he assesses critiques of *Discipline and Punish* by culling only evidence internal to the text, and weighing different passages against one another.

An example that distills the moves involved in this approach to Foucault can be found in Richard Bernstein's essay, "Foucault: Critique as a Philosophic Ethos." Bernstein suggests that we can account for the stronger agency-denying claims in middle Foucault by understanding them rhetorically rather than literally. In these instances we can

> even grasp Foucault's use of that favored rhetorical device of Nietzsche, hyperbole. One might think, for example, that Foucault is heralding the death of the subject, that he is claiming that the subject itself is *only* the result of the effects of power/knowledge regimes, that he completely undermines and ridicules any and all talk of human agency. There is plenty of textual evidence to support such claims. But it is also clear, especially in his late writings when he deals with the question of the self's relation to itself and the possibility of "the man who tries to invent himself," that he is not abandoning the idea that "we constitute ourselves as subjects acting on others."[23]

On the one hand, we are told that a strict adherence to logical argument will cause us to miss the rhetorical strategy of hyperbole, though we are not told what the reason for hyperbole is in this instance. It simply stands in as a trope for rhetoric itself. On the other hand, Bernstein admits that there's plenty of "textual evidence" for a denial of agency—here now limiting himself to the explicit argument, and to formal criteria for assessing logical coherence—but then adds, that it "is also clear" "in the late writings" that he hasn't abandoned agency. How do we answer such a flexible defense? Initially, we are presented with an almost esoteric appeal to rhetoric, then we are expected to simply accede to the notion that Foucault's later utterances have a corrective power over prior utterances, as though early and middle Foucault were simply early and middle drafts, interesting, but needing to give way to the aggrandized intentionality legible in the decisive revision.

The appeal to Foucault himself, the elevation of his own artful rhetoric and self-representation, partakes ultimately of what we might call charismatic fallacy, a version of positive ad hominem. The appearance of this form of argument is instructive, revealing the ways an appeal to ethos here merges with a cult of the theorist's personality, shifting the criteria of argumentation so as effectively to thwart the charges of incoherence. This move confuses the turn to ethos with the elevation of the theorist's personality, the effect of which is to narrow the significance and resources of the former. Rather than understanding Foucault's genealogical project as crucially mediated through forms of cultivated characterology (understood both intellectually and ethically), this framing of Foucault invokes the aura and mystique associated with his person so as to forestall a moment of critique and potential dialogue. A glamorized notion of personality eclipses the more complex mediations involved in articulating the relation between theory and enactment, mediations that Foucault's work itself often works hard to promote. Thus, although Foucault's late work does in key ways constitute a promising, exceptional turn to ethos, both the defining opposition to the Habermasian position and the cult of personality have warped its development.

It should also be noted that the charismatic fallacy, or the cult of the theorist's personality, functions in Foucault's case not only to disable the charges of incoherence associated with the Habermasian critique but also to absorb what is after all a rather dramatic theoretical turn in the late work. It is not simply the case, as in the Bernstein example, that the turn is used to answer critiques of the earlier theories. The late work is accepted and heralded precisely because it is a self-correction by a charismatic figure whose legitimacy derives from his earlier embrace of suspicious reading. Indeed, if anyone else had published the second and third volumes of the *History of Sexuality*, they would have had little to no impact on the theoretical domains of literary and cultural theory in the U.S. academy.[24] More generally, one might say, the enduring identity of the theorist allows the legitimating aura to extend backwards as well as forwards, so that both orientations at once correct for one another and remain somehow untouchable on their own terms. Under such conditions, we don't have far to travel to a work like David Halperin's *Saint Foucault*, which confidently yokes Foucault's later work to the agenda of politically minded theory in the United States, an alliance that would not be easily achieved without the (very much avowed) hagiography driving the study. Indeed, if the work from the two phases of Foucault's career had been done by different individuals, we would never encounter a statement like the following of Halperin's: "Queer politics itself, finally, is a kind of spiritual exercise, a modern practice of the self."[25] Nor would we see a trend of literary scholarship informed by Foucault's late work on "practices of the self" or the "aesthetics of existence."[26]

II

Within the context of the Habermas/Foucault debate, the appropriation of ethos on the part of Foucault and his admiring commentators, buttressed as it is by a cult of personality, works above all to promote the view that Habermas and his followers are somehow locked into a rigid and abstract rationalism that fails to understand not only the workings of power (the abiding focus of the Habermas/Foucault literature) but also the subtle demands of intellectual and political practice. As Foucault himself says when distinguishing his views from Habermas, "The problem, then, is not to try to dissolve [power relations] in the utopia of a perfectly transparent communication, but to give one's self the rules of law, the techniques of management, and also the ethics, the *ethos*, the practice of self, which will allow these games of domination to be played with a minimum of domination."[27] There is a kind of characterological or ethical piety here, an attempt to trump Habermasian criticisms by casting the investment in rational argument or democratic procedure as not simply deluded about the nature of power, but also vulgar and misguided from the standpoint of practice, which requires subtle adjustments, tact, and phronesis precisely because of the ubiquity of power. There is the suggestion, both in Foucault and in the secondary literature, that Habermas just doesn't "get" ethos, and therefore doesn't "get" Foucault. As a consequence, everything that might have seemed inappropriately personal in the earliest poststructuralist reactions to Habermas—the complaints about his "style" or the unreadability of his work—in this context emerges as suddenly salient.

But Habermas's critique of Foucault is by no means reductively limited to the sphere of logos, and it is fundamentally misguided to think that Foucault is somehow the guardian of ethos while Habermas is locked in logos. Admittedly, Habermas holds Foucault's work to standards of coherence, and is critical of the offhand or gestural remark that Foucault's followers would be more likely to treat as living philosophy. After approvingly citing Nancy Fraser's well-known critique of Foucault's failure to give any positive elaboration of the grounds for opposition to the modern power/knowledge regime, for example, Habermas writes, "Once, in a lecture, Foucault addressed this question in passing and gave a vague suggestion of postmodern criteria of justification..."[28] Should we infer from Habermas's frustration here that he adheres rigidly to protocols of formal argumentation and is deaf to the art of negative critique, whose informing commitments will ever remain elusive of outright exposition, appearing, leprechaun-like, in transient forms like the lecture or interview? Habermas's understanding of ethos is far more developed than such an inference would have it—though fraught with ambivalence as well. Habermas's neo-Kantianism defines itself via an intersubjective turn: his notion of communicative reason, the ground on which he mounts the charge of performative contradiction, requires an understanding of the individual speaker as embedded in social relations. But there is a tension in Habermas's conception of sociality. On the one hand, he stresses the value of, and need for, embedded sociality in his emphasis on primary socialization processes and their centrality to moral development, individual autonomy, and the cohesion of cultural groups. On the other hand, Habermas emphasizes the preeminent value of reason's capacity to break free of tradition and custom: reflective distance defines the crowning achievement of modernity. It is true that he to some extent characterizes this achievement as a social and historical development. Valorized forms of communicative rationality derive from specific cultural forms: the public sphere in Enlightenment culture, the conditions of multiculturalism within the democratic state, the pressing current challenges of globalism. Indeed, in a sense one could say that Habermas's insistence on the reflective institutionalization of communicative and democratic principles promotes a practical philosophy that operates, unlike the Foucaultian art of living, at the collective and institutional levels of political life. This is ethos as an emergent democratic culture, not ethos as individual cultivation or charismatic critique. But it also must be acknowledged that in persistently figuring modern reason as an abstractive ascent out of embeddedness, Habermas seems to deny what he otherwise acknowledges as the primacy of the social and historical, insisting more absolutely on reason's transcending power. Reason's capacity to break the bounds of context is, moreover, what for Habermas defines the moral as opposed to the ethical, the universal as opposed to the particular. In sum, Habermas oscillates between wanting to redefine universalism as a new ethos, and wanting to assert universalism over and against ethos, insofar as the latter always seems to fall into some form of blinkered adherence to custom. His detractors tend to emphasize only the latter move, which they see as misguided and off-putting in its deindividuating and decontextualizing drive toward the procedural and the impersonal.[29]

The shape of the received Foucault/Habermas opposition shifts, however, if one explores more fully the positive pole of Habermas's ambivalence toward ethos. In this section I will therefore examine a few important moments where Habermas's own thinking displays attentiveness to the significance of ethos—as a critical tool, as a philosophical stance, and as an integral element of democratic culture. My analysis will continue to acknowledge the limits of Habermas's conception of ethos—the persistent pressure of his ambivalence—while still trying to allow as much space as possible for these more capaciously imagined understandings of ethos. The entrenched opposition between Foucaultian ethos and Habermasian rationality, partly enforced by Habermas's own patterns of expression, has hitherto left these suggestive aspects of Habermas's thought largely in shadow. They are of interest in their own right, as a dimension of his thought, but also insofar as they suggest a dialectical relation of theory to practice, or argument to ethos, that reflectively encompasses individual, collective, and institutional domains. This involves, above all, a demystification of the move that distributes ethos exclusively to negative critique.

Habermas employs ethos as a critical tool in his discussion of Foucault in *The Philosophical Discourse of Modernity*. It is noteworthy that in this text, his most sustained engagement with the critique of modernity stemming from the Frankfurt School through poststructuralism, Habermas's analyses are centered almost exclusively on individual figures; somehow the notion of an individual's life and history is absolutely vital to his sense of how one should understand his or her thought. To be sure, in addition to tracing intellectual genealogy Habermas tends to accord privilege to what we might call historical psychology and ideological forces rather than characterology: there is in fact a leitmotif of historical crisis and political disappointment in the text, which is meant to explain the dark mood of the theorists he criticizes. Thus, Stalinism and fascism are seen to provoke the bleak cynicism of Adorno and Horkheimer, while the disappointment of May 1968 is alleged as key in the development of Foucault's work, as well as in the emergence of the general mood which allowed the success of the postmodernists in France.[30] But Habermas does not restrict his discussion to this form of historical psychology, and indeed implies a far more nuanced understanding of how we might analyze the character of theory when he registers certain excesses or tensions internal to the writing of specific thinkers.

This is strikingly the case in his discussion of what he calls Foucault's cryptonormativism, a form of internal tension that needs to be distinguished from performative contradiction. Indeed, these two charges—performative contradiction and cryptonormativism—are crucially different. The charge of performative contradiction rests upon a prior assumption about communicative rationality, a claim about certain presuppositions built into linguistic use itself: if one does not buy into these transcendental claims, one can quite justifiably reject the notion of performative contradiction, as well as the appeal to the arguably loaded notion of livability that accompanies it. But the charge of cryptonormativism takes on a different hue. Less insistent on the underlying transcendental assumptions of the theory of communicative action, it points rather to internal tension and strain in Foucault, a strain evident precisely in the gap between tone and assertion. It reads Foucault more in the manner that we are instructed to read Victorian dramatic monologue. The charge of cryptonormativism *can be* distilled into a form of logical contradiction or paradox: Foucault's critique of normalization, which gets extended into a critique of normativity tout court, is incoherent insofar as it has to implicitly make appeal to certain norms which it is unwilling to acknowledge or avow. But the *elaboration* of the criticism typically finds the cryptic appeal to norms evident in tone or stance. That's what the crypto in cryptonormativism is: an implicit appeal felt most vividly at the level of tone or rhetorical gesture. For example, Habermas notes the extreme difficulties that arise as Foucault aims to maintain second-order value-freeness in his critique of the false pretense to value-freeness in the human sciences:

> Now this grounding of a second-order value-freeness is already by no means value-free. Foucault understands himself as a dissident who offers resistance to modern thought and humanistically disguised disciplinary power. Engagement marks his learned essays right down to the style and choice of words; the critical tenor dominates the theory no less than the self-definition of the entire work. Foucault thereby distinguishes himself, on the one hand, from the engaged positivism of a Max Weber, who wanted to separate a decisionistically chosen and openly declared value basis from an analysis carried out in a value-free way. Foucault's criticism is based more on the postmodern rhetoric of his presentation than on the postmodern assumptions of his theory. (94)

In building itself out of a recognition of the tension between ethos and explicit claim, Habermas's critique of Foucault in some crucial sense honors the way in which ethos inhabits argument, rather than insisting on a suppression of ethos and the absolute purity of the argument.[31] One might be tempted to read Habermas's critique, reliant as it is on noting the investments of furtive tone and rhetorical shading, as a dedication above all to explicitness and rule-governed coherence. But the attention to the disjunction between tone and assertion seems better understood, within the context of Habermas's larger investment in democratic dialogue, as continuous with those principles of openness and transparency that forward the practices of deliberative debate. Dialogue is stymied or at best asymmetrical when one party to the debate is accorded an exclusive charismatic privilege. If the polemicist "proceeds encased in privileges that he possesses in advance and will never agree to question," the construct that I have called "the ethos-bearing Foucault" proceeds suffused with an aura that he too is seen to possess in advance, one that seems to elude entirely the realm of open questioning.

If Habermas shows an attentiveness to ethos in the critique of Foucault, his tendency to criticize the views of his philosophical opponents partly by appeal to the moods (*die Stimmungen*) they express or provoke reveals, I think, the limits of his capacity to accord the dimension of ethos any positive centrality within the project of communicative reason. This is a habit of thought that extends beyond the recourse to historical psychology that I noted earlier, one that issues from his enduring ambivalence toward anything that seems to attenuate reason's distancing powers. A distinctly negative quality, ethos in the guise of mood appears only as that which undermines or overwhelms moral and intellectual clarity. "Under the sign of a Nietzsche revitalized by poststructuralism, moods and attitudes are spreading that are confusingly like those of Adorno and Horkheimer. I would like to forestall this confusion." Or: "In interviews of the early 1970s, Foucault revealed the vehemence of his break with earlier convictions. At that time, he joined the choir of disappointed Maoists of 1968 and was taken by the moods to which one must look if one wants to explain the remarkable success of the New Philosophers in France."[32]

This pattern mirrors the very opposition that we saw in the Foucault material, where the appeal to ethos involved a rejection of formal argument. Moreover, the discourse of mood plays into—and in part derives from—the ideal of mature moral development as it appears in Habermas's writings on communicative action, reflecting his persistent tendency to apply an evaluative contrast between youth and maturity. In this sense, Habermas might be said to psychologize the contest between philosophical positions.[33] But it is also the case that mood functions in a deliberate contrast with a form of maturity that seems to supersede an investment in psychological depth: the deliberate non-grandiosity of proceduralism. Relevant here would be a discernible

continuity between the critique of republican virtue and the refusal of
the grand gestures and self-indulgence connoted by moods.
Particularly revealing is a statement from an interview with Michael
Haller, in which Habermas responds to a question about whether his
views on political and social changes in Europe have failed to take into
account the profound material inequities between Europe and the
third world:

> But *we* can overcome Eurocentrism only out of the better spirit of
> Europe. Only if we are able to do this will the wounds inflicted on the
> world by Eurocentrism, and the material world culture that grew from
> it, become if not healed, then at least treatable.

> These are somewhat too grand turns of phrase for characterizing the
> completely profane, piecemeal kind of perspectives that we need to
> work from. I've got a tin ear for Heideggerian melodies. 'Only a god
> can save us'—that's the kind of noble tone in philosophy that already
> got on Kant's nerves. Philosophers don't change the world. What we
> need is to practice a little more solidarity: without that, intelligent
> action will remain permanently foundationless and inconsequential.
> Such practice, certainly, requires rational institutions; it needs rules and
> communicative forms that don't morally overtax the citizens, but rather
> exact the virtue of an orientation toward the common good in small
> change.

> If there is any small remnant of utopia that I've preserved, then it is
> surely the idea that democracy—and the public struggle for its best
> form—is capable of hacking through the Gordian knots of otherwise
> insoluble problems. I'm not saying that we're going to succeed in this;
> we don't even know whether success is possible. But because we don't
> know, we at least have to try. Apocalyptic moods sap the energies that
> nourish these initiatives. Optimism and pessimism aren't really relevant
> categories here.[34]

We might call Habermas's modest program an appeal not so much
to the spirit of Europe as to the spirit of proceduralism, here construed
as forms of institutionally bound collective practice that are best

advanced through modes of interaction that downplay extreme affect or, presumably, strong investments in personal style. This conception, too, is an ethos, of course, and the negative charisma that marks the response necessarily exists in tension with the appeal to modest procedure. Habermas here lights up the ways in which romantic notions of opposition and critique have tended to underfund the hard work of institution-building and collective practice: one might distill the point down to the observation that the valorization of individual ethos has undermined the advance of collective ethos precisely by romanticizing politics. This zero-sum conception, whereby affect is conceived as a limited resource whose overspending depletes the reserves of political energy, is surely itself too defended, narrowing ideas of political practice and expression in unwarranted ways. Where it is suggestive, however, is in the challenge it poses to the valorization of individual ethos, and in its willingness to dwell on the more mundane, pragmatic task of promoting simple acts of citizenship.

In addition to the attention to collective ethos, one finds the occasional attempt within Habermas's writings to conceive of his own theoretical stance as *askesis*, as a refusal of various seductions to which others fall prey: the desire to absolutize reason by conflating it with power, for example, or to imagine one could engage in a "final unmasking." The end of the chapter on Adorno and Horkheimer is one such moment, and placed next to the attentive analyses of ethos in his critique of individual theorists, suggests a possible attention to philosophic ethos that might complement his already strongly developed conception of political culture:

> In one respect, ideology critique had in fact continued the undialectical enlightenment proper to ontological thinking. It remained caught up in the purist notion that the devil needing exorcism was hiding in the internal relationships between genesis and validity, so that theory, purified of all empirical connotations, could operate in its own element. Totalized critique did not discharge this legacy. The intention of a "final unmasking," which was supposed to draw away with one fell swoop the veil covering the confusion between power and reason, reveals a purist intent—similar to the intent of ontology to separate being and illusion categorically (that is, with one stroke). However,

just as in a communication community the researcher, the context of discovery, and the context of justification are so entwined with one another that they have to be separated procedurally, by a *mediating* kind of thinking—which is to say, continuously—the same holds for the two spheres of being and illusion. In argumentation, critique is constantly entwined with theory, enlightenment with grounding, even though discourse participants always *have to suppose* that only the unforced force of the better argument comes into play under the unavoidable communication presuppositions of argumentative discourse. But they know, or they can know, that even this idealization is only necessary because convictions are formed and confirmed in a medium that is not "pure" and not removed from the world of appearances in the style of Platonic ideas. Only a discourse that admits this might break the spell of mythic thinking without incurring a loss of the light radiating from the semantic potentials also preserved in myth. (130)[35]

In this dense and difficult passage, Habermas goes a considerable way toward answering the charge that his theory is itself caught up in a blind idealization of reason. And he does so, interestingly, by insisting that it is the rigorously suspicious ideological critics—here, Adorno and Horkheimer—who necessarily assume or project a form of theoretical purism, insofar as they imagine that theory can itself cleanly unmask the workings of ideology. In a complex reframing of the conditions of communicative reason—a form of reason that Adorno and Horkheimer fundamentally did not recognize in their totalizing conception of reason as instrumental—Habermas builds to the notion that participants in communicative reason have the capacity for a self-conscious relation to their own idealizing presuppositions about the reciprocity of dialogue and the communicative telos of mutual understanding. What is striking about this passage is that the discourse participants are reminded not simply of the cornerstone of communicative ethics—that is, the kinds of validity claims that they *have to suppose* when they engage in any form of communicative action—but also of what they *can know* about their own necessarily idealizing presuppositions. Thus, rather than simply reiterating that speech participants implicitly raise and recognize validity claims about their utterances—elsewhere specified as claims of comprehensibility, truth, truthfulness, and appropriateness—Habermas here invokes a higher-level awareness of the import of these presuppositions. He therefore does not simply impose a transcendental claim about the conditions of communicative reason, but rather imagines that the significance and effects of speech conditions are bound up in the attitude one cultivates toward them, the way in which one makes sense of them. Specifically, discourse participants are here encouraged to affirm their idealizing presuppositions in full recognition of the impurity—or profound embeddedness—of all linguistic practice, the impossibility of theory ever operating apart from mediated and embedded practice. This is thus an important moment where Habermas is effectively situating the ethos that animates what others see as his own unthinking purism.

Habermas's stress on the realization and institutionalization of practices of communicative reason, as well as his ethos-infused notion of cryptonormativism and his gestures toward a kind of enabling theoretical *attitude* (in the passage just cited), both interrogate and advance the relation between theory and practice, and they significantly do so at the individual, collective, and institutional levels. But, as I have shown, other elements of Habermas's thought direct attention away from these potentialities, primarily by opposing mature reason to ethos (conceived as either embedded custom or emotional excess). This narrow conception of reason jars with the otherwise firmly held differentiation between the right and the good, and it in part drives the unforgiving charges of mood-driven thought that appear in Habermas's critique of the anti-Enlightenment positions of postmodernism and earlier Frankfurt School theorists. There is no need to understand communicative reason so narrowly, when it can very much encompass a plurality of styles and modes, including, as Habermas seems to suggest, a kind of second-order ability to reflect on the reasons for its own "inescapable" idealizing attitudes. The formal reduction evident in such limiting moments is a problem that recurs in proceduralism more generally: it tends to restrictively imagine the character of public debate, reading it narrowly out of the liberal principle of tolerance, and thereby strangely foreclosing liberalism's dedication to individual flourishing, ongoing critique, and openness to difference (rather than mere toleration of it).

Conclusion

Practical philosophy is always engaged, to one degree or another, in one manner or another, in imagining how it might be lived, imagining its relation to enactment. We have our own versions, that is, of the Victorian attempt to weld character to method. No matter how disavowed the category of ethos or character may be in many philosophies of the present, it tends to come back in shadow forms, haunting the debate through strange displaced appearances, as when a pragmatist is called smug. Or it may make its presence felt more forcefully, as in the case of the charismatic fallacy or the narrow understanding of reason, where a certain style is elevated to endorse, express, or underwrite the theory. These suppressions and displacements emanate from different sources, depending on the theory to which they are tethered, and they clearly have a complex relation to the genealogy of thought on subjectivity, as the case of Foucault is intended to illustrate. It is my contention here that such suppressions and displacements merit scrutiny on a number of levels, and more generally can be said to reflect a failure sufficiently to think through questions of enactment or practice, especially in their relation to value and concrete political realization. My own intellectual affiliations and commitments aside, the most general aim of this essay is to promote an attention to characterology in the analysis of the practical dimensions of much recent theory.

The problem that emerges most pronouncedly in the Foucault/Habermas debate is the tendency to play upon and reinscribe an unnecessary opposition between reason and ethos. I concluded the previous section by summarizing the way this occurs in Habermas; on the Foucault side, by contrast, the appeal to ethos is used to lend an aura or sheen to Foucault, one loosely associated with rhetoric, art, and dissidence, and intended to render moot, even vulgar, the problem of formal coherence in the theory, while at the same time magically claiming ethico-political effectivity.[36] In this way ethos is used to trump or eclipse certain forms of reasoned argument, rather than to imagine more productively the ways in which theory might deliberate upon its relation to practice. Both sides of the debate, and certainly the understanding of the work of both thinkers, suffer from the distorting postures wrought by the defining polemical situation, itself in turn exacerbated by disciplinary and political contests. The form of practical philosophy that is most lost to view in this particular debate is one that would seek to promote a highly deliberative, reason-infused cultivation of ethos, one that, as in one of the more interesting strands of recent virtue ethics, might wed the insights of Aristotle with those of Kant.[37] Such a practical philosophy promotes reflection and deliberation in the cultivation of habit; it also has the potential to accommodate ideals of self-cultivation alongside those of collective deliberative processes. Above all recognizable in the seemingly outmoded "liberal temperament," this dialectical conception attempts to hold to a pluralism while not imagining that it can itself rise above the demands of enactment, which includes an attention to the ways we might actively guide the inevitable layering of character. By foreclosing even the recognition of such a synthesis, the loyal inheritors of the entrenched Foucault/Habermas opposition imagine themselves to be promoting "ethos," when in fact they are cornering it.

Notes

1. I address the particular itinerary of appeals to character in pragmatist thought in "Pragmatism and Character," *Critical Inquiry* 29:2 (2003): 282–301.
2. For an interesting overview of the field of virtue ethics, as well as a critique of its label, see Martha C. Nussbaum, "Virtue Ethics: A Misleading Category?" *The Journal of Ethics* 3 (1999): 163–201. Nussbaum argues that although virtue ethics is standardly distinguished from Kantianism and Utilitarianism, the taxonomy is a confusion insofar as both Kantianism and Utilitarianism contain elements of virtue. Nussbaum then goes on to analyze two divergent strands of so-called virtue ethics, the anti-Kantian and the anti-Utilitarian.
3. For a representative collection, see Marjorie Garber et al., eds., *The Turn to Ethics* (New York: Routledge, 2000). For a useful map of different approaches within literary studies, see especially Lawrence Buell's essay in the collection, entitled "What We Talk About When We Talk About Ethics."
4. Amanda Anderson, *The Powers of Distance: Cosmopolitanism and the Cultivation of Detachment* (Princeton: Princeton University Press, 2001).
5. Habermas of course devoted two chapters of *The Philosophical Discourse of Modernity* to Foucault, whereas Foucault's comments about Habermas were restricted to occasional moments. In this sense the debate is "uneven" since there is a more extensive treatment/critique of Foucault on Habermas's part.
6. According to Habermas, Foucault delivered the lecture "What is Enlightenment?" just prior to suggesting the conference idea to Habermas in March 1983. The conference was to include as

participants not only Foucault and Habermas, but also Richard Rorty, Charles Taylor, and Hubert Dreyfus. In his memorial address for Foucault, Habermas discusses the proposed conference and this lecture's surprising turn back toward the Enlightenment. See Jürgen Habermas, "Taking Aim at the Heart of the Present: On Foucault's Lecture on Kant's *What is Enlightenment?*" in *The New Conservatism: Cultural Criticism and the Historians' Debate,* trans. Shierry Weber Nicholsen (Cambridge, MA: MIT Press, 1989), 173–179.

7. Perhaps the most influential essay within scholarship on the public sphere, one that influenced the fields of literature, history, and political theory, was Nancy Fraser's "Rethinking the Public Sphere: A Contribution to the Critique of Actually Existing Democracy," which originally appeared in *Habermas and the Public Sphere,* ed. Craig Calhoun (Cambridge, MA: MIT Press, 1991), 109–142.

8. To provide an example of how the invocation of Habermas often played out in the theoretical field, I point to the first page of Ernesto Laclau's 1990 book, *New Reflections on the Revolution of Our Time.* Here, and nowhere else in the text, Laclau invokes the name of Habermas. But it is clear that the invocation is carrying a lot of weight. The text reads: "An initial reaction to this new intellectual climate has been to become entrenched in the defence of 'reason' and attempt to relaunch the project of 'modernity' in opposition to those tendencies considered 'nihilistic.' The work of Habermas is perhaps the most representative of this attitude. Our position, however, is exactly the opposite: far from perceiving in the 'crisis of realism' a nihilism which leads to the abandonment of any emancipatory project, we see the former as opening unprecedented opportunities for radical critique of all forms of domination, as well as for the formulation of liberation projects hitherto restrained by the rationalist 'dictatorship' of the Enlightenment." Ernesto Laclau, *New Reflections on the Revolution of Our Time* (London: Verso, 1990) 3–4.

9. See Jürgen Habermas, *The Inclusion of the Other: Studies in Political Theory,* ed. Ciaran Cronin and Pablo de Greif (Cambridge, MA: MIT Press, 1998). Another irony among several is the fact that Habermas is a profoundly engaged public intellectual in Germany and Europe: his work in this sphere considerably complicates his profile, and unsettles the ease with which he can be described as hopelessly idealist. See especially Jürgen Habermas, *The Past as Future: Interviews by Michael Haller,* ed. and trans. Max Pensky (Lincoln: University of Nebraska Press, 1994). See also Max Pensky, "Jürgen Habermas and the Antinomies of the Intellectual," in *Habermas: A Critical Reader,* ed. Peter Dews (London: Blackwell, 1995), 211–237.

10. There are important disciplinary distinctions to be made here. While Habermas "lost" in the arena of literary and cultural studies, the nature of the battle as well as the range of positions was quite different in political philosophy, where the Foucaultians felt disadvantaged precisely because the Habermasian camp was using strong forms of philosophical argumentation. Some of the anthologies on the debate emanating from philosophy are trying to reframe the terms so as to give Foucault a better hearing: the appeal to ethos that I will discuss is at the heart of this

reframing, and has been advanced by political theorists who are in alliance with certain trends in the literary and cultural studies field. See Michael Kelly, ed., *Critique and Power: Recasting the Foucault/Habermas Debate* (Cambridge, MA: MIT Press, 1994); Samantha Ashenden and David Owen, eds., *Foucault Contra Habermas* (London: Sage, 1999).

11. "In his last years, Foucault became more comfortable than he had been in the past with the profession of philosophy, and he proposed that his entire work be approached in terms of its ambition to be a philosophical ethos, a philosophy as life, a way of acting in the contemporary world which manifests both a way of belonging to it as well as a task within it. This ethos is exhibited most prominently in the philosopher's mode of thinking and one of the most striking features about Foucault's last period is the amount of attention which he gives to meditation on thought itself." James M. Bernauer, "Michel Foucault's Ecstatic Thinking," in James Bernauer and David Rasmussen, eds., *The Final Foucault* (Cambridge, MA: MIT Press, 1988), 66. For a fuller discussion of Foucault's lectures on the *parrhesiast*, as well as an example of the investment in a clear continuity between Foucault and his subject matter, see Thomas Flynn, "Foucault as Parrhesiast: His Last Course at the College de France (1984)," in Bernauer and Rasmussen, eds., *The Final Foucault*, 102–118.

12. This phrase is drawn from Bové's foreword to the English translation of Deleuze's book on Foucault. The immediate context is a discussion of Foucault that compares him with R. P. Blackmur, and that stresses Blackmur's "marked effort to resist the possible commodification of even the most ironic stance into a critical program." Paul Bové, "The Foucault Phenomenon: The Problematics of Style," foreword to Gilles Deleuze, *Foucault*, trans. Sean Hand (Minneapolis: The University of Minnesota Press, 1988) xxxv.

13. Michel Foucault, "Critical Theory/Intellectual History," in Kelly, ed., *Critique and Power*, 124; Michel Foucault, "Polemics, Politics, and Problematizations," in *The Foucault Reader*, ed. Paul Rabinow (New York: Pantheon, 1984), 384. Also see Michael Foucault, "Politics and Ethics: An Interview," in Rabinow, ed., *The Foucault Reader*, 375: "If you like, what strikes me is the fact that from the beginning I have been considered an enemy by the Marxists, an enemy by the right wing, an enemy by the people in the center. I think that if my work were essentially political, it would end up finding its place somewhere in the long run." This comment interestingly comes shortly after Foucault states that "The key to the personal poetic attitude of a philosopher is not to be sought in his ideas, as if it could be deduced from them, but rather in his philosophy-as-life, in his philosophical life, his ethos" (374). Ethos for Foucault becomes associated with a kind of singularity and ineffability.

14. I do not mean to suggest that the feature of Foucault's intellectual style described here—and often most strikingly in evidence in the interview format—encompasses the whole of his repertoire or manner of being. There is great variety within the interviews, which also include moments of self-conscious fallibility and marked openness. I am interested here in the ways that the specific polemical field has shaped the emphasis on ethos as negation, ethos as aversion to formal argument.

15. William Connolly, "Taylor, Foucault, and Otherness," *Political Theory* 13 (August 1985); Richard Bernstein, "Foucault: Critique as a Philosophic Ethos," in Kelly, ed., *Critique and Power,* 211–41.

16. Connolly and Bernstein are just two prominent examples. See also Niko Kolodny, "The Ethics of Cryptonormativism: A Defense of Foucault's Evasions," *Philosophy and Social Criticism* 22:5 (1996): 63–84; David Owen, "Genealogy as Exemplary Critique," *Economy and Society* 24:4 (1995): 489–506; David Owen, "Orientation and Enlightenment: An Essay on Critique and Enlightenment," in Ashenden and Owen, eds., *Foucault Contra Habermas,* 21–44; Bernauer; Flynn.

17. For a discussion of Foucault's engagement with such a distinction in "The Subject and Power" (1982), see David Ingram, *Reason, History, and Politics: The Communitarian Grounds of Legitimation in the Modern Age* (Albany: SUNY Press, 1995) 188–97. Despite Foucault's somewhat shifting position on this issue, the question of whether and to what extent power saturates all communicative contexts remains the key locus of difference between the two thinkers, both in the primary and the secondary literature that can be said to constitute the "debate."

18. For a discussion of the explicit embrace of performative contradiction in poststructuralist thought, as well as a general discussion of the intellectual historical context of this Frankfurt School category, see Martin Jay, "The Debate Over Performative Contradiction: Habermas vs. the Poststructuralists," in Axel Honneth et al., eds, *Philosophical Interventions in the Unfinished Project of Enlightenment* (Cambridge, MA: MIT Press, 1992), 261–79.

19. Michel Foucault, "The Ethic of Care for the Self as a Practice of Freedom," trans. J. D. Gauthier, S.J., in Bernauer, *The Final Foucault,* 18. I have emended the translation somewhat. For the original transcription of the interview, see Michel Foucault, "L'éthique du souci de soi comme pratique de la liberté," *Dits et écrits* IV (Paris: Gallimard, 1994), 726–27. For a variant translation, see Michel Foucault, "The Ethics of Concern of the Self as a Practice of Freedom," trans. P. Aranov and D. McGrawth, with emendations by Paul Rabinow, in *Essential Works of Foucault, 1954–1988, Vol I: Ethics,* ed. Paul Rabinow (New York: The New Press, 1994).

20. Foucault, "Polemics, Politics, and Problematizations," 112. For a fascinating reading of Foucault's approach to polemic, see Jonathan Crewe's essay in this volume. It is interesting to note that Foucault's ire about polemics was primarily focused on Marxism, and that Habermas of course is partly associated with this tradition.

21. Michael Kelly, "Foucault, Habermas, and the Self-Referentiality of Critique," in Kelly, ed., *Critique and Power,* 371.

22. See Didier Eribon, *Michel Foucault,* trans. Betsy Wing (Cambridge, MA: Harvard University Press, 1991), 185, 323–4.

23. Bernstein, "Foucault: Critique as a Philosophic Ethos," in Kelly, ed., *Critique and Power,* 223.

24. I would hazard a similar claim about the influential Eve Sedgwick essay, "Paranoid and Reparative Reading; or, You're So Paranoid, You Probably Think This Introduction is About You," in *Novel Gazing:*

Queer Readings in Fiction, ed. Eve Kosofsky Sedgwick (Durham, NC: Duke University Press, 1997), 1–37.

25. David Halperin, *Saint Foucault: Towards a Gay Hagiography* (New York: Oxford University Press, 1995), 101. This book appropriates the turn to ethos but in a particular way that subordinates it to, and legitimates it via, politics (see esp. 106).

26. See James Eli Adams, *Dandies and Desert Saints: Styles of Victorian Masculinity* (Ithaca: Cornell University Press, 1995); Jeff Nunokawa, *Tame Passions of Wilde: The Styles of Manageable Desire* (Princeton: Princeton University Press, 2003); John Guillory, "The Ethical Practice of Modernity: The Example of Reading," in Garber et. al., eds., *The Turn to Ethics,* 29–46. For the purposes of this argument, however, I am far more interested in the work directly on Foucault in this arena, such as Halperin's. The practical criticism is often to be distinguished from the more theory-identified work insofar as it often cites the need to correct for the disciplinary Foucault by turning to the late Foucault. From a longer perspective, I see this phenomenon as related to the claims about legitimating aura that I am making here. But this does not mean that the individual studies enact the same blur that one sees in more strictly theoretical analyses and discussions.

27. Foucault, "The Ethic of Care for the Self as a Practice of Freedom," 18.

28. Jürgen Habermas, *The Philosophical Discourse of Modernity,* trans. Frederick G. Lawrence (Cambridge, MA: MIT Press, 1987), 284. Subsequent page number references will be cited parenthetically in the text.

29. Portions of this discussion are indebted to Richard J. Bernstein, "The Retrieval of the Democratic Ethos," in *Habermas on Law and Democracy,* ed. Michael Rosenfeld and Andrew Arato (Berkeley: University of California Press, 1998), 287–305. Bernstein's more even-handed appraisal of Habermas yields a more balanced, and ultimately illuminating, analysis of ethos in this case than it does in his essay on Foucault. I found it very helpful in thinking through the dual stance Habermas takes toward this concept. I take up the issue of ethos in Habermasian proceduralism, and discuss the particulars of Bernstein's position on Habermas more fully, in the longer project from which this essay is drawn. See Amanda Anderson, *The Way We Argue Now* (Princeton: Princeton University Press, forthcoming).

30. See Habermas, *The Philosophical Discourse of Modernity,* 257.

31. Similarly, a respectful attention to, and even recuperation of, "instructive contradiction" is palpably evident in Habermas's memorial address to Foucault, "Taking Aim at the Heart of the Present: On Foucault's Lecture on Kant's *What is Enlightenment?*" in Jürgen Habermas, *The New Conservatism,* 173–79.

32. Habermas, *The Philosophical Discourse of Modernity,* 107, 257.

33. Two examples are salient here. When discussing what for him is the unappealing moral stance of strategic rather than principled postconventionalism—what Kohlberg designated as stage 4 ½ in his overall schema of moral development—Habermas notes that this arrested stage has its own philosophical counterparts in the value-skepticism of

thinkers in a line from Weber to Popper. See Jürgen Habermas, *Moral Consciousness and Communicative Action*, trans. Christian Lenhardt and Shierry Weber Nicholsen (Cambridge, MA: MIT Press, 1990), 184. And the relative values assigned by Habermas in his use of the concepts of youth and maturity assert themselves somewhat strangely in an acrobatic moment in his analysis of Hegel in *The Philosophical Discourse of Modernity*. Habermas has been showing that Hegel's youthful insights (as manifest in his critique of the one-sidedness of the principle of subjectivity) are replaced, as he gets older, with the misguided notion of the Absolute. But as though unable to distinguish between the literal and the metaphorical in the case of this governing conceptual contrast, Habermas manages to re-cast the youthful insight as maturity relative to the later ideas: "With this concept of the absolute, Hegel regresses back behind the intuitions of his youthful period" (22).

34. Jürgen Habermas, "Europe's Second Chance," in *The Past as Future*, ed. and trans. Max Pensky, 96–7.

35. Translation emended to correct for what was probably a printer's error in penultimate sentence.

36. For a more considered attempt to link Foucault's own writings on the *parrhesiast* with the demands of political practice in the present age, see Paul Rabinow, "Modern and Countermodern: Ethos and Epoch in Heidegger and Foucault," in *The Cambridge Companion to Foucault*, ed. Gary Gutting (Cambridge: Cambridge University Press, 1994), 197–214.

37. See Nussbaum, "Virtue Ethics: A Misleading Category," for a discussion of the strand of virtue ethics that retains a privileged place for reason.

5

Can Polemic be Ethical?

A Response to Michel Foucault

Jonathan Crewe

Polemic has a bad name in the humanities academy. Reasons for avoiding or seeking to discredit polemic aren't always articulated, yet they surely include these: polemic disrupts the shared endeavors of the academy and preempts the civil or technical discourses of professionalism; polemic is a short cut to professional recognition typically chosen by those whose ambition outruns their achievement; conversely, polemic is the last resort of major figures in decline, seeking to maintain their professional dominance; polemic is a cheap, often trivial, substitute for real intellectual production; polemic belongs to the sphere of public journalism, where careers can be made on the basis of verbal aggression alone; polemic caters to the unseemly pleasures of cruelty and malice; polemic tends to become compulsive and consuming. Such reasons, or perhaps only intuitions, suffice to create an aversion to polemic, at least in the U. S. academy; they also tend to render polemic ethically suspect, with whatever intellectual justifications it is pursued. Yet it is not clear that academic disapproval of polemic remains at a steady level. During the past three decades or more—say the post-1960s decades— a trend to devalue, disavow, or, on occasion, disingenuously deny polemic has intensified in the academy.

The claim that there has been such a trend may surprise people distressed by how badly academics often treat each other, or merely those who can call to mind many instances of academic polemic in this period. Nevertheless, post-1960s demands for civility, professional respect, negotiation, and collective endeavor have prevailed to a marked degree over forms of unbridled militancy. The academic warrior-critic bent on annihilation now seems embarrassingly old-fashioned, pathological, or simply out of place. So does the academic revolutionary, seeking to upset the apple cart. The widespread embrace of "critique" as the term defining our endeavors is revealing: however radical critique may aspire to be, its philosophical antecedents temper aggressivity and presuppose some level of respectful engagement with, or even continuing dependency on, the object of critique.

So far, so good. In this paper, however, I want to suggest that the commonsensical reasons I have given for academic aversion to polemic don't sufficiently account for what is disturbing about it. Nor do they sufficiently account for the anti-polemical ethic so forcefully articulated by Michel Foucault in a well known passage from an interview with Paul Rabinow, to which I shall turn shortly. I will suggest that the question of polemic is ultimately and disturbingly inseparable from that of belligerence and violence more broadly: from their effects; from their reasons or lack of reason; from their redemptive potentialities or lack of such potentialities (by which I mean both their wished-for redeeming power or capacity to be redeemed); from their implicating troublesomeness, even when intellectual justification is claimed. It is that troublesomeness I particularly wish to emphasize, fully acknowledging that if Foucault were *less* troubled by polemic than he professed to be towards the end of his life, there would have been no prompting for me, at least, to investigate further. My examples later in this paper will suggest that polemic may strike us as troublesome to different degrees, but for Foucault the question is not one of degree but kind: that is the force as well as a possible limitation of his argument.

In what, then, does the troublesomeness consist? An important part of the answer is suggested by the derivation of the term "polemic" from Greek *polemos, polemikos* (war, warlike). If, in fact, polemic has become increasingly discredited in the academy during the past thirty years, is it just a coincidence that the trend coincided with a broader academic rejection of violence in the post-colonial, post-Vietnam era, to which era Foucault's work distinctly belongs?[1] With the emergence of an anti-war ethos in the humanities academy, an ethos currently challenged both by the war plans of the George W. Bush administration and by a conservative intelligentsia supporting those plans?[2] With an aversion to combat not necessarily restricted to particular instances, such as those currently contemplated by the U.S. government? These questions can only be posed, but they suggest that limited, intra-professional explanations may not suffice.

Foucault does not refer directly to the derivation of the term "polemic," yet, as we will shortly see, his antipolemical declaration is suffused with aversion to war. For that reason as well as others, I will take Foucault's anti-polemical statement as my main point of departure and periodic return. What is at stake for Foucault, and will ultimately be so for me, is an ethic of discourse that takes full account of verbal aggression and combat. More exactly, what is at stake for me is the precondition for such an ethic, the point on which I will disagree with Foucault.

This disagreement—call it polemical if you will—can be meaningful only if I credit as fully as possible the categorical challenge of Foucault's anti-polemical declaration. His challenge calls for a response, not least insofar as we academics might find ourselves drawn to his position. As part of that response, I shall try to do justice to Foucault by drawing on early modern examples of polemic that tend to substantiate his misgivings. I believe those examples confront us with the very issue Foucault wishes us to take seriously, namely the unsettling continuity, despite all buffering or transforming decorums, between verbal aggression and annihilating warfare.[3] Yet I shall use the same examples against Foucault in the end.

Let us then hear Foucault:

> It is true that I don't like to get involved in polemics . . . that's not my way of doing things . . . a whole morality is at stake, the morality that concerns the search for truth and the relation to the other. In the serious play of questions and answers . . . the rights of each person are in some sense immanent in the discussion . . . . The polemicist proceeds encased in privileges that he possesses in advance and will never agree to question. On principle, he possesses rights authorizing him to wage war and making that struggle a just undertaking; the person he confronts is not a partner in the search for truth but an adversary, an enemy who is wrong, who is harmful, and whose very existence constitutes a threat. For him, then, the game consists not of recognizing the person as a subject having a right to speak but of abolishing him, as interlocutor, from any possible dialogue.[4]

Something might be said, and not without irony, about the veiled polemic against Habermas being conducted here, about the obstacles to entry into this game, and about the self-idealization that allows Foucault to forget the inescapably polemical formation of his own intellectual positions.[5] Not to trivialize the issue, however, Foucault's statement, by separating polemic from ethically sanctioned, intellectual discourse—by making polemic, in effect, the Other of such discourse—at once relegates polemic to a lawless outside and paradoxically pre-empts it as an inferior *genre* in which intellectual aggression, *ipso facto* unprincipled whatever its excuses, can be cordoned off, at least in principle. That double move of expulsion and tacit enclosure—a move so foreign, we might think, to the logic of Foucaultian argumentation from *Madness and Civilization* through *The History of Sexuality*—is the crucial one for a radically anti-polemical ethic.[6] It not only constitutes such an ethic as one of non-violence, but precludes any further discussion of what one might call the tempering, regulating, or mediating sub-genres and decorums of polemic.[7]

Foucault's momentous gesture is one to which I shall return in due course, but before doing that I should additionally like to highlight one fairly staggering implication of Foucault's statement. It is that polemic has no constitutive role in intellectual history, or in bringing about intellectual change. Is legitimate intellectual history then also a history of non-violence? Can we just detach ourselves from the apparent fertility and even pleasure as well as the implicating troublesomeness of polemic? How, by the same token, are we to negotiate between the demands of an ethical universal and those of historical understanding, a dilemma that arises, as we shall see, as soon as we turn to texts from earlier historical periods. The logic of Foucault's own arguments regarding the double effect, both oppressive and productive, of disciplinary violence might suggest the need for a more complex view. So might consideration of recent polemic: without feminist, queer, or postcolonial polemics, some of it ad hominem, there would be no academic fields corresponding to those designations. Without polemic directed at the New Critics and all their works, there would be no institutionalized post-structuralism in the U.S. academy.

While change and innovation may not be caused by polemic, they are apparently seldom effected in its absence. In this volume, the important polemics of Foucault vs. Habermas and Kael vs. Sarris are given their due. Consideration might equally be given to Nussbaum or Gubar vs. Butler, Derrida vs. Searle, Derrida vs. Foucault, Chomsky vs. Skinner, Sartre vs. Camus, Leavis vs. Snow, and any number of other modern instances. Both the belligerence and the intellectual momentousness of these polemics call for recognition. Historical examples from classical antiquity through the present are innumerable. Yet in a sense verbal aggression has become so "unfamiliar" to us that it needs to be reconsidered as if from the beginning.[8]

To address both the implicating troublesomeness of polemic in its deepest etymological sense and the preconditions for an ethic responsive to that troublesomeness, I shall turn now, at the risk of producing some disorientation, to two related examples from the late sixteenth century in England. If the unfamiliarity, even strangeness, of these examples creates difficulties, I must ask readers to bear with me since the historical remoteness of the examples will be an element in argument I finally wish to make.

The first example, then, is that of the so-called Marprelate controversy (1588–89). It may initially seem like a counter-example that reveals the separability of polemic from *polemos,* thereby making Foucault's objections seem melodramatically exaggerated (an objection not infrequently voiced about his work in general). The troublesomeness of polemic in the Marprelate instance seems only moderate. My second example, which will be my principal one, is that of Thomas Nashe's *Christ's Teares over Jerusalem* (1594).[9] That text goes a long way towards substantiating Foucault's position and it also brings into question the "harmless" polemic that precedes it.

Briefly, the Marprelate controversy arose in the aftermath of a 1586 Star Chamber decree procured by Archbishop Whitgift of Canterbury, prohibiting publication of any books, pamphlets and tracts not authorized by him or the Bishop of London. Following this decree, a series of unlicensed, anti-episcopal pamphlets were produced under the pseudonym of Martin Marprelate by some gifted English Puritan authors, John Penry and Job Throckmorton generally being credited as the leading ones.[10] So successful were these rambunctious, often hilarious, pamphlets that the alarmed church authorities recruited a number of English university wits, among them Thomas Nashe and John Lyly, to

respond in kind. These recruits, hired guns rather than persons of conspicuous religious conviction, became known as the anti-Martinists.
Nashe, in particular, made his name as an anti-Martinist. The controversy ended only with the closing down of the Martinist press and the
imprisonment of suspected authors, including John Udall and John
Penry.

   This example is to the point here in more than one way. It calls to
mind the religious provenance of the term "polemics" (as distinct from
"irenics") in European usage, a provenance of which Foucault was fully
aware in singling out religion as one of three prominent historical sites
of polemic, the other two being judicial and political (382).[11] The
example also suggests, apparently somewhat at odds with Foucault,
that polemic can be—or has historically been—susceptible to decorous
neutralization, performative transformation, generic regulation, and
medium-specific conventionalization.[12]

   The Marprelate controversy remains widely regarded, in any event,
as a print-facilitated mutation in prior and concurrent religious controversy.[13] Clearly, the Reformation gave an enormous impetus to religious polemic, with acrimonious controversy between Erasmus and
Luther supplying only one example of extremely widespread, multifo-
cal contention. Clearly, too, religious controversy did not begin with
the Reformation, but went back at least as far as the emergence of
Christianity.[14] It was not the fact, however, of conducting religious
polemics through the medium of printed pamphlets that made the
anonymous Marprelate authors different. Rather, in the now established view, it was their conscious exploitation of the print medium,
and even of typographical layout, to popularize and theatricalize mul-
tivocal religious polemic. The narrative of the Marprelate printers'
eventually unsuccessful efforts to evade capture by moving their press
around England on wagons (no mean undertaking given the weight of
lead type and the massive size of printing presses) serves to highlight
the critical role of the print medium at this historical juncture.

   This brilliantly opportunistic hijacking of religious disputation from
its respectable academic and ecclesiastical sites provoked a contemporary scandal, but also made the Marprelate pamphlets a popular success
and (hence) a perceived threat to the authority of the English Church.[15]
The example is one of many in which print culture can be seen at once

to have transformed old spaces of public discourse and constituted new ones. Alexandra Halasz, in particular, has studied the commodification of discourse in early modern English print culture, the pamphlet itself having the character of an unadorned, "authorless" commodity despite authorial signatures.[16] For Halasz, these developments are not the prelude to a general outbreak of lawlessness; rather, they anticipate and enable the formation of a Habermasian public sphere.

In short, although the Marprelate authors were serious enough to court torture and martyrdom, they gave a ludic and even carnivalesque public character to their assault on episcopal hierarchy, thereby alienating some of their allies as well as their antagonists. The innovations of the Marprelate press made religious controversy openly a form of popular entertainment. Moreover, by personifying themselves and their episcopal adversaries, they recast such polemic as robust comedy on what Nashe referred to in another context as the "paper stage."[17]

The Marprelate authors at least partly succeeded, then, in turning the earnest of religious polemic into game and in establishing the enduring "entertainment value" of print polemics. They further established the possibility of becoming a career polemicist and self-fictionalizing celebrity. In this guise polemic, however rough, takes on the curiously utopian character of harmless, comedic violence and makes itself pleasing. Commodification of "harmless" polemic is one legacy of the early modern print economy that has been assimilated, *mutatis mutandis,* into contemporary journalism, TV, and broadcasting. Contemporary academic careers bound to polemics, even when they do not wholly consist of them, tend to take on the same coloration. The careers of Stanley Fish, and more recently of Camille Paglia, might be taken as exemplary. While there are undoubtedly those for whom such careers and their historical antecedents are ethically troubling, for most, such polemics probably do not rise to the level of troublesomeness implied by Foucault's declaration. Yet Foucault's strictures on the theatricality of polemics are particularly severe and uncompromising:

> Of course, the reactivation, in polemics, of these political, judiciary, or religious practices is nothing more than theater. One gesticulates: anathemas, excommunications, condemnations, battles, victories, and defeats are no more than ways of speaking, after all. And yet, in the

order of discourse, they are also ways of acting which are not without
consequences. (383)

Although Foucault's double location of polemic in the category of theater (in which it is vacuous) and in that of action (in which it is extremely dangerous) again produces a sense of contradiction, let us consider a
more troublesome *exemplum,* Nashe's *Christ's Teares over Jerusalem.*

Briefly, *Christ's Teares* is a commodified pamphlet based in part on the
widely-read history of the "Jewish Josephus," Yosip ben Gorion, who
recounts the destruction of Jerusalem in CE 70 by the Roman armies of
Titus and Vespasian. This text links Christ's prophetic mourning of
Jerusalem's impending doom in Luke, 19:41–42 to the actual destruction
of the city by the Roman armies: "And when he was come near, he beheld
the city, and wept over it, Saying, If thou hadst known, even thou, at least
in this thy day, the things which belong unto thy peace! But now they are
hid from thine eyes." *Christ's Teares* also embodies an invented and "per-
formed" oration, based on this and other New Testament passages, delivered by Christ against the Jews who have failed to recognize him, and who
in past times stoned and cast out their prophets.[18] Having warned the citizens of Jerusalem to no avail, Christ can then only consign them to well-
earned destruction. The effect of Christ's compulsively repetitive,
extravagantly hyperbolic diatribe is to exhaust all mercy and justify the
annihilation of the city. After Christ has proclaimed that "Thy sinne
exceedeth my suffering; It is too monstrous a matter for my mercie or
merites to work on," the narrator duly records that "The Romaines, like
a droue of Wild-bores, roote vp and forrage fruitful *Palestine.*"[19]

Like the Marprelate controversy, *Christ's Teares* is to the point in several ways. In the first place, although Christ's inset oration might be
better described as a prophetic diatribe than as polemic, the pamphlet
is, in fact, a layered polemic. It participates in the widespread contemporary anti-Judaic polemic of Protestantism, relevantly and extensively
discussed by Debora Shuger.[20] It engages as well in a "subtextual"
polemic against the city fathers of London,[21] identified with the Jews
of Jerusalem on account of their alleged cruelty and unchristian parsi-
mony (it was a common critique of Puritans that they were really Old
Testament Jews, not Christians). The perception of this veiled attack
caused something of a contemporary scandal.

At the overt level, Nashe's anti-Judaism makes the conflict between Christ and "his" people an essentially internecine one between good and evil Jew. Here, as so often elsewhere, the agency of Rome and the Empire both in the death of Christ and in the destruction of Jerusalem is placed out of moral contention. More precisely, Christ exonerates the Romans in advance for their violence to come since they will be acting for him and his outraged father. In maximizing self-justifying belligerence on the part of Christ, the pamphlet transmutes "ordinary" Protestant polemic into a gigantic continuous monologue of passionate abuse and recrimination, while also establishing a *causal* link between polemic as verbal aggression and *polemos* as war. Both in fantasy and at the level of plot, the second follows from and gives effect to the first.

It goes without saying that Nashe's insertion of this causal link is rendered dubious, at least for us, by its requirement of divine agency and intervention. In this respect, Nashe's text does little to substantiate Foucault's evident concern about a dangerous continuum, not just an analogy, between polemic and *polemos*. Yet in this text both the divinity of Christ and the intervention of his Father remain conspicuously problematic. Nashe ventriloquizes, and no doubt strongly identifies as well, with the "Jewish" viewpoint in the text, from which Christ is anything but a god incarnate: rather, he is " . . . a drunkard, possessed with a diuel . . . [who] cast out diuels by the power of *Beelzebub,* the Prince of the diuels . . . blasphemed, was mad, & knew not what [he] spake" (23).[22] The figure of an all too human Christ becomes one who *wills* an annihilating violence that does not necessarily follow from his words, but that fact does not necessarily render his words harmless either, as cause, effect, or symptom. Let us pursue this crucial point in the light of Foucault's concerns.

In literary-historical terms, *Christ's Teares* belongs to a contemporary "literature of warning" that prophesies doom to great, corrupt cities on account of their transgressions. With Sodom, Babylon, and Jerusalem in the background, these prophecies could be applied to any contemporary European city: Rome, Amsterdam, and, in *Christ's Teares,* London." The declamatory theatricality of Nashe's Christ is thus both historical and generic. Moreover, Nashe emulously equates his figure of Christ with that of Marlowe's Tamburlaine, who used flags to send progressively more threatening messages to the cities he besieged, the black flag denoting pitiless destruction to come. Christ follows suit: "Hauing offered the Iewes the White-flagge of forgiuenesse and remission, and the Red-flag of shedding his Blood for them, when these two might not take effect or work any yeelding of remorse in them, the Blacke-flagge of confusion and desolation was to succeede for the obiect of their obduration" (20). Christ becomes the protagonist-revenger outdoing even Tamburlaine, just as Nashe seeks to outdo Marlowe, in neo-Senecan tragedy. As "mad" revenger, Christ vents the hyperbolic "passion" of the Senecan protagonist in a prose-poem that vies with its blank verse counterparts on stage.[23] If the rhetoric of this performance has sources (e.g., biblical ones) that separate it from its Latin theatrical counterparts, that does not distinguish it wholly from contemporary tragedy or prevent Nashe from marking his text as Senecan: "Like trag-ick Seneca, I . . . tragedize my selfe, by bleeding to death in the depth of passion" (60).

These textual filiations of *Christ's Teares* (and there are many more) suffice to indicate that the text, which a number of critics in the twentieth century considered inexplicably aberrant, would not necessarily have been perceived as such in its time. If the figure of Christ as revenger is that of a "mad" individual, his is a madness that, as is so often the case in early modern tragedy, cannot be fully isolated from the dominant mindsets, rhetorics, and polemical causes of the time. That, indeed, is the broadly implicating menace of Nashe's Christ-figure—a menace of a kind perhaps insufficiently bargained for in *Madness and Civilization.*

The implicating menace of Christ in Nashe's text cannot be confined to theater alone, or even to "literary" contexts, although it implicates many of these. In the most consequential historicization of *Christ's Teares* to date, Shuger argues on one hand that the represented passion of Christ in Nashe's text is typical of Calvinist passion narratives of the time, and on the other hand that these narratives were informed by, just as they informed, contemporary representations of passion in secular drama and poetry, including Shakespeare's.[24] Shuger additionally notes that for Calvinists none of this necessarily compromises the figure of a human Christ, or renders him "unethical," any more than does the oscillation of both Christ and the reader between the roles of torturer and tortured. Nor, at the time of writing, does the text move beyond the outer limits of what might now be called "redemptive violence."[25] However ambiguously, *Christ's Teares* solicits identificatory participation in a cultural violence imagined capable of redeeming itself, together with the world and the world's troubled redeemer, through the ultimate annihilation of the Jewish other. In sum, the performance of ravaged "Christian selfhood" (90) in *Christ's Teares* is exemplary rather than anomalous; the very language of Christ's hystericized passion and sinisterly "blackened" self-image can be paralleled in many contemporary texts, both sacred and secular:

> The fount of my teares (troubled and mudded with the Toade-like stirring and long-breathed vexation of thy venimous enormities) is no longer a pure siluer spring but a mirie puddle for swine to wallow in. Black and cindry (like Smithes-water) are those excrements that source downe my cheekes, and far more sluttish than the vglie oous of the channell . . . my leane withered hands (consisting of nought but bones) are all to shiverd and splinterd in their wide cases of skinne . . . I nowe but fore-telle a storme in a Calme . . . When Heauen (in stead of starres) shall be made an artillery-house of hailstones . . . then shall you know what it is, by saying *you would not, to make your house vnto you be left desolate.* (47)

Even the figure of the compassionate revenger, so impossibly contradictory, constituted an important riddle for Nashe and his contemporaries, as it evidently does to this day in Christian apologetics.[26] In short, it is hard to escape the conclusion that Nashe's text participates, along with the tragedies of Marlowe and Shakespeare, in a widespread, even dominant, Protestant discourse of now-disturbing passion and faith.[27]

If the flagrant theatricality and belligerence of *Christ's Teares,* but also, importantly, the post-Holocaust power it has taken on to appall, lend credence to Foucault's strictures on polemic, their doing so does not wholly depend on Nashe's particular cause and effect sequence. It is quite enough that annihilating violence is willed and articulated since, if a causal connection to any particular historical event cannot be proved, neither can it be disproved. Nor do we necessarily require formal proof to believe that speech can be consequential. Furthermore, the temporal deferral that renders the logic of cause and effect questionable (*post hoc non ergo propter hoc*) also *conserves* the possiblity of effect(s) at practically any temporal remove, thus rendering any presumption of harmlessness premature at best. Finally, a scandalous belligerence of address may already be understood as a mode of harmful violence. As Foucault puts it: "in the order of discourse, [polemics] are also ways of acting which are not without consequences" (383). "Jews" were no mere fictional entity at the time *Christ's Teares* was written; harm was being inflicted. However reluctantly we may accede, then, to Foucault's contention that polemic inherently entails a denial of the rights of the other and has no goal short of obliteration—in other words, that the lure of polemic as *polemos* is always and only that of annihilating, justified power—there is also no safe refuge in decorum or mediation from that charge.[28] It is to the recognition of this state of affairs that Nashe's text lends itself. If we cannot say that this text, or any like it, accounts for a view that Foucault passionately asserts rather than explains, it nevertheless gives us reason to attend seriously to his strictures and helps, perhaps, to elucidate them.

Even if this proposition is granted, however, *Christ's Teaers* may still seem to pose a dilemma of ethical vs. historical response. Scandalized yet uncomprehending twentieth-century reactions to Nashe's text have been no substitute for contextualization and historical inquiry pursued by Shuger and others.[29] Yet in order to embed and elucidate the text historically—or pose it as a cultural artifact, for that matter—a certain suspension of ethical judgment is required; conversely, the very act of historicization leaves questionable the pertinence or power of current ethical judgment vis-à-vis the historical object. Clearly, it is no solution to confine ethical judgment to the present only, leaving history to the historians, yet negotiating between the respective claims of history and ethics remains a difficult task that a text like *Christ's Teares* may continue to impose on us.

If, in reading *Christ's Teares,* we do not wish an ethical perspective merely to be displaced by a historical one, no doubt that is partly because, post-Holocaust, both Nashe's text and the Calvinist ideological matrix of its production assume a character very different from any that could have been perceived by Nashe's contemporaries. We live a different history, but not one wholly discontinuous with that of Nashe and his contemporaries. On the contrary, the early modern and specifically Protestant antecedents of twentieth-century anti-Semitism are well recognized. It is precisely within that continuing history rather than outside it that Foucault's point continues to resonate: "in the order of discourse, [polemics] are also ways of acting which are not without consequences" (383).

I do not suggest that the difficulty of negotiating between the respective claims of history and ethics always has to culminate in an impasse, since historical and ethical perspectives may modify and inform each other, and beyond a certain point both disciplines may look like comparable attempts to grapple with inordinately troubling phenomena. Shuger, for example, cautions that her book deals with "incommensurable materials that do not share the same discursive genealogy and hence should not be lined up as stages along a single trajectory" (192). This caveat notwithstanding, she nevertheless positions her materials on a grand historical trajectory of secularization. Along this trajectory, a shift from spiritual to psychological categories of interpretation occurs, and the extravagant inner and outer life of a sacrificially-based, early modern, religious culture is at once pathologized and subjected to the discipline of what Norbert Elias called the civilizing process.[30] Passion thereby becomes transmuted into neurosis. Foucault is explicitly a shaping presence in Shuger's historical coda, and we are prompted to recall that the extravagant violence of torture with which Foucault begins *Discipline and Punish* belongs to the same world as that of Calvinist representations of the passion. Yet where Shuger narrates an estranging pathologization of the inner and outer life of passionate Christendom, with the turning point coming in the seventeenth century, Foucault, in *Madness and Civilization, Discipline and Punish,* and *The Birth of the Clinic,* narrates an estranging of premodern "madness" and the institution of disciplinary technologies of incarceration and surveillance. Both these narratives have what might be called the meta-historical effect of placing "madness," passion, sacrifice, and "redemptive" violence at a safe remove. Those unassimilable intensities are relegated, not wholly without regret, to diminished worlds within or worlds apart, but they are no longer located in the world in which, as Shuger puts it, persons are [now] at home (196).[31]

It takes nothing away from the work of Foucault and Shuger to say that what this distancing belies is the increasingly perspicuous temporal and geographical *proximity* of so much that they locate on the far side of a chronological divide. The irruption of threatening "residues" into the world of the present will seem atavistic or foreign only if we have assumed, always prematurely, that they no longer characterize "our" world. Insofar as we are repeatedly blindsided by violence and passion, specifically including those animating warfare, it is partly because our historicizations convince us that these dangerous intensities do not belong to our world, or because we are ethically convinced that they shouldn't. It is a short step from there to the enunciation of an anti-polemical ethic that on one hand outlaws all polemic as such and on the other hand subjects it preemptively to generic enclosure and separation.

By now, my own difference with Foucault will seem predictable if not anticlimactic, although I am inclined to think that this is one context in which less is more, even or especially when the threats presented seem potentially engulfing. My view is that the anti-polemical attitude Foucault enunciates with all the categorical intransigence of an ethical fiat is untenable, and not necessarily conducive to the assumption of historical or discursive responsibility. The options of preemptively cordoning polemic off as a genre, of disengaging, or of situating oneself in a position or history of non-violence seem more conducive to denial and disavowal than ethical efficacy. I would therefore suggest that ethical considerations can most profitably come into play after that recognition, not before it. If they do so then, as they surely should, it may be only in the somewhat disappointing guise of ethics as usual, in which ordinary questions of necessity, justification, harm, and the rights of others have to be negotiated. Polemic does indeed remain one object of ethical consideration and action, but not quite as the special case Foucault wants to make it. In any event, it is far from true, as is sometimes apparently supposed, that the participatory acknowledgement of aggression preempts the ethical; on the contrary, it can help to motivate an assumption of responsibility for verbal contention that will be extremely chary of announcing itself as an ethic of non-violence or non-involvement. Perhaps that is the only way in which polemic can aspire to be ethical.

Notes

1. We may speculate that Foucault's ethical rejection of polemic is both post-war in the sense that it continues to repudiate the Sartrean role of the intellectual *engagé* in favor of a fastidious academic role—a repudiation documented by Didier Eribon, *Michel Foucault,* tr. Betsy Wing (Cambridge, MA: Harvard University Press, 1991)—and anti-war in that it belongs to a post-Algeria, post-Vietnam era of Western disillusionment with both the pursuit and the rationales of violence.

2. Whether the academy is constitutionally anti-war, so to speak—whether open belligerency is simply incompatible with academic values and modes of production—appears to be up for consideration again at the time of writing.

3. By this I do not mean "the violence of the letter" as conceived by Jacques Derrida, "The Violence of the Letter: From Levi-Strauss to Rousseau," *Of Grammatology,* tr. Gayatri Chakravorty Spivak (Baltimore: The Johns Hopkins University Press, 1976) 101–18. That concept remains problematic in failing to distinguish, for example, between the magnitude and specificity of Western, colonizing warfare and other modes of belligerence (see Jonathan Goldberg, *Writing Matters: From the Hands of the English Renaissance* [Stanford: Stanford University Press, 1990] 2–7). More to the point, it is a concept that did little—how could it?—to temper or directly justify Derrida's own remarkably aggressive incursions into polemic.

4. "An Interview with Michel Foucault," in Paul Rabinow, ed., *Foucault: A Reader* (New York: Pantheon, 1984) 382.

5. The process can be tracked in Eribon, *Michel Foucault,* especially as regards Foucault's anti-Marxism. On some of the contexts and implications of this passage, see Michael Warner, "Styles of Intellectual Publics," *Publics and Counterpublics,* ed. Michael Warner, (Cambridge: Zone Books, 2002) 151–58. In her English Institute essay, included in the present volume, Amanda Anderson cites the same passage I have cited in connection with polemics between Foucault and Habermas.

6. Michel Foucault, *Madness and Civilization: A History of Insanity in the Age of Reason,* tr. Richard Howard (New York: Vintage Books, 1973); *The Birth of the Clinic; An Archaeology of Medical Perception,* tr. A. M. Sheridan Smith (New York: Pantheon Books, 1973); *Discipline and Punish: The Birth of the Prison,* tr. Alan Sheridan (New York: Pantheon Books, 1977); *The History of Sexuality,* Vol. 1, tr. Robert Hurley (New York: Pantheon Books, 1978). Others may be more capable than I am of explaining this apparent contradiction or of situating it in last phase of Foucault's career. Contradiction of this kind may well be anticipated by Jacques Derrida in "Cogito and the History of Madness," *Writing and Difference,* tr. Alan Bass (Chicago: University of Chicago Press) 31–63, yet Foucault's statement is far from being reduced to a mere mistake by its possible contradictoriness with respect to earlier writings by Foucault.

7. Genre was implicitly in contention on the Polemics panel of the 2002 English Institute, yet it is not clear how a genre of polemic as such can usefully be defined given the multiplicity of its contexts, purposes, and

functions, and given the range it covers from *ad hominem* attack to aggressive intellectual disputation. It might more plausibly be regarded as a meta-genre than as a genre, or as a phenomenon too contextually dominated to lend itself to abstract rule-making. Loosely rule-governed subgenres might, however, include, at the quasi-literary high end, satire, epigram, jeremiad, flyting, diatribe, lampoon, and the critical essay or review, while low-end genres of current journalism and public debate might include letters to the editor, op ed columns, film, TV, and book reviews, works of transitory political and religious debate. All of that, however, appears to be out of contention for Foucault, as, for that matter, are the many "subgenres," decorums, and legalities of warfare.

8. That conviction evidently inspired the organizers of a conference on writing and violence held in 2002 at the intellectually adventurous University of North Cyprus in Famagusta. That conference, too, highlighted the derivation of polemic from *polemikos* and proposed an extensive menu of sub-topics. See http://lists.partners-intl.net/pipermail/academic-resources/2001 November/001191.html.

9. For me, a return to this scene is a revisitation in a double sense, since I have previously written on these materials in *Unredeemed Rhetoric: Thomas Nashe and the Scandal of Authorship* (Baltimore: The Johns Hopkins University Press, 1982). I am, however, moved to reclaim the exemplariness of these materials in a drastically altered frame of reference.

10. Tracts include: *The Epistle* (Oct. 1588), *The Epitome* (Nov. 1588), *Certain Mineral and Metaphysical Schoolpoints* (Feb. 1589), *Hay Any Work for Cooper* (Mar. 1589), *Martin Junior* (July 1589), *Martin Senior* (July 1589), and *The Protestation of Martin Marprelate* (Sep. 1589). The bishops answered with *An Admonition to the People of England* (1589), authored by Thomas Cooper, Bishop of Winchester (the butt of *Hay Any Work for Cooper*). The church's hired writers included John Lyly (*Pap with a Hatchet* [1589]), Nashe (*An Almond for a Parrot*), and Richard Harvey (*Plain Percival* [1589], *A Theological Discourse of the Lamb of God* [1590]).

11. In the currently received view, this controversy had a religious cast yet not a strictly theological one. The attack on English episcopal hierarchy in the service of a more "popular" (Presbyterian) mode of church government made the debate one about ecclesiastical authority and governance more than doctrine. Theological Calvinists could and did participate on both sides. Yet "religion" is still the field of polemic in this episode.

12. See, for example, Raymond Anselment, *"Twixt Jest and Earnest": Marprelate, Milton, Marvell, Swift and the Decorum of Religious Ridicule* (Toronto: University of Toronto Press, 1980); Kristin Poole, "Saints Alive! Falstaff, Martin Marprelate, and the Staging of Puritanism," *Shakespeare Quarterly,* 46, 1. (Spring, 1995) 47–75.

13. See, for example, Joseph Black, "'The Rhetoric of Reaction: The Martin Marprelate Tracts' (1588–89), Anti-Martinism, and the Uses of Print in Early Modern England," *SCJ,* 28 (1997); Elizabeth Appleton, *An*

Anatomy of the Marprelate Controversy, 1588–96: Retracing Shakespeare's Identity and that of Martin Marprelate (New York: Mellen Press, 2001); Leland H. Carlson, "Research on Martin Marprelate," *English Satire*, ed. Leland H. Carlson and Ronald Paulson (Los Angeles: William Andrews Clark Memorial Library, University of California, 1972) 3–48.

14. But apparently not to anything like the same degree in the Roman world, in which disputes over particular orthodoxies or professions of faith were rare. See Mary Beard, John North and Simon Price, *Religions of Rome: Volume 1, A History* (Cambridge: Cambridge University Press, 1998).

15. The "harmlessness" of polemic is always to some degree in the eye of the beholder, the church authorities not being disposed to take Marprelate lightly.

16. Alexandra Halasz, *The Marketplace of Print: Pamphlets and the Public Sphere in Early Modern England* (New York: Cambridge University Press, 1997).

17. Thomas Nashe, "Preface to Sidney's 'Astrophil and Stella,'" *The Works of Thomas Nashe*, 5 vols., ed. R.B. McKerrow (1904–10), revised and reprinted F. P. Wilson, ed. (Oxford: Basil Blackwell, 1966); III: 329.

18. Ben Gorion was translated into English in 1558 by Peter Morvyn under the title *History of the Latter Times of the Jews' Commonweal.*

19. Thomas Nashe, *Christ's Teares over Jerusalem, Works*, II: 35, 63.

20. Debora Kuller Shuger, *The Renaissance Bible: Scholarship, Sacrifice and Subjectivity* (Berkeley and Los Angeles: University of California Press, 1994). "Anti-Judaic" rather than "anti-Semitic" only inasmuch as what we call anti-Semitism continues to be decisively shaped by the racial pseudoscience of the nineteenth century.

21. See G. R. Hibbard, *Thomas Nashe: A Critical Introduction* (Cambridge, MA: Harvard University Press, 1962) 123.

22. Nashe's skeptically "alienated" view of Christ as all too human has something in common with Marlowe's scandalous epigrams: "Christ was a bastard and his mother dishonest," "[Christ] was the sonne of a Carpenter, and . . . if the Jewes among whome he was borne did Crucify him theie best knewe him and whence he Came." *Marlowe: The Critical Heritage, 1588–1896*, ed. Millar McClure (London: Routledge, 1979) 37.

23. And, one might add, threatens to consume the authorial self Nashe tries to constitute apart from the representation of Christ: "I . . . tragedize my selfe, by bleeding to death in the depth of passion" (60).

24. Shuger, *Renaissance Bible*: "All the Calvinist passions are troubling, dark, bordering on the grotesque" (90). "The causal trajectory from the Crucifixion to the fall of Jerusalem partially or wholly replaces the biblical plot" (91); "All Calvinist passion narratives, in fact, dwell repeatedly on Christ's sufferings. It is almost as if the central contrast between gentleness and malice slips over into a still more fundamental contrast between humiliation and power" (96); "The Calvinist passion

narratives disclose the reciprocal metamorphoses of the torturer and the
tortured" (97).
25. I use the term "redemptive violence" for want of a better. The term in
ordinary circulation—as exemplified by numerous Internet citations—
refers primarily to retributive violence, but evidently as well to practically any instance of violence turned to good, or considered productive
of good. I am not aware of any rigorous, technical use of the term. The
sacralization of violence has been rigorously discussed by René Girard,
Violence and the Sacred, tr. Patrick Gregory (Baltimore: The Johns
Hopkins University Press, 1977).
26. See http://www.bible-sermons.org.uk/text-sermon/441-Christ-Weeping-
over-Jerusalem/.
27. Cynthia Marshall, *The Shattering of the Self: Violence, Subjectivity, and
Early Modern Texts* (Baltimore: Johns Hopkins University Press, 2002),
connects intense representations of violence and cruelty, both done and
received, in Elizabethan texts (e.g., Foxe's *Book of Martyrs,* Nashe's *The
Unfortunate Traveler*) to an impulse of self-undoing dialectically related
to the impulse of self-fashioning given so much prominence since the
publication of Stephen Greenblatt's *Renaissance Self-Fashioning: From
More to Shakespeare* (Chicago: University of Chicago Press, 1980).
28. A refuge Nashe himself evidently seeks in his self-characterization as a
stylist only in the Preface to *Christ's Teares*—a preface in which he also
forswears his earlier jousting with Gabriel Harvey and makes a peace-
offering: "Now better aduised, and of his perfections more confirmedly
perswaded, vnfainedly I entreate of the whole world, from my penne
his worths may receiue no impeachment" (*Works,* 2: 12).
29. For instance, Hibbard, *Thomas Nashe*: "It is far and away . . . the worst
thing Nashe ever wrote. Neither dull nor trivial, it has about it all the
fascination of the thoroughly and horribly bad" (122).
30. Norbert Elias, *The Civilizing Process: The History of Manners,* tr.
Edmund Jephcott (New York: Urizen Books, 1978).
31. Both historicizations (although Foucault would no doubt object to its
being called that) are complicated by identificatory solicitation of the
extreme. Foucault displays a certain exhilarated wonder at the stupefy-
ing excess of early modern torture in *Discipline and Punish*; Shuger likewise registers the exhilarating cognitive disruptiveness, hence pleasure,
of heterogeneous excess when she speaks of the *wunderkammerliche*
character of her textual specimens. See in this connection James Miller's
aptly titled *The Passion of Michel Foucault* (New York: Simon and
Schuster, 1993), and David Halperin, *Saint Foucault: Towards a Gay
Hagiography* (New York: Oxford University Press, 1993).

6

Kael's Attack on Sarris

Louis Menand

Pauline Kael's famous attack on Andrew Sarris appeared in the pages of *Film Quarterly* in 1963. Kael was responding to an article Sarris had published the year before in *Film Culture*, "Notes on the Auteur Theory in 1962." That article was not an introduction to auteur theory. By 1962, everyone who read *Film Culture* knew what an auteur was. Even people in Hollywood knew what an auteur was, because they had been reading the interviews with American directors that had been running in *Cahiers du Cinéma* since 1954. By the late nineteen fifties, every American director with any artistic ambition at all dreamed of being called an auteur by some Frenchman. The intention of Sarris's article was to defend an approach to film criticism that he conceded, right at the start, people had begun to get a little tired of.

Sarris, too, was responding to someone else's article. He was answering some objections to auteur theory that had been raised five years earlier in a piece in *Cahiers du Cinéma* by André Bazin, called "On the *politique des auteurs*." Sarris thought that Bazin was the greatest film critic who ever lived, and he gave Bazin's criticisms of auteur theory considerable credit in his piece. Sarris's defense of the theory was not theoretical, or not very theoretical; it was essentially pragmatic. He was trying to explain why the assumptions of auteurism helped critics understand and evaluate movies. "At the very least," Sarris says at the beginning of his article, "I would like to grant the condemned system a hearing before its execution. The trial has dragged on for many years, I know, and everyone is now bored by the abstract reasoning involved. I have little in the way of new arguments . . . . What follows is consequently less a manifesto than a credo, a somewhat disorganized credo, to be sure, expressed in formless notes rather than in formal brief."[1] He would soon wish that he had taken a little more trouble with the form.

Kael's reply to Sarris was called "Circles and Squares." A great deal of the force of Kael's attack was owed to its ad hominem character. Sarris's article was a reconsideration; Kael's was a polemic. She made fun of Sarris's prose, of his brains, and of his taste, and at the end she suggested that auteur theory was "an attempt by adult males to justify staying inside the small range of experience of their boyhood and adolescence—that period when masculinity looked so great and important, but art was something talked about by poseurs and phonies and sensitive-feminine types."[2]

Sarris never completely recovered. Kael had asked the editor of *Film Quarterly*, Ernest Callenbach, to send an advance copy of her article to Sarris, with the suggestion that he might care to reply in the same issue. Sarris passed on that invitation, but he did publish a response in a subsequent issue of *Film Quarterly*, an essay called "The Auteur Theory and the Perils of Pauline." It was a depressive performance. Most of the article was a diatribe against the cinematic taste and editorial standards of *Film Quarterly* itself. "The difference between *Film Quarterly*'s view of Hollywood and *Cahiers*' is the difference between plain subtraction and differential calculus,"[3] is the kind of thing Sarris said. For the rest, he quoted or paraphrased sections of his original article, and he closed by reprinting in its entirety an article on Italian directors that he had written for *Showbill* in 1961. He did not mention "Circles and Squares" once.

"Polemic," like "rupture" and "transition," is a retrospective term. There are many more would-be polemics—that is, pieces that are written with the intention of changing forever the conventional estimation of an artist or a writer or a school of thought, but that fail to do so— than there are pieces that, looking back, can actually be said to mark a distinctive cultural moment. This doesn't necessarily mean that the polemic was itself a cause of change. Often, the critique may seem, to later eyes, unpersuasive, partial, ad hominem, tendentious. Its success is sometimes simply due to the perception that it was necessary, the vague idea that a structure of assumptions was due to be exploded. One might feel this about, for instance, Noam Chomsky's polemic against B. F. Skinner in 1959, or Jacques Derrida's attack on Claude

Lévi-Strauss in 1966. When the author of the polemic becomes associated with the new direction, which is itself always the consequence of multiple causes, we can say that the polemic has been a success. Kael's attack on Sarris fits this description. It is not only the dart that brought down a fortress. It was the first brick in the new edifice.

*****

In 1963, the year Kael's piece appeared, *Film Quarterly* had a circulation of 5,500. The circulation of *Film Culture*, the magazine in which Sarris's original piece appeared, was almost certainly smaller, since it was by then associated with avant-garde, or "underground," cinema. But in 1963, Sarris was also the movie reviewer for the *Village Voice*, and so the story of Kael's attack got picked up and written about in other magazines. Still, most of these were film journals, like *Sight and Sound*, *Film Comment*, and *Cinéaste*. The only two general-interest magazines that covered the controversy in 1963 were *Commentary* and the *Saturday Review*. In 1964, though, Kael got a Guggenheim fellowship, which she used to put some of her pieces, including "Circles and Squares," together in a book. This was *I Lost It at the Movies*, which was published in 1965, and became a bestseller. It sold 150,000 paperback copies, and *Newsweek* ran a story about Kael in the wake of the book's success.

I Lost It at the Movies was one of the most influential works of postwar American criticism, because an important part of its audience was the younger cohort of music and movie and television critics that emerged with the counterculture and that ended up writing for the magazines that covered it, such as *Rolling Stone* and the *Boston Phoenix*. Twenty and thirty years later, still under Kael's influence, they were writing for the *New Yorker* and the *New York Times*. Most of those younger critics had never heard of André Bazin, whose essays were not translated into English until 1967; most had probably never read *Film Culture* or *Cahiers du Cinéma*. They had almost certainly missed Sarris's original article. But they all read "Circles and Squares" in *I Lost It at the Movies*—which is why it is nearly possible to say that the person who introduced auteur theory to America was not Andrew Sarris, but Pauline Kael.

Sarris, of course, never stopped writing about movies, and he never abandoned the auteur theory, either. On the contrary: in 1968, he

published *The American Cinema: Directors and Directions, 1929–1968*,
a work that is unabashedly auteurist, complete with a pantheon of
great directors, and that became the bible for many movie critics who
were either unmoved by Kael's strictures, or who didn't see that they
had to choose between auteurism and some other way of talking about
the movies. People like to rank directors. People like to rank things,
period. Ours is a species in which it is considered normal to have a
favorite color. Sarris reviewed movies regularly, first in the *Voice* and
then in the *New York Observer*, for more than forty years. He taught,
for most of that time, at Columbia University.

He never stopped having to deal with the fall-out from his one-sided
quarrel with Kael—it comes up in virtually every interview with him
and in nearly everything that is written about her—but he also never
really got it. He thought that Kael had misrepresented him, and that
he had been attacked mainly for careless writing. The personal character of her polemic seems just to have buffaloed him. "I was completely amazed that I would be attacked that way," he said in an interview
published in 1991. "I was flabbergasted. And I wish I had had my essay
reprinted after hers, because I think what happened was that more people read her piece than ever read mine. I think if they'd read it, they'd
see the disclaimers, modifications, and so forth. It has flaws. She picked
them out."[4] After "Circles and Squares" appeared, Kael sent Sarris a
note proposing a meeting, but he refused, and over the years, in the
Village Voice, he published some fairly nasty things about Kael. She
never responded. (She had her epigones do it for her.[5]) She always
insisted that her article on Sarris was intended as "good intellectual
fun,"[6] as she put it. "I said what I had to say about his theory twenty-
eight years ago," she said in 1991, the year she retired from the *New
Yorker*. "I've always been a little surprised he took it so personally."[7] By
then, her disciples were everywhere. She knew that she had won.

What is the cultural significance of this story? One of the ways Kael's
attack was understood at the time—it is how Sarris himself initially
characterized it—was as an East Coast-West Coast rivalry. Kael was
from California, and she was still living there when she wrote "Circles
and Squares." She was born in Two Rock, near Petaluma, in 1919.[8]
Her parents were Jewish immigrants from Poland. She attended
Berkeley on a scholarship, where she majored in philosophy, but she

had to drop out, six credits shy of graduation, when she ran out of money. She became involved with a filmmaker named James Broughton. (They were introduced by the poet Robert Duncan.) They never married (Broughton was gay), but they had a child together, a girl named Gina James. Broughton made avant-garde films, which Kael apparently hated. She began by writing plays, and she did not write any film criticism until 1953, when she was thirty-four years old. She was sitting in a coffee shop in the Bay Area, talking with someone, possibly Duncan, about Charlie Chaplin's *Limelight*. An editor of *City Lights* happened to overhear the conversation, and he invited Kael and her friend to review *Limelight* for his magazine. The friend did not produce a piece; Kael did. Because of his politics, as well as what used to be referred to as "the body of work," Chaplin was almost a god among progressive filmgoers in 1953, and progressive filmgoers were precisely the kind of filmgoers who were likely to be reading *City Lights*, a journal named, of course, for a Chaplin movie. Kael thought *Limelight* was the height of pomposity. In her review, she described it as "the richest hunk of gratification since Huck and Tom attended their own funeral."[9] A star was born.

Kael quickly got a show talking about movies on KPFA, Pacifica public radio, and she became the manager of the Cinema Guild and Studio, a twin-screen repertory house in Berkeley, where she wrote the program notes and married the founder, a Viennese émigré named Edward Landberg. She started writing on movies for *Sight and Sound* and *Partisan Review*. By the time she wrote "Circles and Squares," she had quit KPFA because they wouldn't give her a salary (none of the hosts at the station was paid a salary; Kael evidently believed that she should be an exception), and she quit the Cinema Guild and Studio soon after. She also divorced Landberg. Her reputation had by then made it virtually impossible for her to get a job as a movie reviewer in San Francisco. "San Francisco is like Ireland," she later said. "If you want to do something, you've got to get out."[10] So in 1963, the year of "Circles and Squares," Kael was forty-four, a single mother, and unemployed. It is possible she imagined that an attack on the movie critic of the *Village Voice* was not the worst career move a person in her position might come up with. There was not a huge downside. A year later, she got the Guggenheim; a year after that, *I Lost It at the Movies* made her name as a writer; and in 1967, when she was forty-eight, she became a movie critic at the *New Yorker*.

Despite Sarris's belief that Kael's attack on him had something to do with West Coast *ressentiment*, the important fact in Kael's biography is probably not her place of birth, but her date of birth. Like most people who fall in love with the movies, she succumbed when she was a teenager, and this meant that the movies she first loved were the genre movies of the nineteen-thirties—newspaper pictures like *The Front Page*, comedies like *Million Dollar Legs* and *Duck Soup*, and, especially, the screwballs, which began appearing in 1934, "the year," she later wrote, "when *The Thin Man* and *Twentieth Century* and *It Happened One Night* changed American movies."[11] Nineteen thirty-four was also the year Pauline Kael turned fifteen. Those thirties genre movies had two important features. First, they were designed as entertainment; they were not "message" pictures or art-house films. They lacked, almost completely, the theatrical pretensions of the silents. Second, they were distinguished by the quality of the screenplays and the acting.

Sarris was ten years younger than Kael.[12] He was born in Brooklyn in 1929. He went to Columbia, where he was an indifferent student. After he graduated from the college, in 1951, he spent some time in the Army, then returned to the graduate school, in English, with the thought of becoming a theater director. He also took some classes at Teachers College. It was at Columbia that he met Jonas Mekas. Mekas was a Lithuanian émigré with artistic aspirations who, because his English was so poor, had decided to become a filmmaker instead of a writer. When Mekas started the journal *Film Culture*, in 1955, he asked Sarris to join as an unpaid editor and contributor. In 1958, a friend of Sarris's, Eugene Archer, went to Paris on a Fulbright, and his letters home introduced Sarris to the French movie scene—to the Cinémathèque Française, the movie house where the New Wave critics and directors hung out, and to their journal, *Cahiers du Cinéma*. When the New Wave first broke on the world's shores, at the Cannes Film Festival in 1959, where *The 400 Blows* and *Hiroshima mon amour* won prizes, Sarris and Archer were almost the only American critics who understood what New Wave filmmaking was all about. That knowledge was Sarris's ticket. In 1960, he became film critic at the *Village Voice*. (The *Voice*'s first movie columnist had been Jonas Mekas.) In

1961, Sarris went to Paris himself, where he became converted to a belief in what he later called "the sacred importance of cinema."[13]

Sarris therefore grew up watching not the movies of the nineteen-thirties, for which he was too young, but the movies of the nineteen-forties and fifties—the period of George Stevens and Raoul Walsh, Vincente Minnelli and John Ford, Otto Preminger and Douglas Sirk, Stanley Kramer and Elia Kazan. The big movies that came out when Sarris was fifteen, in 1944, were *Laura, Lifeboat, Going My Way, Meet Me in St. Louis,* and *Arsenic and Old Lace.* The big movies that came out in 1949, when Sarris turned twenty, were *She Wore a Yellow Ribbon, I Was a Male War Bride,* and *The Fountainhead.* Sarris had a completely different kind of movie to try to work himself into an interesting critical relation to. Unlike the movies Kael grew up with, films of the nineteen-forties tended to have messages and to have ambitions beyond entertainment.

There is no need to summarize auteur theory.[14] It was not originally meant to be a full-dress theory; it was a *politique*—a policy, a critical orientation. It arose from the confluence of two premises that were shared by the members of the French New Wave group. One was that film is a medium of personal expression, which is the view that had been promoted since the late nineteen-forties by Alexandre Astruc and by Bazin. The other is that it is the *mise-en-scène*, rather than the story or the "message," that constitutes the essence of the movie experience. This was a view promoted by the co-founder and long-time director of the Cinémathèque Française, Henri Langlois. What these premises enabled Sarris to do was to rescue Hollywood directors from their own material. Sarris imagined those directors—the ones whose movies he admired—to be expressing themselves against, or in the interstices of, the generic stories and settings they had been given to work with by the studios. Auteurism was a way to bracket the "givens" of mass-culture entertainment and to uncover what Sarris referred to as (in a phrase Kael remorselessly picked apart) the "interior meaning." As Kael summarized it in "Circles and Squares": "[the] ideal auteur is the man who signs a long-term contract, directs any script that's handed to him, and expresses himself by shoving bits of style up the crevasses of the plots."[15] This is why Sarris considered George Cukor a better director than Ingmar Bergman: unlike Bergman, Cukor didn't have to struggle with the quality of his ideas. There is a sense in which auteur theory enabled Sarris to take seriously movies he could not honorably take seriously in any other way.

Sarris considered himself a scholar of film history. He believed that you cannot make a judgment about a director until you have seen all of that director's work—which is one of the *a priori* assumptions of auteur theory. Auteurism is all about "the body of work." Individual movies are not judged individually, but as aspects of an oeuvre. Sarris regarded Kael, therefore, as anti-intellectual. "*I Lost It at the Movies* functioned as an unending diatribe against film scholars and film scholarship," he said in 1980.[16] He was not mistaken. Early in her career, Kael was invited to attend a panel at Dartmouth, which was planning to introduce film studies into the curriculum. "People who think that education can't ruin movies," she said, "don't know the power of education."[17]

Why did Sarris want to eliminate content, though? Or rather, why did he want to relocate content from, using his dubious metaphor, the "exterior" to the "interior" of the film? Why did he want to mystify the movie experience in this way? To answer this, we need to go back a little farther. There were two generations of New Wave critics and film-makers in France.[18] The older generation was Kael's generation, born between 1918 and 1925—Bazin, Alain Resnais, Eric Rohmer. The younger generation was Sarris's, born between 1928 and 1932—Jean-Luc Godard, Jacques Rivette, Claude Chabrol, François Truffaut. Bazin's notion of French film was formed during the "classic" period of French cinema; he was nineteen at the time of *Grand Illusion*, in 1937, twenty-one at the time of *The Rules of the Game*, in 1939. Then came the Occupation, and it was during the Occupation that the younger generation—Godard and Truffaut—was introduced to film.

French film was regulated under the Occupation, of course, and Jews were purged from the film industry.[19] The Nazis did not allow American movies to be shown—no one in France saw *Gone with the Wind*, for example, until after the Second World War. French movie-goers were restricted to German and Italian imitations of Hollywood musicals, and similar fare, and to the French movies that managed to be produced under the ideological restrictions of the Nazi occupiers. These restrictions turned out not to be all that insuperable. Two hundred and twenty movies were made in France between 1940 and 1944. This was certainly a falling off: in the decade before the war, France had produced an average of a hundred and twenty movies a year.[20] The United States, by comparison, produced 2,212 movies between 1939 and 1944—ten times as many.[21] But there were new French movies made during the Occupation, and those are the movies that Truffaut and Godard and their generation went to see.

The Cinémathèque Française was started by Langlois and Georges Franju in 1936, but the number of movies they could show was limited by very strict regulations on screening rights.[22] After the war, in 1948, the Cinémathèque opened a new screening room, on the Avenue de Messine, and it became the place where young cinephiles went to see movies of all types and from all periods. Langlois was the society's programmer, and he had a theory of programming. All of his programs were mixed genre; he showed silent films without music; and he showed foreign-language films without translation. Langlois was careful not to explain the basis on which he had chosen the particular selection of films on a given night, and this encouraged his audience to detect patterns of resemblance in films of different periods and genres. The lack of translation put the emphasis on the *mise-en-scène*, rather than the story. If you have only a vague idea of what the characters are saying, the visual elements—the cutting, camera placement, lighting, and so on—will be where your attention is engaged. Early moviegoers at the Cinémathèque had seen enough German and Italian knock-offs of Hollywood movies to recognize the real thing when they saw it; that those movies exerted a grip on their imaginations without being translated naturally led them to privilege technique over story.

This fit in perfectly with Bazin's aesthetic line—that cinema is a medium of personal expression—and he became the patron saint of New Wave film criticism.[23] The Germans banned film societies in France, but Bazin was an exception. He and his friend Jean-Pierre Chartier were allowed to run a film society during the Occupation. Bazin had many friends in the Resistance, but he was always careful not to give his film society a political profile. Bazin was a man famously pure of heart. He was not protecting his film club; he just believed that art should be divorced from politics. And he himself, though sympathetic to the Resistance, tried to remain above party throughout the Occupation and, for that matter, all his life. He was married to cinema.

After the war, Bazin wrote mainly for the film journal *L'Écran français*. *L'Écran français* had split off from the magazine *Lettres françaises* at the time of the Liberation.[24] *Lettres françaises* was the magazine of the French Communist Party. By then, French film criticism was starting to split between an aesthetic, or formal, approach, and a political approach along lines laid down by the French Communist Party. Bazin and Astruc became the champions of the formalist position, and in 1949, when *L'Écran français* was reabsorbed by the Communist press, Bazin lost his job. He went to work for the Bureau de Travail et Culture, a government-supported cultural and educational association, and it was out of Bazin's office at the Bureau that the New Wave group coalesced and that *Cahiers du Cinéma* was born. The New Wave was thus a reaction against the politicization of art as represented principally by the French Communist Party.

Kael and Sarris faced exactly the same problem, which was the politicization of cinema, and what is interesting about their quarrel on this level of analysis is that they were basically on the same side. For Kael's attack on Sarris does bear all the signs of an outbreak of the narcissism of small differences. What had killed Hollywood after the nineteen-thirties, in Kael's view, was moralism and didacticism. She thought moralism and sentimentality were the bane of silent cinema, which she never liked; that those excrescencies had been effectively banished from the screen by the great entertainments of the thirties; and that they had reemerged after the war in the form of liberal and fellow-traveling kitsch on the one hand and patriotic propaganda on the other.

Sarris took the same position—that is, he wanted a style of film appreciation without political obligations—but he was constrained by his fondness for a canon of work saturated with political and moral intention. So far as it enabled him to neutralize the political content of the films he admired, auteurism was a way of avoiding the whole mess of ideology. The catch was that in order to accomplish this, Sarris had to explain why Otto Preminger's movies are art. Kael had a simpler idea, which was to fault the content. If the movie was offensively preachy or moralistic or politically pious, if it cut corners or tricked the audience into a false sentiment, she said so. This is why she was able to skewer Charlie Chaplin. She wasn't locked in to a politics of appreciation. There is a sense in which her appeal as a reviewer was based on one fundamental technique: she showed viewers when they had been fooled. That's why people read her. For the truth is that people, at least educated people, like not to like movies, especially movies other people like, even more than they like to like them.

The irony in Kael's attack on Sarris and auteur theory is that the movie that enabled her to launch her career at the *New Yorker* was a deliberate attempt to imitate New Wave style. This was *Bonnie and Clyde*.[25] *Bonnie and Clyde* was dreamed up in 1963 by two people at *Esquire* magazine: David Newman, who was an editor and writer there, and Robert Benton, who was the art director. Newman and Benton were inspired by *Breathless*, which was released in the United States in 1961, one of the after-effects of the New Wave triumph at Cannes the year before. Newman was from New York, but Benton was from Waxahachie, Texas, a place where, on Halloween, kids used to dress up as Bonnie Parker and Clyde Barrow. He and Newman decided to write a screenplay based on their story. The person they hoped would direct the movie was François Truffaut. Truffaut spent a month in New York, in 1964, discussing the project with them. He liked the screenplay, but he was reluctant to make a movie in the United States because his English was so bad (which is a reminder of the extent to which Truffaut's understanding of American movies was mainly visual). In the end, he turned down *Bonnie and Clyde* and directed *Fahrenheit 451*, which he had already been offered, instead. Truffaut sent the screenplay to Jean-Luc Godard, who was also interested in directing it, and who also met with Newman and Benton, but the deal fell through. Leslie Caron wanted to be cast in *Fahrenheit 451*. She arranged to meet Truffaut for lunch. Caron happened to be going out with Warren Beatty at the time. She brought Beatty along; Truffaut mentioned Newman and Benton's script; and that is how *Bonnie and Clyde* got made, with Beatty as the producer and the star.

Bonnie and Clyde was widely panned when it opened in September 1967. Jack Warner, of Warner Bros., who had been persuaded to finance the movie by Beatty, hated it, and the movie was booked into only twenty-five theaters. Bosley Crowther published two attacks on it in the *New York Times*, where he called it "a cheap piece of bald-faced slapstick comedy that treats the hideous depredations of that sleazy, moronic pair as though they were as full of fun and frolic as the jazz-age cut-ups of *Thoroughly Modern Millie*."[26] The movie was also panned by Richard Schickel, in *Life*; Hollis Alpert, in the *Saturday*

Review; Joseph Morgenstern, in *Newsweek*, and Richard Gilman, in the *New Republic*. Charles Samuels, in the *Hudson Review*, called it a "bunch of decayed cabbage leaves smeared with catsup."[27]

Kael disagreed. She was then writing for the *New Republic*, and she composed a seven-thousand-word response to the reviews of Gilman and the rest. The *New Republic* killed it. She showed it to the *New Yorker*, and in one of the most unforeseeable decisions in magazine history (among other things, the magazine had already run a favorable review, by Penelope Gilliatt), William Shawn bought it. By the time Kael's piece came out, *Bonnie and Clyde* had closed. But Morgenstern, at *Newsweek*, had already written a retraction of his original negative review, and in December, *Time* ran a Rauschenberg collage of images from the movie on its cover. *Bonnie and Clyde* was re-released, and it went on to become, for a while, one of the twenty top-grossing movies of all time. It was the first film of the Hollywood New Wave—the movement that produced Martin Scorsese, Francis Ford Coppola, Robert Altman, Brian De Palma, Roman Polanski, Paul Mazursky, Hal Ashby, Paul Schrader, and Robert Towne. That was the generation of directors and writers that Kael made her career by championing. They rescued Hollywood for international cinema, and they all recognized Kael as their critical mediator. She stole the New Wave from Andrew Sarris.

For many people, *Bonnie and Clyde* didn't kill moralism at all. It just resituated morality on the wrong side of the social spectrum. It sentimentalized criminality. That had been Crowther's point, and to say that Crowther was just being square is a little obtuse. Newman and Benton had self-consciously set out to duplicate what Godard had done in *Breathless*, which was to seduce the audience into identifying with the criminals in the beginning of the picture in order to force them into a uncomfortable moral position later on. Bonnie and Clyde turn out to be killers, but it's too late to disapprove—just as it's too late to disapprove in the *Godfather* movies, in *Mean Streets*, and so on. If you try to reduce the experience of those movies to the *mise-en-scène*, you are ducking the very basis of their appeal.

The usual thing to say about *Bonnie and Clyde*, and the movies that came after it, is that it suited a time of rebellion and nonconformity—that it was a movie of the Vietnam era, and expressed the distrust of government and the establishment that many Americans felt. "At last

Hollywood had grown up," is the general idea. Movies were finally being made to express the filmmaker's personal vision, rather than the studio's notion of what was socially acceptable or politically inoffensive. Movie art was at last free to criticize, to challenge, to provoke. This now seems to miss the point of what was happening.

*****

The reason the Germans permitted the French film industry to produce movies relatively uncensored was because Goebbels was not interested in destroying France. France was just another country the Nazis had to run, part of the New Europe. Though the French movie industry would be subordinate to the German movie industry, Goebbels thought that French movies would continue to be made by Frenchmen, and in their national character. Goebbels's chief concern was to maintain control of European cinema after the war. This meant two things: promoting national cinemas under Nazi supervision, and excluding American movies.

Thus the divided effect of the German Occupation on French cinema. On the one hand, the industry produced a number of films in the tradition of classic French cinema. *Children of Paradise*, for example, was made during the Occupation. On the other hand, the price of continuing to make such movies was to renounce the politics of resistance—to become, if only in a passive sense, a collaborator. The shadow of collaboration therefore fell over the whole of French cinematic production from the Occupation period, and, by virtue of that cinema's stylistic continuities with pre-war French cinema, over French film in general. Truffaut's notorious essay "A Certain Tendency in French Cinema," partly composed while he was in prison for military desertion, and published in *Cahiers* in 1954, was an attack on the whole industry.

It is impossible not to read movies like *Breathless* and *The 400 Blows* as allegories of the Resistance. They are movies about French shame, and their break with both classic French cinema and the so-called "tradition of quality"—their rejection of the postwar French industry style—is of a piece with their politics. It is, in fact, how they express their politics. The industry style had itself become a signifier for collaboration and denial, and for the politicization of cinema. The jump cut was a form of protest. In 1962, after the New Wave was more or less finished as a movement, Truffaut said: "We are proud to have been and to remain a part of the New Wave, just as one is proud to have been a Jew during the Occupation."[28] This is why the apolitical attitude of the *Cahiers* critics is so misleading, and why it misled Sarris. Like all formalisms, New Wave theory *was* a politics.

Liberation for France was not liberation for French film. Having survived one system of cultural imperialism, French cinema found itself confronting another. In 1946, France and the United States concluded a treaty, the Blum-Byrnes Pact, concerning the repayment of French war debt and the extension of American loans for the modernization of the French economy.[29] As it did with Great Britain, as well, the United States tied its forgiveness of war debt and its extension of postwar loans to the lifting of trade barriers to American movies. Just as Germany had during the war, the United States wanted to dominate the European film market. Overseas rentals had always been crucial to profitability in the studio era. Nazi occupation and war had deprived Hollywood of access to European markets for six years, and the studios were desperate to get back into those markets, and to take advantage of the depression in European film production by dumping its oversupply on the European exhibition market, which was eager to have something to exhibit.

In the nineteen-thirties, France had set up barriers at home to protect its film industry from foreign competition. Before the war, France had reserved seven weeks out of every thirteen for the exclusive showing of French-made movies. After Blum-Byrnes, this was reduced to four weeks out of every thirteen. Employment in the French film industry immediately dropped from 2,132 in 1946, the year of the accord, to 898 in 1947. American films flooded the French market. They were also, at first, more popular than French films. When De Gaulle had tried to impose import restrictions on American films in 1945, French exhibitors protested. "If you want to stab America in the back," the president of the French Exhibitors Association told De Gaulle, "you shall not do it in our cinemas."[30] By 1951, 50 percent of the movies playing in France on a given day were American. In Western Europe as a whole, the figure was 61 percent. The damage to the French film industry was widely protested in France, in demonstrations led by French Communist Party. It inspired an animus against American movies, and that animus was the main reason Bazin, the champion of American cinema, lost his job at *L'Écran francais*.

The American government did a favor to Hollywood with the Blum-Byrnes Pact because the dissemination of American cultural products in Western Europe was a key element of postwar foreign policy. The target of that policy was much more selective than it may seem—and this is a point about cultural warfare that is sometimes missed. The American government wasn't interested in winning the hearts and minds of the average Frenchman; it was interested in winning the hearts and minds of the French élite. Cold war cultural policy was directed at European intellectuals and opinion-makers—people who might have philosophical, rather than economic, reasons for tilting toward the Soviet Union. The American government thus did not want to present an image of conformity and domesticity; it did not want to export "Ozzie and Harriet." The image it sought to present was one of personal freedom and cultural sophistication. This is why, for example, Jacques Barzun turned up on the cover of *Time* magazine in 1956: a transplanted French intellectual who was there to say that the intellectual life was good in America, which is exactly what he does say in the story inside. The United States wanted Jean-Paul Sartre to think that there was more to American civilization than the pursuit of money.

In the early years of the cold war, the American government did not have a very clear idea how to go about using film as a weapon. In 1955, the Navy and the National Security Council organized a secret campaign to insert the theme of "freedom" into Hollywood movies. The idea was to plant a specific phrase—"militant liberty"—in Hollywood screenplays, in such a way that foreign audiences would have the impression that the phrase was a popular slogan that had arisen spontaneously from the American people. In 1956, the producer Cornelius Vanderbilt, on the advice of the CIA, announced plans to produce what he called an "American series" of films. "I want to . . . show our people their country," he said, "and to make certain that the rest of the world learns more about us." The first movie Vanderbilt produced in this series was *The Searchers*, directed by John Ford.[31]

But American patriotism doesn't play very well overseas, and big surprise. Non-Americans don't respond all that favorably when we show what a terrific nation we are by waving our flag in their faces. That was one problem with the cultural policies of the early cold war period. The other was a domestic one. For in the nineteen-fifties, many educated

Americans did not think much of Hollywood movies, either. Educated Americans went to the movies, but they had been taught by their own intellectual opinion-makers to condescend to them. In 1960, Lionel Trilling wrote an essay praising Ingmar Bergman, in which he admitted that, because of a general aversion to the cinema, he had never actually seen any of Bergman's movies.[32] This disaffection was not lost on Europeans, and the HUAC investigations of Hollywood did not exactly burnish the image. So the first step in transforming American movies into a high-end propaganda weapon aimed at European intellectuals was to persuade *American* intellectuals to take them seriously. Sarris played a role in this project. Kael played a larger one, and the reason has everything to do with Shawn's decision, in 1967, to bring her to the *New Yorker*.

In 1967, the *New Yorker* was the most successful magazine in America.[33] It owed its prosperity to a formula that can no longer be duplicated: it was a general-interest commercial magazine for people who disliked commercialism and who rarely subscribed to general-interest magazines—a magazine, essentially, for people who didn't read magazines. For in the nineteen-fifties and sixties, a literate and unstuffy anticommercialism was still a cherished ingredient of upper-middle-class taste, and by catering to it, the *New Yorker* was able to deliver to advertisers several hundred thousand well-educated and affluent people who could be reached through almost no other medium. It did so with an editorial product rigorously manufactured to avoid any semblance of the sensational, the prurient, or the merely topical—any semblance, that is, of the things educated people could be assumed to associate with commercial media. It also avoided, less famously but with equal diligence, anything that hinted at cultural pretension, and this policy, too, was based on a genuine insight into the psychology of its audience. For *New Yorker* readers, though proud of their education and their taste, were culturally insecure. They did not need to be told who Proust and Freud and Stravinsky were, but they were glad, at the same time, not to be expected to know anything terribly specific about them. They were intelligent people who were nevertheless extremely wary of being out-browed.

The *New Yorker* was enormously attentive to this insecurity. It pruned from its pieces anything that might come across allusive or knowing, and it promoted, in its writing and cartoons, a sensibility which took urbanity to be perfectly compatible with a certain kind of naïveté. The *New Yorker* made it possible to feel that being an anti-sophisticate was the mark of true sophistication, and that any culture worth having could be had without special aesthetic equipment or intellectual gymnastics.

Kael made it possible for people to feel this way about the movies, and although that sounds like a modest accomplishment, it was not. It required disarming both of the phobias in the sensibility the *New Yorker* had so successfully identified: the fear of too low, and the fear of too high. It meant overcoming the intelligent person's resistance to the pulpiness, the corniness, and the general moral and aesthetic schmaltz of Hollywood movies, but without refining those things away by some type of critical alchemy, as Sarris, for example, might be considered to be trying to do. The *New Yorker*'s readers did not want an invitation to slum. But they didn't want to be told that appreciating movies was something that called for a command of "the grammar of film," either—that they had to pay attention to something called the *mise-en-scène* if they wanted to grasp the meaning of a movie. They needed to believe that it was possible to enjoy the movies without becoming either of the two things *New Yorker* readers would sooner have died than be taken for: idiots or snobs. This was precisely the approach to movies that Kael had devoted her pre-*New Yorker* career to perfecting. She heaped scorn on the moguls, and she heaped scorn on the cinéastes. She joined the magazine at the moment the movies seemed to many people, with *Bonnie and Clyde* and *The Graduate*, to have caught up with the rest of American culture. She kept the attention of the magazine's readers during a time when movies seemed to mean a great deal to them.

The problem Kael undertook to address when she began writing for the *New Yorker* was the problem of making popular entertainment respectable to people whose education told them that popular entertainment is not art. This is sometimes thought of as the high-low problem—the problem that arises when a critic equipped with a highbrow technique bends his or her attention to an object that is too low, when the professor writes about *Superman* comics. In fact, this rarely is a problem: if anything profits from (say) a semiotic analysis, it's the comics. The professor may go on to compare *Superman* comics favorably with Tolstoy, but that is simply a failure of judgment. It has nothing to do with the difference in brows. You can make a fool of yourself over anything.

The real high-low problem doesn't arise when the object is too low. It arises when the object isn't low enough. *Meet the Beatles* doesn't pose a high-low problem; *Sgt. Pepper's Lonely Hearts Club Band* does. Tom Clancy and "Who Wants to Be a Millionaire" don't; John Le Carré and "Masterpiece Theater" do. A product like *Sgt. Pepper's* isn't low enough to be discussed as a mere commercial product; but it's not high enough to be discussed as though it were *Four Quartets*, either. It's exactly what it pretends to be: it's entertainment, but for educated people. And this is what makes it so hard for educated people to talk about without sounding pretentious, as though they had to justify their pleasure by some gesture toward the "deeper" significance of the product. It was in just such an act of pretension that Kael believed she had caught Andrew Sarris when she wrote "Circles and Squares."

One of Hollywood's best-kept industrial secrets is that the movies are entertainment for educated people, too. This was a finding that surprised the studios when, in the nineteen-forties, they undertook to analyze their audience: frequency of movie attendance increases with income and education.[34] Even today, when people complain that they don't make movies for grown-ups anymore, the percentage of people who say they are "frequent moviegoers" is more than half again as great among people who have gone to college (31 percent) as it is among people who have only finished high school (19 percent). The belief that education makes people snobbish about moviegoing is the opposite of the case: 20 percent of people who have been to college say they "never" go to movies, but the figure is 39 percent among adults who have only finished high school and 57 percent among adults with even less education than that.[35] Kael didn't persuade *New Yorker* readers to go to the movies; they were already going. That wasn't the problem. The problem was teaching them how to think critically about the experience.

One way to think critically is to have a theory. Kael had devoted her entire pre-*New Yorker* career to scorning that approach. She hated theories. She didn't oppose only auteur theory: she opposed all theoretical preconceptions. "Isn't it clear that trying to find out what cinema 'really' is, is derived from a mad Platonic and metaphorical view of the universe," she wrote, in an unreprinted essay, in 1966, "—as if ideal, pure cinema were some pre-existent entity that we had to find? Cinema is not to be found; but movies are continuously being made."[36] And, more famously, in "Is There a Cure for Movie Criticism?," an attack on Siegfried Kracauer: "Art is the greatest game, the supreme entertainment, because you discover the game as you play it . . . . We want to see, to feel, to understand, to respond in a new way. Why should pedants be allowed to spoil the game?"[37]

Kael seemed to make it possible to like movies without feeling pompous or giddy by showing that what comes first in everyone's experience isn't the form or the idea but the sensation, and that this is just as true for moviegoers who have been taught to intellectualize their responses to art as it is for everyone else. The idea that a movie critic needs to work from sensations was not new with her. James Agee's persona as film critic for the *Nation* had been that of the ordinary intelligent guy who just happens to love going to movies (and who also just happens to write like James Agee). Robert Warshow, who wrote about movies for *Commentary* and *Partisan Review* in the nineteen forties and fifties, warned that the critic who trucks a load of sociology and aesthetics into the movie theater will end up missing the show. "A man watches a movie," as he once famously, and perhaps a shade sententiously, put it, "and the critic must acknowledge that he is that man."[38]

When Warshow wrote about *Scarface* and Agee wrote about *National Velvet*, they didn't have much trouble being that man. But that is because the high-low problem doesn't kick in with *Scarface* and *National Velvet*. It kicks in with a movie like *Monsieur Verdoux*, Chaplin's black comedy about a serial killer, which very few people have patience for any more, but which Agee and Warshow both went solemnly bananas over, as did Sarris. Agee and Warshow and Sarris thought that Chaplin had something important to say in movies like *Monsieur Verdoux* and *Limelight*, and they bent over backwards to give him credit for his good intentions. Warshow compared *Limelight*, the movie Kael had begun her career by ridiculing, to Kafka and *King Lear*.

Kael's contention that "serious" movies should meet the same standard as pulp—that they should be entertaining—turned out to be an extremely useful and widely adopted critical principle. For it rests on an empirically sustainable proposition, which is that although people sometimes have a hard time deciding whether or not something is "art," they are rarely fooled into thinking they are being entertained when they are not. It was Kael's therapeutic advice to the overcultivated that if they just concentrated on responding to the stimulus, the aesthetics would take care of themselves.

*****

By opening the French market to Hollywood, the Blum-Byrnes Pact Americanized French movies. But that is not the significant part of the story. For it also Europeanized American movies. Truffaut and Godard, by making movies like *Breathless* and *Shoot the Piano Player* in "the American style," did for Hollywood movies what the Beatles, at about the same time, did for rock 'n' roll: they validated it for a culturally insecure people. The United States dumped a commercial mass-market product on Europe after 1945. Fifteen years later, it got back a hip and sophisticated pop art form. The Beatles taught educated Americans how to love Elvis Presley; the New Wave taught them how to love James Cagney and Humphrey Bogart and *The Postman Always Rings Twice*.

The analysis has one more twist. For of course *Bonnie and Clyde* is not a New Wave movie at all. It's a Hollywood movie of a perfectly conventional type, right down to the ending. Bonnie and Clyde are criminals, and they are therefore not permitted to survive the picture—just like in *Scarface* and *Little Caesar*. Apart from obvious surface similarities, Arthur Penn's movie is nothing like *Breathless*. Like almost every Hollywood movie, *Bonnie and Clyde* wants one thing above all: it wants to entertain you. So do most of the movies of Coppola and Altman and Scorsese. Entertainment was not one of Godard's principal ambitions. It is significant that most of Truffaut's advice to Newman and Benton about their screenplay had to do with making the story conform more closely to generic and narrative conventions.[39] And Beatty, of course, is the consummate Hollywood figure. Like Coppola, Steven Spielberg, George Lucas, and Stanley Kubrick, he is an artist who believes he is a better businessman than the executives. The screenplay of *Bonnie and Clyde* originally indicated a sexual ménage between Bonnie, Clyde, and the Michael Pollard character, C. W. Moss. (Newman and Benton had been great fans of Truffaut's *Jules and Jim*.) Beatty is supposed to have announced that he could not play a bisexual, and the idea was dropped.[40] The French idea of the jump cut was one thing. The French idea of erotic *frisson* was another matter.

There is a great oddity in the critical literature on what is now referred to as cold war culture. Most of the books imagine the cold war as something that came to an end around 1965. It is as though the exposure of the CIA's involvement in *Encounter* and the demise of the Congress for Cultural Freedom marked the end of the symbiosis of art and ideas on the one hand and American foreign policy on the other. But the true goal of every imperialism is to be invisible, an imperialism that will run by itself. The period when a bunch of ex-OSS men tried to orchestrate Hollywood movies and intellectual journals was a politically primitive time. Movies like *Bonnie and Clyde* make for far more effective propaganda than movies like *The Searchers* or *The Green Berets*, which are really expressions of isolationism. *Bonnie and Clyde* has the phrase "militant liberty" practically written all over it. So does *The Graduate* and *The Godfather* and *Dog Day Afternoon* and many of the other Hollywood New Wave movies of the nineteen-sixties and nineteen-seventies. Militant liberty is what these movies are selling. Movies that to Americans like Bosley Crowther or William Bennett read as anti-American and subversive read differently in other societies. For it doesn't matter whether the heroes of these movies are conventionally good or bad, and it doesn't matter whether the social order they defy is American or Eastern European. They are still allegories of resistance. That is how fantasy works.

*****

Assuming, as we have so far, that polemic is a genre defined more by its cultural function than by its formal elements, what speculations does the story of Kael's attack on Sarris support? First, that a polemic is likely to be the product of what Freud called the narcissism of small differences. Several features we would expect to find in a polemic—features likely to be recognized by, and important to, its contemporary readers, readers "in the know"—are, first, the sense that the polemic is being used as a weapon in a struggle for primacy in a particular field of endeavor, and, just as crucial, the sense of a surprise attack (much as the attack on Kael herself by Renata Adler, in *The New York Review of Books*, in 1980, owed the attention it received mostly to the fact that it was so unexpected: one *New Yorker* writer savaging another). It is the turn against a figure people had counted as, if not a friend, at least an ideological ally, that gives a piece the notoriety required in order to rise to the level of a polemic. If Kael had written an unmodulated attack on Bosley Crowther, the piece might have been read with pleasure by her admirers, but it would have been ignored by everyone else. Of course Pauline Kael disagrees with Bosley Crowther, would have been the response. But Sarris and Kael wrote for the same sorts of journals; they shared many likes and dislikes, including an admiration for the French New Wave; they had no apparent political differences; even the differences in their literary styles were not great. The polemic announces a break where no one had suspected a fissure. Kael's polemic gave her an instant identity, and saved her from being lumped with Sarris in conventional lists of serious film critics: she was, eternally, the not-Sarris.

Second, the polemic must rest on a substratum of, as it were, shifting sociological plates—political, institutional, demographic, even geopolitical—none of which it needs to address or even to acknowledge. A piece that begins by musing on impersonal, large-scale movements in art and ideas, or the needs of national security, and the like, is not a polemic, even if it goes on to throw some person into the dustbin of history. It is precisely its triviality that makes the polemic a polemic, and not a reconsideration, or an editorial, or a scholarly intervention. There needs to be something scandalous, a scorched-earth quality, as well as something personal and petty, to distinguish the polemic from these ordinary markers of cultural change. Still, when we peel away the trivial surface of the polemic, we should be able to see pretty far into the workings of cultural change.

Third, the writer who tries to live by the polemic must be prepared to die by the polemic. A failed polemic is a self-inflicted wound, often a mortal one; as Emerson said, when you shoot at a king, you must kill him. The great polemicist is, after all, taking on the conventional wisdom, and must bank on changes in the larger culture no one, including the polemicist, can entirely see. If Hollywood had continued to turn out Otto Preminger movies, Kael might have remained a voice in the wilderness. Events over which she had no control thrust her into a position to dominate movie criticism for a generation of film-goers, which gave, retrospectively, her attack on Sarris the status of a turning point. Most of the reviews Kael wrote before 1967 were negative and filled with sweeping complaints against contemporary film culture. Then, unexpectedly, film culture changed.

Finally, the story always has, eventually, a bookend. This appears when it is possible to see the polemicist as him or herself caught in the grip of forces invisible at the time. No law is more dutifully observed in cultural history than the law of unintended consequences. Kael did not imagine that by condemning film theory she was helping to reconcile educated Americans to their popular culture. She certainly did not imagine that the kind of movies she championed sped the globalization of American film far more effectively than the sort of moralizing and didactic movies she disdained. But it wasn't her business to imagine these things. Her business was to see movies and write what she thought of them, which, unquestionably, she did.

Notes

1. Andrew Sarris, "Notes on the Auteur Theory in 1962," *Film Culture* (Winter 1962–63): 1. A good account of the dispute is Raymond J. Haberski, Jr., *It's Only a Movie: Films and Critics in American Culture* (Lexington: University Press of Kentucky, 2001), 122–43. See also William D. Routt, "L'Evidence," *Continuum: The Australian Journal of Media and Culture*, 5 (1990). Parts of the present essay draw from my essays "The Popist: Pauline Kael," *American Studies* (New York: Farrar, Straus and Giroux, 2002): 180–97, and "Paris, Texas," *The New Yorker* (February 17&24, 2003): 169–77.
2. Pauline Kael, "Circles and Squares: Joys and Sarris," *I Lost It at the Movies: Film Writings, 1954–1965* (Boston: Little, Brown, 1965): 319.
3. Andrew Sarris, "Auteur Theory and the Perils of Pauline," *Film Quarterly*, 16 (Summer 1963): 28.
4. Quoted in George Hickenlooper, *Reel Conversations: Candid Interviews with Film's Foremost Directors and Critics* (New York: Citadel, 1991), 9.
5. See, e.g., Greil Marcus, "The Critics' Inquisition," *Rolling Stone* (September 4, 1980): 26.
6. Quoted in Philip Lopate, "The Passion of Pauline," *Totally, Tenderly, Tragically: Essays and Criticism from a Lifelong Love Affair with the Movies* (New York: Doubleday, 1998), 235.
7. Quoted in Will Brantley, ed., *Conversations with Pauline Kael* (Jackson: University Press of Mississippi, 1996), 135.
8. On Kael, see Lopate, 219-50; Francis Davis, *Afterglow: A Last Conversation with Pauline Kael* (Boston: Da Capo, 2002), 1–28; Lawrence Van Gelder, obituary, *New York Times*, September 4, 2001: C12.
9. Pauline Kael, review of *Limelight*, reprinted in *Artforum*, 11 (March 2002): 124. The story that she referred to the movie, in her review, as "Slimelight" (see Van Gelder) is false.

10. Quoted in Lopate, 236.
11. Pauline Kael, "The Man from Dream City," *When the Lights Go Down* (New York: Holt, Rinehart and Winston, 1980), 6.
12. On Sarris, see Haberski, 122–27; Hickenlooper, 3–16.
13. Quoted in Haberski, 123.
14. On auteur theory and the French New Wave, see Antoine de Baecque, *La Nouvelle Vague: Portrait d'une jeunesse* (Paris: Flammarion, 1998); Jean Douchet, *French New Wave*, trans. Robert Bonnono (New York: DAP, 1999); Richard Neupert, *A History of the French New Wave Cinema* (Madison: University of Wisconsin Press, 2002); Michel Marie, *The French New Wave: An Artistic School*, trans. Richard Neupert (Oxford: Blackwell, 2003).
15. Kael, *I Lost It at the Movies*, 302.
16. Andrew Sarris, "Sarris vs. Kael: The Queen Bee of Film Criticism," *Village Voice*, July 2–8, 1980: 30.
17. Pauline Kael, "It's Only a Movie," in *Film Study in Higher Education*, ed. David C. Stewart (Washington, D.C.: American Council on Education, 1966), 137.
18. See Douchet, 13–22; François Truffaut, "Introduction: André Bazin, The Occupation, and I," in André Bazin, *French Cinema of the Occupation and Resistance: The Birth of a Critical Esthetic*, ed. Truffaut, trans. Stanley Hochman (New York: Frederick Ungar, 1981), 3–21.
19. See Evelyn Erlich, *Cinema of Paradox: French Filmmaking Under the German Occupation* (New York: Columbia University Press, 1985). Also Colin Crisp, *The Classic French Cinema, 1930–1960* (Bloomington: Indiana University Press, 1997), 43–63; Alan Williams, *Republic of Images: A History of French Filmmaking* (Cambridge, MA: Harvard University Press, 1992), 245–71; Rémi Fournier Lanzoni, *French Cinema: From Its Beginnings to the Present* (New York: Continuum, 2002), 103–42.
20. Richard Pells, *Not Like Us: How Europeans Have Loved, Hated, and Transformed American Culture Since World War II* (New York: Basic Books, 1997), 216.
21. Serge Guilbaut, *How New York Stole the Idea of Modern Art: Abstract Expressionism, Freedom, and the Cold War*, trans. Arthur Goldhammer (Chicago: University of Chicago Press, 1983), 137.
22. On Langlois, see Penelope Gilliatt, "Of Henri Langlois," *Three-Quarter Face: Reports and Reflections* (New York: Coward McCann and Geohegan, 1980), 73–88; Richard Roud, *A Passion for Films: Henri Langlois and the Cinématheque Française* (New York: Viking, 1983); Glenn Myrent and Georges P. Langlois, *Henri Langlois: First Citizen of Cinema*, trans. Lisa Nesselson (New York: Twayne, 1995).
23. On Bazin, see Dudley Andrew, *André Bazin* (New York: Oxford University Press, 1978).
24. See Olivier Barrot, *L'Écran français, 1943–1953: Histoire d'un journal et d'une époque* (Paris: Editeurs Français Reunis, 1979).
25. See Sandra Wake and Nicola Hayden, *Bonnie and Clyde* (n.c.: Lorrimer, 1971); Peter Biskind, *Easy Riders, Raging Bulls: How the Sex-Drugs-and-Rock'n'Roll Generation Saved Hollywood* (New York: Simon and Schuster, 1998), 23–41, 47–49; Antoine de Baecque and Serge Toubiana, trans.

Catherine Temerson, *Truffaut: A Biography* (New York: Knopf, 1999), 210–12; Lester D. Friedman, *Bonnie and Clyde* (London: BFI, 2000).

26. Bosley Crowther, "*Bonnie and Clyde* Arrives," rpt. in Friedman, ed. *Arthur Penn's "Bonnie and Clyde,"* 177.
27. Charles Thomas Samuels, "*Bonnie and Clyde*," *Hudson Review*, 21 (Spring 1968): 22.
28. Douchet, 172.
29. See Irwin M. Wall, *The United States and the Making of Postwar France, 1945–1954* (Cambridge: Cambridge University Press, 1991), 113–26; Patricia Hubert-Lacombe, *Le cinéma français dans la guerre froide, 1946–1956* (Paris: L'Harmattan, 1996), 151–65; Jean-Pierre Jeancolas, "From the Blum-Byrnes Agreement to the GATT Affair," in Geoffrey Nowell-Smith and Steven Ricci, eds., *Hollywood in Europe: Economics, Culture, National Identity, 1946–95* (London: BFI, 1997); Jens Ulff-Møller, *Hollywood's Film Wars with France: Film-Trade Diplomacy and the Emergence of the French Film Quota Policy* (Rochester, N. Y.: University of Rochester Press, 2001). The degree to which the Blum-Brynes agreement (later amended) damaged the French film industry is a matter of dispute.
30. Quoted in Frank Costigliola, *France and the United States: The Cold Alliance since World War II* (New York: Twayne, 1992), 56.
31. See Frances Stoner Saunders, *The Cultural Cold War: The CIA and the World of Art and Letters* (New York: The New Press, 1999), 284–86.
32. See Lionel Trilling, "Bergman Unseen," in *A Company of Readers: Uncollected Writings of W. H. Auden, Jacques Barzun, and Lionel Trilling from The Readers' Subscription and Mid-Century Book Clubs*, ed. Arthur Krystal (New York: Free Press, 2001), 205–11.
33. See Gigi Mahon, *The Last Days of "The New Yorker"* (New York: McGraw-Hill, 1988); Mary F. Corey, *World Through a Monocle: "The New Yorker" at Mid-Century* (Cambridge, MA: Harvard University Press, 1999); Ben Yagoda, *About Town: "The New Yorker" and the World It Made* (New York: Scribner, 2000). Also my "A Friend Writes: The Old *New Yorker*," *American Studies*: 125–45.
34. Robert Sklar, *Movie-Made America: A Cultural History of the Movies*, (New York: Random House, 1979), 269.
35. Data from Motion Picture Association of America surveys, 1992.
36. Kael, "It's Only a Movie," 143–44.
37. Kael, *I Lost It at the Movies*, 292.
38. Robert Warshow, *The Immediate Experience: Movies, Comics, Theatre and Other Aspects of Popular Culture* (Garden City, NY: Doubleday, 1962), 27. The words were written in 1954.
39. Matthew Bernstein, "Perfecting the New Gangster: Writing the Script for the 1967 Film *Bonnie and Clyde*," *Film Quarterly*, 53 (Summer 2000): 16–31.
40. There are contradictions in the recollections of this incident. See Biskind, 32, and Arthur Penn, "Making Waves: The Directing of Bonnie and Clyde," in Lester D. Friedman, ed., *Arthur Penn's "Bonnie and Clyde"* (Cambridge: Cambridge University Press, 2000), 18. In my interviews with David Newman and Arthur Penn (2002), Newman insisted that Beatty refused to play a "fag" and Penn insisted that he did not.

7

"What is Enlightenment?"

Gayatri Chakravorty Spivak Conversing with Jane Gallop

New York. June 7, 2003

JG: A year and a half ago you suggested that we do Kant's "What is Enlightenment?" for the English Institute. We all agreed it was a good idea, but we didn't talk about *why* it was a good idea.

GS: The immediate reason was that someone showed me this book edited by James Schmidt, *What is Enlightenment?: Eighteenth-Century Answers and Twentieth-Century Questions.* I knew that I had to read it. So, I proposed it. I felt I had to read it because "what went wrong with the best of the Enlightenment?" is a question crucial for our time. I think the French Enlightenment is more intellectual and the German more political. These kinds of very broad generalizations can always be broken down, but . . . in a certain sense, intellectual movements that have been given a name do not happen as such. You can always say the Enlightenment happened with the Peace of Westphalia, that Kant wrote "Perpetual Peace," the very late text, because of the Treaty of Basel. Those treaties and peaces happened. But if you're thinking of an intellectual movement, how do you pin-point it exactly? This is a little bit different from Habermas saying the project of modernity is unfinished. I'm not saying something is unfinished. I'm just saying it doesn't happen in some sort of phenomenal sense. So, therefore, it seemed to me that, whatever it was that the German Enlightenment thought about the public sphere, itself so centrally involved with imperialism, needed to be revisited and that the German essays, written in response to a newspaper competition, were much more accessible to general political thinking than great philosophical texts.

JG: Can you say a little bit more about "our time?" What do you mean by "our time?" What's the span of "our time?" Or, what makes you want to go back to that?

GS: During the roundtable I mentioned Ho Chi Minh's answer to the question "What are the consequences of the French Revolution?" and his profoundly philosophical answer, "It's too soon to tell." "Our time" is a very flexible concept. I don't quite know where I would begin them, or where I would end them.

But let me give you a parable. You know that in Cincinnati there's this 35.6 million dollar, wonderful museum that has just opened. It is designed by Zaha Hadid, an Iraqi-American architect of extraordinary, extraordinary brilliance. In this museum there is now an extraordinary collection of art. There's a Japanese "Chappi 33," thirty-three life-size girl dolls in jumpsuits and hard hats. There are six disco balls by John Armleder called "Untitled (Global V)." There is Marjetica Potrc's "El Retiro Roundhouse," recycled materials designed to be quickly built by relief agencies, and so on. This is a response to our time as a time of terror—and a war against terror. Now this extraordinary museum, the Rosenthal Center for Contemporary Art, and the architect Zaha Hadid, Iraqi-American—are on one side. And I applaud it, I celebrate it, I will undoubtedly go to it soon. Full of contemporary conceptual art relating to the war on terror. On the other side is the destruction of the great museum in Baghdad, the library burned and looted. When Rumsfeld was asked about this he said they were just carrying out vases. There was vase after vase. In other words, for him one vase was the same as the other. One of my colleagues went to Kraków, and they took him to Copernicus's house and they showed him the instrument with which Copernicus looked into the heavens and they said to him, of course there's one in Kraków and the other used to be in the museum in Baghdad. That's my parable. Imperialism has become racialized in a new way. Extraordinary diasporics are being used to give support to the idea that the United States is going to save the world. On the one side military intervention, on the other side human rights. And that saving is made in the name of principles that sound a lot like the principles in these essays about the Enlightenment. At the discussion itself, I had brought George W. Bush's "National Security Strategy of the United

States: September, 2002." And I had read some stuff from it: "People everywhere want to be able to speak freely." "We seek to create a balance of power that favors human freedom." And then there are other kinds of things: "The United States will use this moment of opportunity to extend the benefits of freedom across the globe." "We are increasingly united by common values." "To build a world the international community has the best chance since the rise of the nation state in the seventeenth century"—Peace of Westphalia—"to build a world where great powers compete in peace instead of continually prepare for war." I had said at that point that rather than engage in the sport of liberal Bush-bashing, let us take into account that these words, if we didn't know where they were coming from, would still resonate. We are still, indeed, in that stuff. My parable is not yet over. I am still putting together the ingredients for our historical moment. I don't yet have a definition. I have just received a notification from the . . . GOP. The Republican Party sends this document. They think that I am . . .

JG: . . . a GOP supporter.

GS: . . . a GOP supporter. There are many things here that are very interesting in terms of the census document questionnaire. One of them is "do you think that U.S. troops should have to serve under United Nations commanders?" Now, obviously, they want the stalwart GOP person to say "no." "Do you support the use of air strikes against any country that offers safe harbor or aid to individuals or organizations committed to further attacks on America?" Now this is, this is . . . the Republican Party census. And here is Kant's material on perpetual peace where he is saying "no nation shall forcibly interfere with the constitution and government of another" and "no treaty of peace that tacitly reserves issues for a future war shall be held valid." Where did the best of the political enlightenment go wrong?

JG: I guess the other question is—I don't know if it was when you originally proposed it, or whether it was shortly thereafter—you said that you wanted as a text not only Kant's "What is Enlightenment?" but also Foucault's "What is Enlightenment?" as part of the original reading material. And this argument for Kant is also an argument for going back to the eighteenth century, taking this quite popular text, and looking at the Enlightenment and trying to see where it's going. Why did you insist on having Foucault there?

GS: Because of the way in which Foucault and the whole pomo thing is understood as being a critique of the Enlightenment. Finally, I did read a little bit of Habermas, as well. I wanted to put it there because I felt that all our colleagues at the English Institute might not have thought of Foucault as someone who really had twice commended Kant on the idea of, not just the Enlightenment, but the *Aufklärung*. Mendelssohn's response is "Was heisst aufklär*en*?" What is it to enlighten? It relates more to explaining, *erklären*, and so on. Foucault begins his essay in the usual way, writing in French, but right at the end he says I did not dare, I did not have the courage to give . . . the title that this piece should have had which is "Was heisst Aufklärung."

So that's why I wanted to put in Foucault. Now here is today's *New York Times*, where Thom Collins, Senior Curator of this Rosenthal Center, is talking about this collection of wonderful contemporary conceptual art. He's calling it a "gentle manifesto." Now, you remember what I said, the parable that I made between Iraq and Iraqi-American stuff. And so I don't think that it is indeed a time for a gentle manifesto. But he says that the traditional white-cube gallery, I quote, "the traditional white-cube gallery . . . a site of cultural ritual, having to do with isolation of art objects from the outside world, and of individuals from other individuals—a pure Kantian notion of aesthetic extremes." I'm quite sure Mr. Collins knows something that I don't know about Kant. I wouldn't doubt that he's speaking in an informed way. But I can't know to what this refers. And the next, and also I don't know in what way this museum in Cincinnati is going to be not isolated from the outside world—if I know anything of the state of industry there, the state of unemployment, Cincinnati as another typical mid-level city in the general midwest of the United States. I do not know how the museum is not isolated, it's wonderful, but it's certainly isolated, but that's another thing. But then he goes on to say, "the idea was not utopian but heterotopian, a sort of communal self-examination of society" the United States society, OK? "to paraphrase the French philosopher Michel Foucault whose 1967 essay 'Of Other Spaces' Mr. Collins has included in the exhibition catalog."

Here you get the general idea of how people think Foucault relates
to Kant. Somehow Foucault's lucubrations of the sixties apply to the
United States of 2003, as opposed to Kant's—the word Enlightenment
is hovering on the tip of my tongue—Kant's enlightenment bourgeois
idea of the enclosed white space of the old museum. These are the
clichés. I wanted to question that. This is why I put Foucault in there,
so that the binary opposition between the Enlightenment and pomo
could be . . . shook up a bit.

JG: You remember one of the talks at the English Institute was a talk on
the debate between Foucault and Habermas, right? And I hadn't at the
time actually connected that to what you were doing but I see that it is.
This is Amanda Anderson's talk, but it's actually in the piece in which
she tries to evenhandedly make Foucault and Habermas closer together, and go beyond the polemic, at the same time that she gets back into
that polemic. I see that part of what you were doing is to show that
when we oppose Foucault to Kant we see Habermas as in the place that
we put Kant, and as the kind of continuation of that line . . .

GS: Mmm.

JG: as opposed to Foucault.

GS: By the merest chance. By the merest chance. And indeed I did not
want to place this attempt on my part into that polemic. The idea of
making one intellectual win or lose is questioned by our politics of
reading.

JG: What was the Habermas piece you were reading?

GS: It was from *Nachmetaphysisches Denken*, postmetaphysical thinking, and it's included in James Schmidt's book and I believe it's called
. . . "The Unity of Reason in the Diversity of Its Voices" in the English
translation. What he was doing was, as in the case of Foucault, too confined to the European example. It's not Eurocentric, simply too confined to the European example. I'm at the moment engaged in
finishing a thing called "Foucault and Najibullah." In 1996 *The New
York Times* had the picture of the last communist president of
Afghanistan, Najibullah, hanging from a lamppost and his brother
hanging from a lamppost and people behind them, and I remembered

the way in which *Discipline and Punish* opens with a public execution. I began to ask the question what happens if we don't take Europe confined within its boundaries as an example. In the two pieces that Foucault has written on Kant's essay, he is completely confined to Europe. In the first one, it's Baudelaire whom he chooses as the example of the modernity that Kant's essay heralds in. And in the second one, of course, he's really talking about the idea of the critique. When I read the Habermas essay I pointed out that the English translation had tried to. . . make of the Habermas essay a more multicultural communicational enterprise. First, by mistranslating certain words, introducing certain words in there. And secondly, by omitting a really difficult sentence which certainly would not allow one to think—

JG: It actually omitted a sentence from the German?

GS: Yes. Yes. Yes.

JG: I'm shocked. [laughs.]

GS: Yes, so am I. The omitted sentence would not have allowed us to think that this was a multicultural enterprise. In terms of that debate between Foucault and Habermas, neither one of them in their different ways was thinking about the problem of our moment when imperialism is becoming racialized through the . . . highly placed diasporics claiming the moral entrepreneurship of the international civil society "saving the world" without any social contract or any kind of democratic back-up, at all. Destroying the states of the global South. Neither Habermas nor Foucault was responding to our world. Whatever their differences, they are in the same camp. It's not altogether fair to Foucault, he died before the phenomenon became exemplary. And Habermas is now among the intellectuals claiming a new Europe in the name of Kant. But you and I must keep our conversation within its limits.

JG: This is an aside, and I don't know whether this should go in the text or not. When you say "Imperialism is being racialized," which means it wasn't being racialized before, what does that mean?

GS: The emperor is racialized now, because the emperor's troops are highly placed diasporics of many colors.

JG: I see what you mean.

GS: Of course it was . . . it was . . .

JG: It was *racial.* [laughs.]

GS: Right. It was altogether racial.

JG: Right, that's why I was surprised.

GS: Oh, sorry. I'm glad you asked the question.

JG: Yeah. OK . . .because I took an aside I forgot where the main line of the argument was.

GS: Polemics. Habermas.

JG: Right. Thank you. [laughs.] So, one of the things that comes out in Amanda Anderson's piece is that, and again I can't quote it because I don't have it here, but Foucault says of Habermas, "I'm a bit closer to Habermas than he is to me." Right, which is a kind of wonderful, very complicated statement. And I actually see in that, for whatever reason, a move like your move of trying move out of our easy conceptions in which we see Foucault as the opposite of Kant. Right?

GS: Yes. And I think all of the . . . all of the . . . so-called postmodernists—Lyotard, Derrida—they've all in fact said they're closer to Habermas. Habermas is a learned man. His one book on the postmodernists, if you look at the documentation, you will see that most of the documentation on the Derrida chapter, for example, is coming from Jonathan Culler's book *On Deconstruction.* It was unfortunate that he was pushed by *The New Left Review* interviews and so on, to give an opinion on this group of writers with whom he has no sympathy in terms of intellectual style. Indeed, their intellectual styles are so different that that's what has come in to vitiate this whole thing into a useless polemic. But that's not what I was really focusing on. Can I take a moment to talk about what Habermas' project, I thought, was in that essay?

JG: [pause.] Yeah.

GS: It's a good project. It's a postmetaphysical thinking type project, right? Now, one of the most interesting things about Kant's notion of the public sphere, and you won't get this in the "What is Enlightenment?" essay, because Kant is not writing there as a philosopher. He always says the question of the Enlightenment is not a philosophical question. The Enlightenment comes in as a digression in section 40 of *The Critique of Judgment*. The essay on perpetual peace is also not written "as a philosopher." Kant's real idea of the public sphere comes out in what I, and I believe some others, have called the fourth critique: "Religion Within the Boundaries of Mere Reason": *blosse Vernunft*. Which takes its place with pure reason, practical reason, and the power of judgment.

JG: Um-hmm.

GS: In that essay, in that magnificent work which is very late, 1792 I believe, he tries to look at an idea of the public sphere which does not derive from the binary opposition between public and private, but, from the idea that reason is one. You see now Habermas' title, "Unity of Reason?" Incidentally, because Kant is not grounded in that binary, people have difficulty with his examples of free and bound behavior in that essay.

JG: Uh-huh.

GS: OK. Reason is one in the human being, and therefore the telos of humanity is collective, therefore the public sphere. You understand? And it's like, obviously I'm not going to summarize that extraordinary, complex, wonderful text. It's also about how can there be a secularism without an intuition of the transcendental. These are questions that are very important for our time because the ones who talk secularism these days have privatized the transcendental like going to the bathroom. But, at any rate . . .

JG: [laughs.]

GS: Let's get away from that hobbyhorse. When Habermas tries to look at this he makes it postmetaphysical by saying that he's going to base himself on the fact of language. That maybe languages are diverse, but all languages are made to be understood. So this is his rewriting of Kant's idea that reason is one. To be made to be understood really has something to do with translation and therefore it's a pity that the translation plays those games. Habermas uses the word *Verständigung*, which is not really only being intelligible. It also means the possibility of having "understandings," which of course implies the political. If you look at our idea of human rights, that still relates to where Kant is putting his faith: Reason is one. Therefore, everyone has the same inalienable rights. On the other hand, we know that, although we must assume that you and the most disenfranchised aboriginal in the wastes of the global South have the same rights, practically speaking, that's not true. The rich and the poor are not equally free to sleep under the bridges of Paris. In order to go to that challenge, the challenge of what to do with the idea that reason is not one, that the reason-effect is produced, that the human being is not culpable where he—and in Kant it is he—where he is not reasonable . . . . What to do with those kinds of ideas, in the moment that I just described? We still have to use what Kant is talking about, this public sphere without a distinction between public and private. That's where the usefulness of these texts comes in. Mendelssohn was the only respondent, Mendelssohn the Jew, who brought in the point which is extremely important in the context of human rights. His title, remember, was—What is it to *aufklären*? To enlighten? And he brings up the difference between the human being and the citizen. In that difference lies the problem with the idea of reason being one, and therefore, you and the totally disenfranchised having the same rights. If, historically, you go further along this line, you will see that the division between public and private, which is something that people always think about in terms of the public sphere, is not shared in the same way by the rest of the world. And, therefore, if we move into a revisiting of an idea of the public sphere based on some commonality, in the case of Kant—reason, some commonality shared by all human beings, an immense effort is required, because the public sphere is not present everywhere in the same way. That's an historical argument into which I will not now go. But, we can begin to touch polities, and civilizations, and societies that are not European, because the division between public and private, which is a historical division, is not shared by the rest of the world in the same way at all. Therefore at our discussion I empowered myself by putting myself within the novel *The Rape of Shavi* by Buchi Emecheta, the Nigerian novelist. Although criticism has not noticed it, she in fact revises and rewrites the punishment of Agamemnon by Clytemnestra, which leads to the first presentation of a trial by jury in the European tradition and the declaration that it is a punishable murder, whereas Orestes' murder of his mother was a punishment, and not a murder. We are looking here at a displacement of what Europeans think of as private and public into crime and punishment. Today I would add another text to this—Patricia Grace's (she's a Maori writer) *Baby No Eyes*, which takes up the notion that Kant has of the enlightened voice. Kant says it's the *Gelehrt*, it's the scholar. In his moment in time, that's the best he can do in terms of the reasonable person, you know, who knows that reason is one in the human being. And how does this scholar behave in an enlightened fashion? He publishes. And what kind of publication does he make? He makes a publication which would be good for all time and all places. Now, Patricia Grace's novel *Baby No Eyes* takes us through a certain discourse, where the public-private distinction is irrelevant in terms of the socialization of the Maori. I'm not going to summarize that excellent novel here, but what is most important is that at the end it is the Maori child who is now a student at a university. A modern university, which, as Derrida has suggested—although there are things to be said about that—is generally on the European model. Any democratic state has that university on that model. A modern university where he is turning his own history, which is a Maori history, a history which Mr. Thom Collins would call "the self in the social world." In Patricia Grace's novel, the hero, the young Maori, now is wanting to understand others. Understand others. As my mother said at the Indian Consulate a couple of years ago when she was asked to give her opinion because she was the oldest person present at a meeting on South Asian leadership, she said with an inimitable smile, "you should think about people other than South Asians." See?

JG: [laughs.]

GS: So that particular move, the *Gelehrt*, writing for all time and all people, you can also see that in Patricia Grace's novel where the Maori worldview comes earlier, in the earlier generations. And that worldview, as for example critics like Caroline Sinavaiana described, that worldview has a notion of the community which is not based on the division between the public and the private. I feel that it is useful for us to revisit Kant and, in the way in which history offers the possibility of a correction, a revision of Kant in today's world rather than take a bad faith position of the Enlightenment defined as a time in history where bourgeois capitalism began to rule the world. Or what is worse, Europeans trying to rule the world (better than the Americans) in the name of Kant. That's what I was trying to save, the best in the German Enlightenment contained accessibly in those essays written in response to a newspaper competition.

Is this making sense?

JG: It is making sense. It's hard. [laughs.]

GS: I don't think it's that hard actually.

JG: [laughing.] Well, I know *you* don't, but you're thinking it.

GS: [laughs.] I mean the work is hard.

JG: Following the pieces of it is hard, and it's hard particularly because I think you have worked out a notion of Kant which I don't have worked out. So part of following you involves following that.

GS: But isn't that why one writes, because one has a . . .

JG: I'm not saying it's bad, I just said it's hard. [laughs.] That's all.

GS: . . . because one has a newish idea?

JG: I don't use "hard" critically, I know people do. I'm just trying to keep with you.

GS: Good. Thank you.

JG: In order to ask good questions.

GS: Thank you. But what I'm saying, I mean you are surely, of course you will understand, I mean surely you are understanding what I am saying. I mean, come on.

JG: I'm both trying to follow what you're saying and I'm also making connections.

GS: Good.

JG: And that's probably part of what makes it hard, too. I'll just try to figure out what I want to ask. I'm thinking of a couple things and they all seem to go in different directions. I'll just say one of them. . . . I don't think this is where you are going which is why I hesitate to say it, or that it's even where you are coming from, but, it's one of the things I was thinking about.

Amy Hollywood gave this paper that is based in her work on this fourteenth-century mystic and her paper is also about reason. And so when you're talking reason, I'm thinking about that reason, and reason in opposition to some kind of belief, some kind of faith.

GS: Faith.

JG: Right. As well as love, all these kinds of terms. I was trying to think about the relation between reason there, which would also be described in Hollywood's text as mere reason because of its limitation in a way that is related to the way that Kant limits it. For her, it involves questions about the limitations of reason and, therefore, our protocols and assumptions as scholars. And, because she's in religious studies, trying to understand religion and trying to respond to religion. I was trying to think about mere reason and its relation to the religious.

GS: Yes.

JG: But I couldn't at the same time think about that and figure out where that was in what you were saying. That's my question.

GS: That's a hard question, but that is the question to be asked. And let me put it this way, you know Kant does not just think mere reason. He thinks also pure reason and practical reason. Certainly the fourteenth-century mystic is not thinking that way, and I know that Amy Hollywood would completely understand that. But for people who trivialize the Enlightenment in bad faith, they don't always distinguish between rat choice, you know, rational choice, self-interested choice, you know, game theory by which the market is . . . predicted, and so on and so forth, and these ideas of reason. OK? They conflate the two. Now, the real problem is that there *are* historical lines of conflation. So that's why we are talking about the rethinking and revisiting and revising and so on. Redoing effort-fully so that that is brought into political activism.

Now, what is really difficult in Kant's text, and that's I think its strength, one does not know which kind of reason he values most. He values each in its own sphere, and keeps insisting that reason is one. His three-sided reason is never and always working together, never continuous. If I can make a digression that's *completely* a digression, and I will not pick it up, yet I hope it will be included in the essay. I have a subterranean argument that Marx shares things with Kant. Marx's notion that everything can be expressed, his word always, or represented in various different ways, most famously capitalism itself in its three circuits, reminds one of this three ways of reason as it were. When Kant is talking about mere reason, he talks about *parerga*, you know, work outside of the work of mere reason. And he speaks of moral labor, to which mere reason is not given. Mere reason finds moral labor troublesome. He's an eighteenth-century man, right, so his idea of mere reason is much like, not like a clock, but it's like a machine with little screws and stuff. Which is very badly translated from the eighteenth century on and turned into a psychodrama. What Kant calls *Triebfeder*, which is like little things with which you wind toys and clocks. These little *Triebfedern* seem programmed to go wrong, so that the work of moral labor can happen. When something goes wrong, mere reason tries to put a plus in the place of a minus, you know. It sounds to me very much like the way in which people work at human rights. Frighten the state, change the law, make a little stop-gap something and then run off, etcetera. So mere reason tries to put a plus in the place of a minus, turn the screw the other way, etcetera. But that is not what is required in the programming of the human. What is required is moral labor. And therefore, of all the *parerga* that cannot be discussed, in terms of mere reason, the one that Kant thinks is useful is to give a little room—*einräumen*, this is also mistranslated—to give a little room for the inscrutable in the structural picture of mere reason. And what would be the inscrutable thing that pure reason would not be able to theorize? It's the effect of grace. Unless one presumes that, practically one doesn't go into moral labor. And the entire last section of the book is involved with why any kind of established church may be necessary but it is not a good thing. It has to be laundered into philosophy, into secularism.

Now, Derrida's . . . excellence here is that in his *"Foi et Savoir,"* faith and knowledge, he talks about what Kant calls, in the very first section, *Nebengeschäfte*, tasks that are all side-tasks compared to the noble real task of moral labor. This is about people—there are some extremely funny footnotes—believing that by saying prayers right at the last moment after a life of completely dissolute behavior you get into heaven, etcetera. So he makes many jokes, and Derrida says that these are no longer . . . these should not be though of as *Nebengeschäfte*, in fact, these should be taken seriously as something that comes with the religious. I think he's thinking in terms of global terrorism justified by reward in heaven. How people can be made to be suicide bombers, by promises of rewards. I don't know that he is actually thinking this, but this would be my guess. I think that it is a good idea to imagine that the stuff that Kant dismisses as adventitious to the truly religious, as the calculative merely reasonable notion of salvation, should not be put out of court. But nonetheless, I don't think that's the way to use the Kantian notion of the three kinds of reason and its relationship only to the effect of grace without giving a name to religion. Just taking into account that any religious impulse brings in those kinds of crude things, calculative beliefs in how to get salvation is fine, but we should realize that as Kant thinks religion, he is also theorizing the public sphere. When the early subalternists spoke of religion brought to crisis as militancy, they were on their way here.

JG: Right.

GS: And so, what I'm interested in is how to revise the idea of the reasonable. In Kant there are two problems. One of them being that Christianity at all costs is the best example. And the idea of a peaceable world as patriarchal. It seems to me that when we are looking at multiplicity, and when we are looking at reasonableness being multiple, it's not just saying "look here, religion *will* bring with it the other stuff that we should also concentrate on," but rather to look at it the other way—that reason is produced and not one. And, if I may just say this to bring you back to the fourteenth century, the idea in Kant, then, is that faith is not opposed to a reason understood minimally as mere reason. But faith, not faith so much as grace is allowed to be thought as the inscrutable that will allow moral labor. Today we would say "radical alterity." This is allowed to be thought so that the merely reasonable may move into the practically reasonable of moral labor without being able to define it through the purely reasonable of theory. That's the model in Kant. And what we would say is that reason is not, even when broken up into three in this way, reason is not the only thing. That would lead us into a holding-concept of gendering which is what allows religion to flourish. All negotiations between the sacred and the profane are generally negotiated in terms of gendering because the creation of life is a kind of hierophany and all that stuff—you will find that all over the place. And there, to bring myself to my last sentence on this issue, but it will lead to other work, there I think the person, I'm a Europeanist, the person within the European tradition whom I find extremely useful is Melanie Klein. Melanie Klein who makes us understand the biological as the fractured ground of semiosis, ethical semiosis. I will use that as far as I can in order to get into what I only know vaguely which is outside of Europe. You know what I'm saying? So, that's a *huge* answer to your question about Amy Hollywood.

JG: Yeah, and it also points into a different direction.

GS: Yeah, but, I think . . . it needs to be said.

JG: Yeah.

GS: I think this is getting very hard now. I think we should just say "good-bye, have a good time."

JG: [laughs.] Do you want to stop?

GS: No, I don't particularly want to stop. Do you? I could go either way.

JG: No, I think we should keep going for a while.

GS: For a little while.

JG: . . . see what happens.

GS: Little while, little while. One hour is enough I think.

JG: Yeah, it's fine. So, I think I would like you to say a little bit more—and, again, this is a while back but it's also what you did in

September—about the move from the question of how do we go back and look at what was going on in the Enlightenment—what was going on with Kant, going back to that sort of moment, thinking about not a clichéd version but an actual valuable version. . . . Where do we want to go with that? How do we want to use that? OK. And then you make a move to Emecheta's novel.

GS: And then also Patricia Grace's novel.

JG: And now you've added Patricia Grace's novel.

GS: I've added it. I've added it because I hadn't read it then.

JG: Right. And you also see Emecheta's novel as a rewriting of—

GS: Certain values. You know, trial by jury and the decision by jury on what is crime and what is punishment.

JG: This is what my question is: How do we get from this question about *What is Enlightenment?* to Emecheta's novel. And you did it again fast.

GS: Yes.

JG: You may have done it slower last September, but I don't remember it.

GS: No, I didn't do it slowly, because what I had said, and I didn't want people to think that I was going off the point. It was also because I absolutely did not want to hear the slightest suspicion that I was making a kind of third world bleat. You know?

JG: Bleat?

GS: Bleat. Like . . .

JG: Like a. . . like a sheep?

GS: Like sheep, yeah, yeah. That is so boring! Like, you know, there is an essay here in this collection, which I did read, a passage which I did read where the trivially true point is made that third world women are not considered by Kant. Of course third world women are not considered by Kant! And here I am, now, talking about the fact that the emperor is now racialized and sexualized. I found it to be an insulting sentence: "We may be heir to a tradition that constrains our ability to think the unthought, but nonetheless, we must respond to the demand to create a new future shaped by the contributions of women and third world people whose history is the underside of Enlightenment tolerance." I mean . . . I mean Mendelssohn would not particularly have commented on European Enlightenment tolerance, either. You know I read that little contemporary account of Mendelssohn coming into Kant's classroom and the students snickering. So we are not talking about Enlightenment tolerance here. I read a lot from Hamann because Hamann had already seen that Kant's essay insulted women.

JG: Who is Hamann?

GS: Hamann is a contemporary philosopher. Johann Georg Hamann. He worked at the customs house and I made the comment that he was a scrivener [laughing] like Bartleby. [still laughing] A throw-away comment. But, nonetheless, he had already written at length on that.

JG: Can I interrupt just a second to see if I'm right or wrong? First of all, you brought in Foucault in order to get rid of the simple opposition in which Foucault proves that Kant is wrong, or whatever, some dumb thing like that, and then you brought in Emecheta. But what you didn't want was to bring in Emecheta as the opposite of Kant. That somehow proves that we've gone over to some other side.

GS: Yes. What I was saying was that I wanted to think again about the usefulness of the best of the Enlightenment. And I was empowering myself, because I'm a teacher of fiction, by intercepting Emecheta's implied readership. In Emecheta there is a moment when the young woman who makes the *Eumenides* impossible receives a bitter knowledge that contradicts her own women's culture by way of a rape by a foolish European: that a woman can't be penetrated unless clitorized. Yet this knowledge leads to no sustained historical change. How to be the implied reader of this allegory of the Enlightenment? I was placing myself within her fiction, as it were. That was my place. I was speaking as a reader of fiction that takes on the same kinds of insights, you know, trial by jury, crime and punishment, knowledge and violation, the scholar of other civilizations (I'm bringing in Patricia Grace), as it's thought through . . . as these things are being thought through by writers who are not just content to take the banal oppositional position toward an enlightenment that is there in the very declaration of human rights, and that is there in our historical necessity to have an abstract public sphere. That's what I was trying to do with these folks, you know what I'm saying? I was trying to find a subject position for myself as a reader of such texts. I'll tell you something about Toni Morrison. It's a slightly . . .

JG: It looked like that was a very quick non-sequitur.

GS: Yeah.

JG: [laughs.]

GS: It's slightly oblique because Toni Morrison is African-American. But, I believe that her epigraph—she has two epigraphs—one is about the continuation of racism continuing beyond Emancipation. But, the other is from Saint Paul's epistle, I believe, to the Corinthians, where she is—and I must and will believe this, nothing in the text tells me anything to the contrary . . .

JG: By the way, these are epigraphs to what book?

GS: *Beloved*. OK? Two epigraphs. And the second one is where Saint Paul is talking about the fact the Jews are changing into Christians and that is a much bigger deal than just the original chosen people, and those who were not beloved will be beloved. Change from Africa to African-America. It is so clear that that's where Denver is. Otherwise why this peculiar epigraph? Why does she have an epigraph from Saint Paul? It's the same kind of impulse that makes these writers take on the revisiting of what we have come, as through a code-word, to call Enlightenment principles. The best of the Enlightenment. To save it from the history of European capitalism. See what I mean? That is where I was putting myself.

JG: Um-hmm. Um-hmm.

GS: Fiction is an experience of the impossible, to coin a phrase.

JG: [laughing.] Therefore . . .

GS: [laughing.] The effort that is involved in this will never succeed. But on the other hand, can one not make the effort if one has thought this? No.

JG: OK. I have another question which goes in a different direction. There is this focus on these newspaper articles. Kant's newspaper article, this competition. Mendelssohn, etcetera.

GS: And *The New York Times*, yes.

JG: Right, and *The New York Times*, exactly. So can you talk about your interest in going to the newspaper as a way of talking about this?

GS: Yes. You know, public opinion, what the newspaper stands for, and how the newspaper is already not only archaic but also residual, to use Raymond Williams' words, also *attempting* to be residual by this redefining of itself as infotainment and so on and so forth . . . . I've talked about this at much greater length in an interview with Mary Zournazi that appeared in a book called *Hope*, but you know, [laughing] I'm always talking hopefully.

JG: [laughs.]

GS: Yes, I'm very interested in the way in which a newspaper is a *lieu tenant* for public opinion, which is a *lieu tenant* for the preferred subject. . . . It's supposedly a representation of the undifferentiated subject of the public sphere. The newspaper writes as if from the correct ideological subject of the public sphere to the correct ideological subject of the public sphere. On the other hand, there is a difference between these two subjects, putatively, because it also supposedly forms public opinion which supposedly then allows the construction and the up-keep of the democratic public sector. The public sphere. Now this is of course a simulacrum in so far as the newspaper still repeats this residually straight-line communication which is the condition and effect of the public sphere, and it is a performative contradiction. You've heard this criticism on the street. But the argument of how then the Internet and cyber-literacy and telecommunication—the movement of data—have come in to supply the lack of the democratic impulse that's the allegory of the newspaper, that is another story. But, yes, I'm *very* interested in the newspaper.

Now, when I began I said that intellectual movements, strictly speaking, do not take place. But the Enlightenment is a code-word for us. Now, they do not take place also because of the distance between the putative subject writing and responding to the newspaper and reading the newspaper and the general public, let us say, and in Kant's day *more* supposedly than in ours. See what I mean? So, that little bunch of—

JG: In Kant's day there was more of a gap?

GS: More of a. . . more of a gap. I am not making a complicated argument here, I am talking about mass education. And when Kant is talking about the *Gelehrt*, he's talking about the scholar, the university educated scholar, he's really talking about people who publish. So, in fact, there is an understanding in Kant that the subject of the Enlightenment is not everyone. You know?

JG: Right.

GS: Today we tend to forget it because our idea is that everyone should be educated. But Kant's idea of education, to speak for all time and all place, not education but specifically publication, is rather different from our idea of education which we see as vocational and as an instrument of upward class mobility.

JG: Um-hmm.

GS: See, these confusions also have to be brought up when we are talking about enlightenment.

A little story. You know, people always complain about the fact that Kant is . . . so nice to Frederick the Great and, in this essay, he says that in your job you should always obey. And people say "come on, academic freedom, ta-da." But you know that day that I came in to do the roundtable I had had my research assistant e-mail me the security statement, OK? And I got it and I had printer paper with me and I printed it out, OK? And, as it happened, there were two cover sheets—I mentioned this—there were two cover sheets so that there were two title pages. And since I'm clearly a foreigner, dressed in foreign clothes, and, in fact I'm a green-card holder . . . I was about to drop one of the sheets in the wastepaper basket. I did not want to do it. You know, that paranoia which is 200 years after Kant wrote, more than 200 years, it's still there. This idea of being afraid in the public sphere and, indeed, also there were discussions almost at the same time of not calling a certain conference by a certain name because the president of the institution might think it was too radical, and so on and so forth. And might not give money. So when we fault Kant we forget that we live in the same kind of world, and that our civil liberties which are supposedly greater than what Kant's world had, are in fact, in effect, they are not there for everyone. And, of course, now even less and less.

A postscript. There was a moment when it was suggested that Asia could say no in terms of Confucianism. I would like to say here, once and for all, that that is a meretricious argument. The way in which Confucianism is brought up by the Asian moral values folk like Senior Minister Lee Kuan Yew and others in Korea never ever looks at anything textual. It's much like the argument made by moral majorities everywhere in support of capitalism and it really provides us with the managerial class all across the globe today in globalization who are many colors, again racialized. If the empire is racialized so is capital. And it seems to me that we should not think that Asia is saying no. It's a way of avoiding the simplest human rights obligations. The entire story of being oppressive to the underclass is recoded as Asia saying no to Europe by giving Confucius in place of Kant. I would like to say that if one actually *read* Confucius carefully, then one would be able to find family resemblances. Just the way I've been saying that there are family resemblances with non-European ways of thinking which do not share the public and the private division. So I would, just as I had said on the occasion of Emecheta and Patricia Grace, that I do not want to be understood as bleating for the third world woman, so indeed, I do not want to be understood as a cultural conservative who criticizes the idea of reason from the point of view of some fantasmatic Confucianism or Hindutva. I think this is a good place to end.

JG: I want to ask you a question now. Why is "bleating" the word that you use? The first time I heard it I wasn't even sure that I heard it. I'm surprised. It's a shorthand, clearly.

GS: Because I always feel that the sort of . . . sort of anthropological goodwill that is shown toward an ethno-cultural agenda that is always kept there as in these politically correct situations . . . is much like Little Bo-Peep. And the pastor, you know, I mean, behind the sheep is also the entire Christian imagery—

JG: Of the pastor and his flock.

GS: Yeah, and also the person being nice to the herd, the one sheep, kind of making a noise out of the whole herd. I mean it's . . . I haven't really thought it through but I *always* think of it as that kind of *ahhh-hhh* [imitates sheep]. That noise. You see what I mean?

JG: Yeah.

GS: That's why.

JG: [laughing.] Uh-huh. I like the image though.

Notes on Contributors

Amanda Anderson is Caroline Donovan Professor of English and Department Chair at Johns Hopkins University. She is the author of *The Powers of Distance: Cosmopolitanism and the Cultivation of Detachment* (2001) and *Tainted Souls and Painted Faces: The Rhetoric of Fallenness in Victorian Culture* (1993). She has also coedited, with Joseph Valente, *Disciplinarity at the Fin de Siècle* (2002). She is currently working on a book entitled *The Way We Argue Now*, from which her contribution to this volume is drawn.

Jonathan Crewe is Professor of English at Dartmouth College, where he also directs the Leslie Center for the Humanities. His primary publications are in English Renaissance literature and its modern sequels. He has recently edited five plays and the narrative poems for the New Pelican Shakespeare, and is currently working on a book on Elizabethan romance.

Helen Deutsch is Associate Professor of English at UCLA. She is the author of *Resemblance and Disgrace: Alexander Pope and the Deformation of Culture* (1996), and has coedited, with Felicity Nussbaum, *"Defects": Engendering the Modern Body* (2000). She has published numerous essays linking the fields of eighteenth-century studies and disability studies, particularly through an ongoing exploration of the connection between literary authorship and physical difference. She is currently completing a book, *Dr. Johnson's Autopsy*, forthcoming from the University of Chicago Press.

Jane Gallop is Distinguished Professor of English and Comparative Literature at the University of Wisconsin-Milwaukee. She has published extensively on psychoanalysis, sexuality, and the history of feminism. Her most recent books are *Living With His Camera* (2003) and *Anecdotal Theory* (2002).

Amy Hollywood is Professor of Theology and History of Christianity at the University of Chicago. She is the author of *Sensible Ecstasy: Mysticism, Sexual Difference, and the Demands of History* (2002) and *The Soul as Virgin Wife: Mechthild of Magdeburg, Marguerite Porete, and Meister Eckhart* (1995).

Louis Menand is Professor of English at Harvard University. His book *The Metaphysical Club* won the Pulitzer Prize in History in 2002. He is also the author of *American Studies* (2002), and *Discovering Modernism: T. S. Eliot and His Context* (1987; new edition 2004).

Gayatri Chakravorty Spivak is Avalon Foundation Professor in the Humanities at Columbia University. She is the author of *A Critique of Postcolonial Reason: Toward a History of the Vanishing Present* (1999), *Outside in the Teaching Machine* (1993), and *In Other Worlds: Essays in Cultural Politics* (1988).

Michael Warner is Professor of English at Rutgers University. His publications include *Publics and Counterpublics* (2002), *The Trouble With Normal: Sex, Politics, and the Ethics of Queer Life* (2000), and *The Letters of the Republic: Publication and the Public Sphere in Eighteenth-Century America* (1992). He is the editor of *Fear of a Queer Planet: Queer Politics and Social Theory* (1993).

Index